BAKER & TAYLOR

Shipwreck Hunter

Deep, Dark & Deadly in the Great Lakes

Gerald Volgenau

ANN ARBOR
MEDIA GROUP

917.7
V
c-1

ANN ARBOR
MEDIA GROUP

All inquiries should be addressed to:
Ann Arbor Media Group
2500 S. State Street
Ann Arbor, Mi 48104

Printed and bound in the United States of America.

1 2 3 4 5 6 7 8 9 10

ISBN 13: 978-1-58726-430-6
ISBN 10: 1-58726-430-7

Library of Congress Cataloging-in-Publication Data

Volgenau, Gerald, 1940-
    Shipwreck hunter : deep, dark & deadly in the Great Lakes / Gerald Volgenau.
        p. cm.
    Includes bibliographical references.
    ISBN-13: 978-1-58726-430-6 (hardcover : alk. paper)
    ISBN-10: 1-58726-430-7 (hardcover : alk. paper)
  1. Fader, Danny. 2. Scuba diving--accidents--Great Lakes (North America)
3. Shipwrecks--Great Lakes (North America) 4. Underwater exploration--Great Lakes (North America) I. Title.

  G525.V56 2007
  917.7--dc22

                                                        2007004711

To Christopher and Teresa
Two of the bravest people I know

Contents

CHAPTER 1

No Air

Somehow none of this made any sense. No sense at all.

This was supposed to be about treasure. Real underwater treasure hidden in a safe. Maybe gold. And Danny Fader was no rank amateur. No warm-water wuss who once a year bubbled down among the coral to look at all the pretty fish. He was a veteran wreck hunter, a member of one of the world's most elite teams of deep-diving wreck hunters.

Compact with hard muscles, curly hair, and full of boyish laughter, the 48-year-old Danny dared to go where 98 percent of recreational divers would never consider going, certainly no divers with any conventional sense of safety. His hunting preserve—and that of his team led by David Trotter, one of the world's most proficient finders of lost ships—was the Great Lakes. For wreck divers, the Great Lakes are a dangerous nirvana.

"Nothing will ever happen to me," Danny had said. Maybe he was bragging, a bit of hubris. But more than anything, Danny felt like he was just stating the facts as he knew them.

By some estimates, more than 6,000 ships have foundered in these lakes. Some say as many as 10,000. Certainly some lost vessels today are no more than a pile of boards on the bottom, but others—the kind divers cherish—are virtually as intact as the day they sank.

At least until recent years, sinking a ship in the big lakes was almost equivalent to encasing a bug in amber. Near-perfect preservation. Lake divers regularly have found 150-year-old wrecks with wooden decking, masts, and bulkheads that were almost unsullied. Caulking still lay between the boards. Ships' bells could be rung. Even hemp rigging could still be found. But divers pay a price to explore these wrecks.

Experienced divers have called the Great Lakes some of the world's most inhospitable waters. Especially when the diving is deep. Almost every year, divers are lost in these waters.

And Trotter's team dives deep. Very deep. Often 200 feet down, and more. Recreational divers are discouraged from going below 130 feet. Diving at these depths is called technical diving for its sheer complexity of equipment and underwater dangers.

Why dive so deep? Put in another context, a reporter once asked Willie Sutton why he robbed banks. "Because," he said, "that's where the money is." For Trotter's team, the logic is the same. Deep is where the wrecks are.

Most of the shallow-water shipwrecks have been found already, Trotter says. Those were the "low-hanging fruit." So for those divers who now would be the very first to swim along long-vanished decks, no other choice remains. Go deep. And then go deeper still.

Here the waters below the thermocline are finger-numbingly cold, and vital equipment can freeze and fail. And the light is all but gone. Underwater hand lights help. But they can quickly become as useless as car headlights in a mountain winter whiteout, for the lake waters are silty. Visibility typically can run five feet or less. And it can get worse in a hurry when an errant flipper teases up mud from the bottom or bubbles from a regulator shake lose debris from a cabin ceiling.

For wreck explorers, some wrecks seem benign, as easy to pick as daisies. Others can be truculent, seeming to resent intrusion. These do not lightly suffer fools or foolish divers. Like tantalizing Venus flytraps with a witless bug, these wrecks can—and do—kill scuba adventurers.

But still the most intrepid of divers come.

The reasons are many and varied. Perhaps they come to test their mettle, to prove their manhood in a way that's hard to manage in a modern world outside of war. Perhaps they need to be distinguished—in their own minds if for no other reason—from the faceless millions. Perhaps they follow a promise of treasure—if not gold then some fascinating historical loot, some of the world's hardest-to-get souvenirs.

And in a world where being first counts, the wreck hunters get to be first. First to see. First to touch. Nothing can quite match the experience of swimming along a deck or into a cabin that no man has seen for decades or even a century or more.

But to enter a sunken ship is to swim through a film noir. Danger can lurk in every dark corner. Hulls and bulkheads can collapse with a touch. At profound depths, a diver's brain can fog with a buildup of nitrogen. Judgment becomes flaccid, unsure. And indecision worsens when the silt begins to swirl. Which way is right? Or left? Where is the hatch you entered only minutes ago? And then there are cables and wires and monofilament fishing line. Like grasping fingers, they reach out to snag any passing flippered foot or air tank or regulator.

Like the witless fly, the wreck diver can be trapped by the underwater flower of a shipwreck. And once trapped, he can be held in a deadly embrace until all breath is gone. But Danny understood these dangers.

He had faced them not just once or twice, but again and again almost every weekend during the diving season not just for months, but for years on end. He had faced them on what is regarded as the most perilous wreck in the Atlantic and on wrecks in the South Pacific. So watery depths were his comfort zone. His place of wonder. His place of pride. His dangerously safe place, far from an often all-too-pressing and depressing daily life on land.

His marriage, once a joining of laughter with the happiest woman he ever knew, had soured. He wanted to fix it, but somehow could not find the way. His son looked at him like a stranger. He yearned to fix that, too. His illness-ravaged daughters were an emotional and financial black hole of neediness. Though he had tried and prayed and prayed some more, none of this seemed anywhere nearly as fixable as the pipes he worked with on his job at Ford Motor Company.

But here underwater, he was a master. His fellow divers respected Danny and his skills. Here all was quiet, an enthralling, green-black sanctuary. Here he understood the dangers; he knew how to command them. Everything was under control. Always.

That's why none of this made sense.

It was an October Sunday in 1994. Up on the surface, divers squinted into a sun that played happily across the water. But Danny was now down 160 feet below them, down where almost no light could penetrate. And he had suddenly found himself undone, as though caught in some terrifying hallucination. But this was real.

When things go wrong underwater, they usually go wrong in a rush. One evil piggybacks on another, until the dangerous weight comes crushing down.

He had stayed 26 minutes, most of that time at 200 feet below the surface at the bottom. He had been struggling to move the 200-pound safe off the deck of an 1840s side-wheel steamer called the *Detroit*. This mission had exhausted too much time and too much effort. More than he had planned on. Now he had risen to the topmost part of the ship and reached for the mooring line that would lead him back to the silvery surface far above and the dive boat.

But then things went bad. And they went bad in a hurry. One of his three tanks had just gasped its last bit of gas. He reached for a second regulator and that one froze open. Divers call it a free flow. And he could only watch in horror as his air rushed out in an uncontrolled flurry of bubbles. He had a third tank. He reached for the regulator and sucked hard. It was dry.

Suddenly Danny Fader felt like he was out of options.

It made no sense.

Danny was a pro, as comfortable underwater as Jacques Cousteau. If this situation was not about to kill him, it would be just embarrassing.

But now only one thought dominated his brain. Air. He needed air. In this moment he could not do the one everyday thing that most of us take for granted. He could not breathe. His dive partner was too far away to help. Fear burned through his veins, flooded his sinews, swamped his already nitrogen-addled brain.

Darker than these deep, deep waters, life's end waited just minutes away.

And it made no sense.

CHAPTER 2

Fated Day

In the predawn darkness of Sunday, October 16, 1994, the slight breeze off Lake Huron still carried enough real chill to make Danny Fader tuck his chin inside his collar.

Bleary-eyed yet giddy with excitement, he and the rest of David Trotter's team of wreck hunters made their way down the small wood dock at Grindstone City harbor and up onto the 28-foot dive boat *Obsession*.

Their mission, for such they called it, was not one that would logically come to mind for anyone who was not a wreck hunter. They were heading out not to find a sunken treasure. They had already found one—or at least what looked like one. On this trip, they were out to hide it.

They could see from the sky where the stars had yet to fade that it would be one of those rare fall days in the Midwest. Cloudless, compass-point to compass-point blue skies. Danny Fader loved to dive on fall days. And this one would be a standout. The sun soon would rise, pale and sharp-edged. The sky's blue would be straight out of the Crayola box. And the lake seemed to cooperate. Waves of less than a foot would be slapping against the hull. To be sure, down below— deep down below—the sun made little difference. There in the liquid darkness, the temperature hung at a steady 39 degrees.

Unlike the steamy days of August, in the fall Danny could pull a dry suit on over long underwear—essentially like putting on a water-proof snowmobile suit with glue-like neck and wrist seals—and not have the trapped heat of his body turn his face to scarlet.

The slow rise back from the bottom would be good, too. It would take an hour of decompression stops for his body to rid itself of the accumulated nitrogen and helium. He would already be badly chilled from the frigid waters below. But as he approached the surface above the thermocline, the water would still hold much of the summer's warmth. So hanging out at 20 and then 10 feet would not leave his teeth chattering on his regulator.

The thermocline is a layer of water below the surface where the temperatures suddenly get colder as you go deeper. Because water is not perfectly transparent, virtually all the sunlight is absorbed nearer to the surface. Winds and waves move this layer about, mixing it. Once deeper than the thermocline layer, the water temperatures continue to get colder but at a slower rate.

Scuba divers can actually see the thermocline where the temperature change is, say, six or so degrees. The water takes on a look of wrinkled glass, like that used for bathroom shower stalls.

The *Obsession* slid down the rails of its trailer, dipping into the dark water almost as soundlessly as a toe into a loafer. Trotter took the wheel and with a quick turn of his head glanced around the tiny oval harbor at Grindstone City.

In this case, the term *city* was an out-and-out exaggeration. Grindstone harbor was not much more than a divot in the shoreline near the tip of Michigan's thumb. The harbor was surrounded by a scattering of vacation homes, a trailer court, and a little store selling sundries, prepackaged sandwiches, sodas, beer, and bait.

But most importantly, Trotter saw no other boats gearing up to leave. Nothing was moving in the harbor except for the slight breeze and a few somnambulant ring-billed gulls. The summer boaters had fled to their suburbs weeks before. Most of the slips were empty. He saw no fishermen, but more to his concern, he saw no other dive boats. No one would follow him.

Trotter gave a grim smile, cranked the wheel, and slowly the *Obsession* muttered its way toward the open water of Lake Huron. On this of all days, he certainly wanted no company.

On this Sunday, the Trotter team was headed to dive on a sunken steamship the team had found earlier that summer. It was the *Detroit*, a pre–Civil War side-wheel steamer that had gone down in 200 feet of water. They had tied a mooring line to the superstructure and marked it with a small float. The ride out would take about an hour and a half, so Danny Fader and the other four divers settled into the pre-dive routines. Some napped, some chatted, others like Danny sat sorting, checking, and testing their deep-water dive gear. This mission was something special; something they never anticipated when they started diving on the *Detroit*.

They had discovered the steamer in June while the *Obsession* was "mowing the lawn" in search mode. The team uses sophisticated side-scan sonar equipment to examine the lake bottom. The technique is to follow a straight-line course, say, eight miles in one direction then coming back on a parallel but somewhat overlapping path—just the way grass is mowed. And pass after pass, they learn what is on the lake bottom.

Trotter's team takes this lawn mowing seriously. Most other groups may search for a few hours over a day or two or even a week.

The side-wheel steamer *Detroit* as it sits on the bottom. David Trotter along with his team including Danny Fader discovered this well-preserved steamer in 1994. The ship was built in 1846 and went down in 1854 after a collision with another ship in Lake Huron. Inside divers found a locked strongbox. They could not know what dangers it held. Illustration by Robert McGreevy.

Every year, Trotter's group will survey every weekend for three-plus months, often working night and day around the clock.

By the year 2006, they had scanned more than 2,000 square miles of Lake Huron bottom lands.

On that June day in 1994, a dark spot—little more than a smudge, really—scratched onto the sonar's paper readout.

"Bingo." That was Trotter talk. They'd spotted a wreck.

In the coming weeks they dove many times on the *Detroit*, with each visit gathering more details about the ship. For weeks, they were not even sure of its name. But after extensive library research and consulting Dr. Charles Feltner, a Michigan-based expert, they finally were able to put a reliable name on their discovery. It was the *Detroit*, first launched in the mid-1840s. What they already knew was that this steamer was a wreck diver's dream.

The 157-foot wooden vessel was almost entirely intact, even though its sinking had been caused when another ship accidentally rammed it on a foggy day in May 1854. An upper deck had collapsed. The smokestack had jerked from its moorings and fallen to one side. But the steam engine was unscarred. And high above the deck, the walking beam—a device used to translate the up-down action of the engine to turn the side wheels—was pristine. The side wheels themselves were unharmed, although their covers had fallen off. Trotter later joked that with a little tune-up, it probably could have motored away.

Two anchors hung from the bow. The nickel alloy on the ship's bell was still bright. And, best of all, the *Detroit* was standing upright, like some toy galleon in a child's fish tank. Perfect for exploring.

But then after numerous dives Trotter's team found something that set every diver's heart to pounding onboard the *Obsession*.

Strongbox

Rocky Arsenault, now in his second year with the team, sputtered to the surface to announce that he had found what looked like a strongbox. It was tucked away in one of the *Detroit*'s aft cabins, maybe the purser's office.

Imaginations soared. This discovery was almost unthinkably cool. Unlike the Caribbean with its scores of gold-laden galleons, the Great Lakes have never had much in the way of treasure ships. While the Caribbean shipping lanes could boast the sea-going equivalent of armored cars, the Great Lakes were—and are—the highways for semis and Greyhounds. They were working ships. They hauled lumber, coal, copper, limestone, wheat, fish, taconite iron ore, and automobiles. And yes, lots of people. In the nineteenth century, the big lakes were the highway west, carrying thousands of America's newcomers and its most adventurous to the wonderful new untouched lands and opportunities.

In follow-up dives to examine the strongbox, the team discovered first and importantly that it was not only heavy—perhaps 200 pounds—but locked up tighter than Al Capone's cell door. So it might hold anything. Documents. Jewelry. And maybe, just maybe, gold coins. That seemed like a real possibility. In the pre–Civil War era, when the *Detroit* was sunk, people still used currency you could bite, not the paper stuff that would come later. It was called specie, and a prolonged dunking was unlikely to hurt it a bit. Also they reasoned—and not unreasonably—that the ship was headed toward Sault Ste. Marie, where locks were being built to connect Lake Superior to the lower lakes. The *Detroit* could have been carrying a payroll for the workers.

From a practical if somewhat pessimistic point of view, they also had to admit that the box could be empty. They had learned it took almost an hour for the ship to sink. The captain would have had time to pull out anything valuable. But if so, why was it locked? Why lock a safe with nothing inside? What's the point? Especially if you are trying to cope with a sinking ship.

So far, the *Detroit*'s strongbox had kept its secrets. Now, sitting on a deck 180 feet below the surface, no diver could budge its door.

At this point, Trotter's team faced another emerging problem. They realized that the *Obsession*, as it hovered over the *Detroit*, had been spotted by another dive boat. That meant other divers might soon be headed down to explore the old steamer—and would likely find the strongbox.

As a result, the team now gave itself a new mission. They would make that strongbox disappear. If they could not pry it open or raise it to the surface, they sure were not going to leave it lying there for someone else to grab.

Trotter knew what to do. He had seen such situations before. And he also knew from hard, past experience that competing wreck hunters might not be far behind him in the discovery of the *Detroit*.

Trotter was already an established star among lake wreck hunters. He held—and continues to this day to hold—a reputation as the premiere shipwreck sleuth in the Great Lakes and one of the best in the world. He was not the first in the Great Lakes to find virgin wrecks. But year after year, he has continued to find them, a lot of them. Trotter, an angular 6-foot-2 with a shock of red-brown hair and an easy smile, seemed to find lost ships as though someone had left the lights on just for him.

Every year Trotter would show up at the annual divers' conferences around the Great Lakes to announce the new wrecks that he'd discovered with his team. He showed slides and later videotapes with increasingly sophisticated artwork and filming technique. In these programs he'd spin out the history of the ships, tell of the ill-fated last days, and share what the divers found. Sometimes he'd talk about not just one, but two, three, or even more ships that he'd found that season. And the savvy divers in the crowd knew that Trotter, the man with the side-scan, had actually discovered even more than he had let on.

He vowed to come back to some of these discoveries. Others he simply ignored because they were little more than "a pile of boards" strewn on the bottom—too boring to dive. In fact, if other divers could have found these "too-boring wrecks," they probably would have jumped on them and called it a fine adventure.

Keeping Secrets

By the end of 1994, Trotter had found some 45 shipwrecks. By last count in 2006, the number jumped to nearly 90—including not just ships, but airplanes, scows, and other things. (A tradition exists among Great Lakes sailors to call any vessel in the inland seas a "boat"—oreboat, steamboat, propeller boat—but divers call them ships. So this book will refer to them as ships.) Trotter indeed knew his stuff.

While Trotter's celebrity as a wreck hunter had some pleasing aspects, it also had some disconcerting ones. It meant that people— state government officials and especially other wreck divers—wanted to know what he had found. So they spied on him.

They wanted in on his discoveries. Some lurked like claim jumpers in the Old West, just waiting for Trotter to hit gold. Then, when he turned his back, they'd anchor on his claim and dive.

After all, it was far cheaper and easier to follow him around than to buy a boat-load of expensive equipment, gain enough experience to actually use it effectively, and then spend three months of weekends every year watching for boat-like smudges to appear on a side-scan readout.

The State of Michigan was especially cranky. It did not want Trotter out there messing with bits of history. Those wrecks belonged to the state, officialdom believed. Not to David Trotter.

Other wreck divers wanted to be like Dave, just like young basketball players once wanted to be like Michael Jordan. They wanted the stardom, the glory, the chance to be the first on a wreck. They wanted bragging rights. So they tried to follow him.

Over the years as he shoved off from the Michigan Thumb, he'd often spot another dive boat in his wake. Usually the stalking dive boat would lay back, trying to be inconspicuous. The boat might hang off on the horizon for hours at a time, just waiting for Trotter to stop and tie into some new wreck. They monitored his radio calls hoping for clues. And on several occasions, they even followed him in helicopters. Once they'd gotten the loran/GPS coordinates for his site, it was simple. They would just drive up, tie off on Trotter's mooring line, and then scavenge everything they could find.

Some of those dogging Trotter's wake were commercial dive boat operators. For them, being able to advertise a dive on a newly discovered wreck was almost akin to, say, Ford coming out with a snazzy new model. Paying customers—lugging their air tanks and regulators—would line up with their VISA cards in hand.

Trotter got very good at spotting them. It was exasperating. It was a waste of time and fuel. But he became deft at throwing them off the scent. He'd zig and zag. He'd simply go for a boat ride, going in no particular direction except away from the wreck he was diving. Or he might just sit for a long time at some random spot on the water and let them think what they wanted. And sometimes Trotter and his team would start in the early morning darkness or late at night when the charter boats were snoozing at the dock.

If Trotter is known in the Great Lakes as the greatest of wreck hunters, he also has another reputation. He is a secret keeper. And his team is expected to be closemouthed as well.

Trotter's mantra: "Never tell 'em where you're going, where you've been, or what you've found."

You might call it a sort of divers' *omertà* or a version of the Las Vegas notion—what happens on the water stays on the water. In Trotter's view, the intellectual property—the exact locations of sunken ships—belongs to those who find them.

Trotter never gives away the loran or global positioning system (GPS) coordinates for a wreck. Not to anyone. Not months later; not years later. This secrecy might strike some as curious, especially since Trotter's team—once it had thoroughly explored a wreck—rarely, if ever, goes back. He simply protects his finds. Early in his career, he learned some hard lessons about not spilling secrets.

One day he dove on a classic wreck, the *Cedarville*, a 588-foot steel freighter that went down after a collision in the Mackinac Straits. Trotter's experience was limited at that point, but still he dropped down inside the ship, swam into the engine room, and followed some pipes to the bulkhead. And "By God, I found gauges. I was fascinated," he said. Trotter took nothing, even though in this early era, stripping wrecks was just part of the thrill of wreck diving. Every diver did it.

"When I got back on shore, I got to talking with the guys around the dock," he recalled. "Apparently other divers had not found these gauges. It wasn't two days later, I went back and there wasn't a gauge left."

Some time later Trotter got his first loran-C—a device similar to a GPS that can locate your exact position. He was the second civilian on Lake Huron to own one. Using the loran in combination with the sonar, Trotter was able to make his first big finds. They were the bow half of the *Daniel J. Morrell* (the stern had been found almost immediately after it went down in 1966) and also a fine little schooner called the *Emma Nielson*.

Sometime later, Trotter got a call from John Steele, who was the granddaddy of wreck finders in the Great Lakes. Steele had grappled onto scores of virgin wrecks before many wreck hunters even got started. His reputation was legend. Steele was held in awe by virtually every wreck diver who had struggled into a dry suit on the lakes. Steele and Trotter had a personal relationship. They dove together on the *Kamloops*, which had sunk off Isle Royale in Lake Superior.

During the telephone call, Steele asked Trotter for the locations for the *Morrell* and the *Neilson*.

"I felt obligated to give him the loran numbers," Trotter said.

"Then, one or one and a half years later," Trotter said, "I discovered that the numbers were all over the place. I told him [Steele], 'Those numbers did not belong to you.'"

Trotter said he remained friends with Steele, but never gave him numbers again. At that point, Trotter decided no more gift numbers. Not to anyone.

Other divers, of course, have mixed feelings about Trotter's secret keeping. On one hand they respect him for keeping his confidences. On the other hand, they resent it. After all, aren't they fellow divers in the Great Lakes wreck-diving fraternity? Shouldn't he, as a fraternal member, let them in on the action?

Trotter's answer: "Well, no." His view is that Great Lakes wreck hunting is "an equal opportunity adventure," available to anyone who wants to spend the time and money and gain enough experience to actually find virgin ships. Also, Trotter is no wreck stripper. He goes to shoot photos and make videos.

That's not to say, Trotter admits, that neither he nor any of his team has never taken souvenirs off a wreck. But, he said, they certainly do not dive down with the goal of hauling up steering wheels, compasses, figureheads, port holes, or—as some have done—going down with car jacks and even dynamite to blow loose something they wanted.

"I respect him," says John Polacsek, former maritime curator of the Dossin Great Lakes Museum on Detroit's Belle Isle. "He takes only pictures and leaves only bubbles."

Yes, Trotter keeps his secrets. And if there ever was a secret to be kept, it was the location of the steamer *Detroit* and the strongbox sitting on its starboard deck. But as the late summer of 1994 neared, the team unhappily realized they had been "jumped" on the *Detroit*.

They were almost sure they had been spotted by a dive boat captain who sailed out of Grindstone City. This was not good. Trotter had already initiated talks with officials at two local museums about raising the strongbox and examining the contents. What's more, with fantasies raging, the team even imagined an on-TV strongbox opening, something like Geraldo Rivera opening Al Capone's safe in Chicago. To lose the box now was unthinkable.

This Sunday was to mark the end of their diving for the year. Fall could bring the lakes' most dangerous storms. It was time to pack it in for a few months. But the team agreed it could not just motor away for the winter and still have any real hopes of finding the strongbox when they came back in the spring.

Bringing the box up was impossible at that point. Along with other complications, they did not have the right equipment to haul it up. So they decided to hide it.

Treasure on Ice

In one respect, hiding the strongbox would be easy. All they had to do was move it out into the muddy bottom about 30 or 40 feet away from the wreck.

Houdini could not perform a better disappearing act. Two hundred feet down from the surface, the water temperature is only in the high 30s. It's very dark and silty. Visibility on a good day might only be four or five feet. Given the depth, any intruding diver would have, at most, 15 or 20 minutes to look around.

"And who," Trotter asked rhetorically, "is going to go wandering off into dark, silty waters to look for heaven knows what when they have a perfectly good wreck to explore?"

In another respect, hiding the strongbox would not be very easy at all. That strongbox was a lug. It was not big. It measured only about 15 to 18 inches on each side. But it was iron and very, very heavy. The team estimated it might weigh 200 pounds.

Now, moving a 200-pound weight with a hand truck on land is one thing. But it's quite another to even budge it 200 feet below the surface, much less move it any great distance.

Also at that depth, a diver can only stay on the bottom for a short time, especially a diver who was working hard. The team figured about 20 minutes at the most. After that, the diver would need more than an hour of decompression time (stopping at several levels) to rid his body of the nitrogen and helium gases.

It was tricky, too, because while they are underwater, divers try to conserve their air or gas mix as much as possible. To sip air rather than gulp. So they try to stay as calm and relaxed as possible. To use too much gas on the bottom is to risk not having enough for the long return. The exertion would also lengthen the amount of time needed for decompression. And it dangerously increases the nitrogen load that fogs judgment.

Moving this strongbox would definitely be work—muscle-straining, exhausting, air-devouring work.

On the day before, Saturday, Danny and Rudy Whitworth, a veteran diver and Trotter's right-hand man, swam down to the *Detroit* and moved the strongbox from the doorway of a cabin to the edge of the deck. They wanted to put it into position so they could attach lift bags to the handles. As the name implies, a lift bag is a strong bag that is tied to an object and then filled, much like a hot-air balloon, so the object can be lifted.

On that Saturday, Danny wrote in his dive book: "I got there first and tried to lift (the strongbox) upright in order to have it positioned properly for a lift bag. I couldn't lift it up all the way without Rudy's help."

Now on Sunday, a different two-man team would go down, attach a lift bag, and try to move the strongbox away from the ship. That was the mission. So as the *Obsession* headed northeast into Lake Huron, Danny Fader figured he could relax. On this trip, he had no major role. The strongbox movers would be Rocky Arsenault and Jeff Moore, two relative newcomers to the team.

Danny would go down next with Werner Wahl, a jovial nuclear chemist and entrepreneur whom the team called "the Doc." It was a good pairing. At 64, the Doc, while a competent and experienced diver, had a little too much paunch and an incipient heart condition. The other divers quietly felt he was the one diver who, at least physically, might get into deep-water trouble.

But so as far as he could tell, Danny had only one mission on the *Detroit* that day, if it could be called a mission. He would go back to the bow of the *Detroit* and retrieve a line and reel that he had left there the day before.

But within hours, all that would change.

CHAPTER 3

Danny

As a boy and even in high school, Danny Fader never really stood out.

He was fast. He could sprint like a Michigan Avenue drag racer. But he was not big or tall. And not particularly muscular or agile. So forget about going out for high school football. Or basketball. Or baseball. Or any sport that was likely to elevate a regular kid into a high school "somebody," the usual way for any boy to distinguish himself from the locker-slamming masses or to catch that girl's eye in algebra class.

Nor was Danny a standout student. Studies came hard, and he hated math. And no, he didn't edit the school yearbook or run for class president.

He was just another kid, like most of the other kids, who regularly showed up for class and fooled around with his buddies on weekends.

Sports for Danny were pickup games with friends in empty lots and backyards. No fancy uniforms with big numbers on the back; no dad/coaches who were wannabe Knute Rocknes. The kids just played whatever sport was in season. Back then, professional and college sports actually were played in specific seasons. Football in the fall, baseball in the spring and summer, and hockey in winter. Danny really liked hockey. His dad came from Canada and loved to skate. So it seemed natural that Danny would love it, too. He liked hockey's nonstop action, the push and shove. And prophetically enough, he took to swimming. He especially loved the quiet, almost surreal world of being underwater, where swimming was almost like flying.

Two or three times a week during summer vacations, Danny and his pals would bike over to Dearborn's Hemlock Pool. They would stage contests on who could hold his breath the longest. Danny got so he could swim underwater the entire length of the pool and halfway back before gasping to the surface.

He always was more a follower than a leader. Always a little happier doing things on his own than in a group. Danny exuded a boyish charm, a wide-eyed openness and a heartfelt delight when good things came his way. It was a joyousness that he never lost. Perhaps because of this almost giddy sense of wonder, he never outgrew the name Danny. He was never Dan or, like his son, Daniel. He was forever the boyishly enthusiastic Danny.

Taking Big Risks

Taking a broader view, Danny's background as being just another kid is not unusual among wreck divers, at least not for those who dive where it's deep, dark, and very dangerous.

Nor is it unusual for many high-risk adventurers. Most, like Danny, walked through their early years as just one of the faceless crowd in the school lunchroom. It was often later that they would find a sense of personal definition in daring-do. Such slow-starting tempters of fate include many mountain climbers, polar explorers, downhill ski racers, half-pipe boarders, and people who single-hand sailboats around the world and the like.

Outside their ranks, many in the world have no understanding of why these people take the risks they do. As Danny often heard about his quite calculated wreck dives, "You must be crazy to do that" or "Do you have some kind of a death wish?"

Those who frequent the edges of danger are often tempted to answer this way: "If you don't understand it, I can never explain it to you." But a death wish? No. Certainly not. Nor can these risk-takers be called crazy.

For Danny and the others who do deep wreck diving, often called technical diving, it is not a matter of risk taking, but of risk *managing*. Yes, they do get a buzz when a risk is taken and safely achieved. It is a euphoria. In physiological terms, it's a shot of dopamine to the brain.

Tim Cahill, one of the funniest and smartest adventure writers, wondered recently in an article whether as someone who tries lots of risky things he "lacked something that others took as a matter of course." He answered, "As the Scottish say, 'Some men are born two drinks short of par.' Maybe I was born short in the euphoria department."

It's certainly an apt way to describe adventurers. It also might be said that risks are not always what they seem.

What looks absolutely lethal to the uninitiated might seem relatively tame to someone with more experience, training, and preparation. For example, if you drive your car at 130 m.p.h. out on Interstate 80, that's dangerous. It really can kill you. But if you are an experienced, professional race car driver, 130 m.p.h. is pretty much every-day stuff.

The same holds true for diving. Most recreational divers—the equivalent of everyday drivers—almost never dive as deep as 100 feet. They use only compressed air in their tanks. They almost never are at risk of the bends. They do not try to wiggle their way inside the cabins and holds of sunken wrecks. So for them and for nondivers, technical diving might well seem "crazy."

But it is also true that risk-takers, in addition to coming up short on their euphoria quotient, also can share a number of other characteristics. Some of them, not so flattering.

If these characteristics or personality traits are kept under control, then the adventurers—and we're talking about most of them—can have a great time and still keep from splattering themselves on a mountain side, drowning at 165 feet, or screwing up their personal lives beyond recognition. But if these characteristics run amok, death and disaster await.

Some of the personality traits, as sketched in the perceptive book *Strange and Dangerous Dreams* by Geoff Powter, include:

- Many adventurers show a certain selfishness and an egocentrism. The attitude is: It's all about me. Expedition mountain climbers, the ones who try to scale peaks in the Himalayas, often seem to care little about the widows and orphans they might leave behind. And in the extreme, their sense of self-confidence can outweigh good sense.
- They can be stubborn, even bullheaded. They tend to go ahead even when others retreat. They will ignore the odds, the pain, the discomfort to reach their goals. Of course, this is the very stuff of adventuring—walking a very thin and moveable line. The key, of course, is knowing exactly where that line lies.

If you succeed—and that is a key factor for the public—then you are a hero. If you fail, if you die or end up with a debilitating injury, then people feel justified in calling you "nuts."

Edmund Hillary, the first to climb Mount Everest, is a hero. Those climbers who die every year or so on the comparatively less difficult Mount Rainer are considered nuts.

- On a still darker side, some adventurers have been known to chase a dangerous dream as a way of escaping other, more serious troubles in their lives. No matter how irrational it may seem, many such risk-takers hope that somehow, some way the difficulties and dangers of their adventures will remedy their other problems. Such an adventurer might think that if I can just sail solo around the world, I will be a hero and as a result my disastrous family life will be happier.

- Adventurers often have a strong need for approval. Maybe this is the sort of approval they missed as children. Dad never said, "Great going, kid!" They were invisible in school. Now as adults, often in a subconscious way, they believe that by pressing the limits of danger they can achieve the approval, the applause they so desperately long for.

Along with this need for approval often comes a powerful feeling of obligation. It's not only that they want to please some important person in their lives—a parent, a teacher, a mentor, a master sergeant—but they feel they *owe* it to him.

A classic case involved Meriwether Lewis, of the famed Lewis and Clark expedition. As described in *Dangerous Dreams* Lewis would never have signed up for such an arduous and probably life-threatening trip on his own initiative. His goal—more than discovering new lands and new plant and animal life—was to please his mentor, President Thomas Jefferson.

In capsule it might be said that risk-takers often are willing to suffer any hardships and danger to achieve the promise of heroics, acclaim, and redemption.

Redemption is a key concept here. This is the sense that by taking the risk, they will be saved. Their mentor will be pleased. Their problems will be solved. They will be beloved. And they will cease to be just another anonymous face in the office pool or in the school lunchroom.

Four in a Bed and Radio Prayers

As it turned out, even if Danny had been interested in playing halfback or point guard for the St. Alphonsus Arrows, there was no time.

"I had to work. There was no question," he said. After all, he was the oldest son. He had responsibilities.

Starting in the eighth grade, Danny got himself an after-school paper route delivering the *Detroit News*. He also picked up short-term jobs. He was a good kid, a hardworking kid from a good, hardworking family. He mowed lawns, did chores, and, by age 13, was never without some way of making a few dollars. By the ninth grade he was paying his own tuition at St. Alphonsus, a glowering, dark brick Catholic school that his mother had attended. He also could buy some of his own clothes once in a while. The rest he saved. He never had a steady girlfriend.

Danny grew up as the oldest of three boys and three girls in a family that, today, might be called "working poor." To live in the Fader household was to scrimp.

All the kids wore hand-me-down clothes, he remembered. Being the oldest, Danny did have the advantage of getting to wear the clothes before the others.

The first home he remembered was a tiny, two-bedroom house stuck in the back of a lot in Dearborn, Michigan. At the time, the children still numbered five. The two parents slept in one bedroom. Four of the kids jammed into the second bedroom, where they all slept in one bed. A crib was set up in the living room for the baby.

Danny described his family as very close. Certainly in a physical sense, they were on top of each other at home.

When the sixth child showed up, the Faders moved next door to a somewhat larger house. Dark red brick with a small porch out front, this house had three bedrooms—one for the parents, one for the girls, and one for the boys. Unfortunately, and one can only imagine the grousing and complaining, it had only one bathroom. A second bathroom was later added in the basement.

Today, much of Dearborn is populated by immigrants from the Middle East. But when Danny was young, the town, located just west of Detroit, was a mix of European stock—Germans, Italians, Scots, Irish, and Poles. Everyone was white. Dearborn had no blacks. Mayor Orville Hubbard, who not so much held office but reigned from 1942 to 1976, permitted no black people to live inside the city limits.

Also, and importantly, Dearborn was a company town, a Ford Company town—lock, stock, and four-barreled carburetors. Relatives, neighbors, friends, just about everybody the Faders knew had some connection to the massive automobile manufacturer.

In Danny's growing up years, locals called Ford Motor Company "Ford's," as in "I work at Ford's" or "He got hired at Ford's Rouge plant." The term was possessive and personal. It was Henry's company after all. The verbal quirk lingers among locals to this day. Many still say they work at "Ford's" and call the nearby Interstate 94, "Ford's Freeway."

His mother Lucille was a housewife and mom. She came from German farming stock that had worked fields in the Dearborn area for three generations. His grandmother often recalled that Henry Ford himself, lean and angular in a grey suit, used to come by once a week with a big bag of groceries for the family. And he always brought a chicken.

The food donation really helped, she said, "But after awhile, we got so we really hated chicken."

His father, Borden Fader, also of mostly German stock, worked the midnight shift as a janitor at the Ford Rotunda. That meant he had to sleep during the day, no doubt a real challenge in a house full of high-energy kids.

"Somehow he got his sleep. He never complained," Danny said. "We had to scrimp, so he often worked overtime to put food on the table. He was a good man, a disciplinarian," Danny was to recall with admiration. In words that would become particularly poignant he added, "Sadly, I did not get to see as much of him as I wanted."

Danny's dad also did something that was relatively rare for that era. He did a set of daily exercises. Danny grew up in the late 1940s and early 1950s, a time when exercise and muscle-building had something vaguely to do with that Charles Atlas guy on the matchbook covers. Regular men with real jobs had no time for such things. They were too busy scratching up enough money to make payments on the family car and buy a loaf of Wonder Bread, a bag of oleo, and the occasional chicken.

His dad would exercise faithfully every day. He called it his ten-minute workout. His oldest son noticed and was impressed.

But perhaps more importantly, the father commanded real respect as a good, religious, prayerful man. All of the Faders, in fact, were good, religious, prayerful people. They were Catholics in the most devout sense. Danny had described himself as "a cradle Catholic."

The house had a statue of the Blessed Mother in the front yard. They also had some pictures of saints, a cross, and some statues of saints in the house. The family prayed a lot—not just before meals, but after, too. All the kids attended St. Alphonsus school, which started each morning with a daily Mass. And at 8 p.m. each evening, the Fader family would gather by the radio to listen to the Rosary broadcast by a Catholic station.

No one ever missed the 8:45 a.m. Sunday services, or wanted to. While St. Alphonsus Church was in walking distance, Danny remembered that "Mom and Dad would pack us all in the car to make it faster when my brothers and sisters were small. It was a given that you went to Mass on Sunday."

Religion always would play one of the most important roles in Danny's life.

Coming to the Waters

Danny was not bookish. After graduating from high school in 1964, he did try studying business at nearby Henry Ford Community College, but he never really got the hang of that.

He was a physical young man. He loved action, actually doing things. Using his hands. Building things. So what grabbed his attention and ultimately set him on a solid career path was the Henry Ford Apprentice Program. He took classes, studied hard, and became a plumber-pipe fitter. He officially joined the Ford workforce in August of 1965.

Now in his early twenties, Danny came to a pivotal moment in his life. He discovered scuba. He first started hearing about skin diving during his apprenticeship at Ford. It was almost destiny. The kid who loved to swim underwater would soon become the adult who loved scuba.

He felt safe and happy underwater. He loved the profound quiet of the depths, the feeling of flying solo.

The famed Jacques Cousteau, one of the inventors of the Aqua-Lung and a media star of the 1960s, said as a boy he frequently dreamed of flying, but once he began scuba he never had another flying dream. He'd in fact found his own way to fly—underwater. And so had Danny.

Danny joined the Ford Seahorses, the company-sponsored dive club. He took classes and was certified through the Professional Association of Diving Instructors (PADI). He took other courses and became a master diver and before long was assisting in teaching dive classes to beginners. Now the kid who had always been a follower began to take on leadership roles in the club. He soon was organizing club dive trips as the activities director.

In 1969, Danny married Mimi, a woman he met on a blind date. The marriage lasted six years. The ending came as a shock to Danny, but in time he felt a real sense of relief to have it over with and to discover that he had a life beyond that marriage. But a hefty problem remained.

The couple had two girls, Kristie and Barbara. Sometime after the break up, doctors told the couple that both girls had muscular dystrophy and other associated problems. Danny knew obligation when it confronted him. He well understood the two girls would need lots of special care and attention. And his responsibility would soon get bigger. It turned out that Mimi had myotonic dystrophy, so she would be of little help caring for the girls.

If this was the down side, other parts of Danny's life were on the upswing.

He loved his job. He loved the hands-on work and especially the climbing up high among the pipes, a little bit of hard-hat adventure. He found he liked working on projects by himself.

As for scuba, almost nothing would change his life more. He had started diving while he was still married in the early 1970s, and every year he did more dives in more places and went deeper and tested himself further.

Initially he just dove in quarries in nearby Ohio. Then his watery horizons began to expand. He ventured into the big lakes and to the Caribbean with its eye-popping corals and lollipop-colored fish. At Grand Cayman he bubbled a long way down the famous wall, which drops from about 30 to nearly 1,000 feet. At Mexico's island of Cozumel, he went drift-diving where the current carries divers along to ogle the underwater formations and fish. These were destinations on almost every diver's want-to-go-to list.

And he made dicier dives—winter dives under the ice in Michigan—and probed some of the underwater coral caves off Florida's coast. And he dove off the California coast, down through the vinelike kelp, which is beautiful but constantly threatens to snag and foul your tank and hoses.

He was getting stronger, training at the local YMCA three days a week. His ritual was more rigorous than his dad's ten minutes a day. He was running three miles at a time, three times a week. He lifted free weights, sweated with aerobic exercises, and stretched. And in the winter, he took up skiing. He loved the speed. His body got leaner and harder.

Then, sometime after the sharp pain of the divorce started to subside, Danny began dating, going to dances, and having fun.

Now in his thirties, Danny—who'd never had much of a social life—was living large. Diving. Skiing. He made 19 parachute jumps. He was a single guy with bucks in his pocket.

He grabbed at his new lifestyle as though it was a long-lost lover that he'd never really met before. The women that he met, well, they weren't all shy little Catholic schoolgirls with their polished Mary Jane shoes. A few of the women could make your toes curl and your eyelashes go straight.

And then, too, Danny's diving cranked up a notch. He started diving wrecks. For a young hot-shot diver on the Great Lakes, it was *the* thing to do. Basically, diving wrecks always has ranked as one of the few things of real interest in the big lakes; that is, once you get past admiring your own bubbles.

In and of themselves, the Great Lakes have little of allure for a diver. Unlike the ocean, the lakes offer poor visibility and not much to see even if you could gaze beyond five or six feet. The bottoms are mud. No pretty coral. No neon fish. For the most part, lake fish come in one basic, troutlike shape. Their color—mostly brown.

But as a graveyard for sunken ships, the lakes are endlessly fascinating. So it was almost inevitable that Danny would gravitate toward exploring wrecks. They're interesting to look at, speak silently of history and human tragedy, and, what's more, they fairly ooze a sense of danger.

He traveled most often with the Ford Seahorse groups. Among his first wreck destinations was Tobermory, a picturesque harbor village at the end of Ontario's Bruce Peninsula across Lake Huron from Michigan. In the Great Lakes, Tobermory is a Mecca for beginning wreck divers. Without ever leaving the protected harbor's unruffled waters, they could bubble down just 20 or 40 feet to see the remains of boats sunk long ago.

In these early days of his diving, Danny admitted being a bit timid about going deeper than 100 feet to see a wreck.

"Man, I'm not going that deep," he said. "I'm staying in the 40- to 60-foot range. I can stay shallow and still see a lot of stuff."

That timidity would not last. Before he left Tobermory, he motored out on a group charter to dive on the *Arabia*, a ship that lay some distance outside the harbor.

It was a tough trip. That day the lake, as the local captains say, "turned snotty." The temperatures dropped, rain lashed down, and the chartered dive boat was slamming up and down in the waves. None of this was good for Danny.

Like many divers, Danny was prone to seasickness. Underwater he was fine. But his stomach turned into a food processor set on *high* when big waves slapped the boat and he started careening from gunwale to bulkhead. It also turned out that diving played hell with his sinuses. He'd get fierce, almost debilitating headaches.

On this trip—as he would on many to come—he managed to make the dive despite a slamming headache and the threat of stomach eruptions.

"It was kind of deep for me," he said, but it was a thriller.

The *Arabia* was a three-masted 131-foot bark that was toting 20,000 bushels of corn when it sank in a storm in October 1884. It was a sad occasion at the time. But for today's divers, it is one of the best wrecks to visit in the lakes.

The *Arabia*, still very much intact, was a Canadian ship built in 1853. It sat upright at a depth of 120 feet. There was a lot to see. The wheel lay to one side, ropes and chains still hung from the dead eyes, and a large anchor still lay waiting to be cast off from the bow.

Divers discovered the *Arabia* in 1971 after a local fisherman snagged his nets on it. Such fisherman finds were often the way—especially in Canadian waters—that ships were discovered in the years before wreck hunters came along with their side-scan sonar equipment. Danny, even though he was still a newbie wreck diver, went down on the *Arabia* the very next year.

"I was so nervous, I forgot my weight belt," Danny said. Someone had to pass it to him in the water.

"I remember it being so dark down there. But it was so clear. As I came down I could see the whole shape of the ship in front of me. Wow! I could see the whole wreck." His enthusiasm was boundless. "I could see the hatches on the deck, a belaying pin, a block and tackle."

But the *Arabia*, for all its charms, has proven dangerous. Over the years, seven divers have died while exploring the nineteenth-century vessel.

Then Danny moved on to exploring more wrecks, and then more. He ventured to Lakes Superior, Huron, Michigan, and Erie. He followed mooring lines down on ships off the Manitou Islands in Lake Superior, on wrecks off Grand Island at Munising, and a mail boat near Manitoulin Island in northern Lake Huron.

Two among his favorites of the early dives were the S.S. *America* and the *Cedarville*.

The 185-foot S.S. *America* has been called "a barely sunk ship." The *America* was a passenger ship that ran aground in 1928 just outside the Washington Island Harbor, on the north side of Isle Royale. Now only a dozen or so yards of water cover its highest point. At its deepest, the *America* is at 80 feet. It had been a multipurpose ship that carried passengers, fish catches, and supplies on runs between Duluth, Minnesota, and Thunder Bay, Ontario, with stops along the way at Isle Royale and many settlements on nearby islands and the north shore of Lake Superior. Since the *America* lies in such shallow water, it is a hugely popular destination for recreational divers. Perhaps five hundred a year come to dive down to explore the fascinations of the ship's ballroom, galley, and engine room.

The *Cedarville* also is a recreational divers' favorite. The ship was a relatively modern steel freighter that went down in the Straits of Mackinac following a collision in a fog east of the Mackinac Bridge on May 7, 1965. A Norwegian freighter—sailing blind—crashed into the *Cedarville*. Neither ship pilot had time to maneuver away. Loaded down with limestone from Rogers City on Lake Huron, the *Cedarville* went down in a hurry. Ten people died in the accident.

Like the *America*, the *Cedarville* was never lost. Boaters and divers quickly found it lying on its starboard side, the upper portions under only 35 feet of water, the superstructure and cabins at 75 feet, and 105 feet at its deepest. As a result, the ship was heavily salvaged. No dishes, cups, gauges from the engine room, or much of anything else was left to be carried away. But the ship's structure is largely intact. So divers like Danny could go into the cabins and, with some care, go down into the engine room. And, as Danny said, with a length of 588 feet, almost two football fields, the *Cedarville* is "Bi-i-i-i-g."

In 1978, Danny took his most exotic dive trip, flying off to Truk Lagoon, now called Chuuk Lagoon, in the islands of Micronesia. For divers, this is almost the equivalent to the experience of travelers coming upon the ancient Mayan pyramids of Uxmal in Mexico's Yucatan or the Incan temples of Machu Picchu high in the mountains of Peru.

On February 17, 1944, American bombers surprised the Japanese fleet tied up at Truk, raining down 400 tons of bombs. The planes knocked out 40 ships and thousands of men died. Then ten days later, the bombers came back with a second hit, sinking another dozen ships.

Truk supposedly was impregnable. Called "The Gibraltar of the Pacific," it was the major Japanese military center of operations for the South Pacific during World War II. Japan's combined fleet and its Fourth Fleet were based there. It also had five air strips. The Japanese used it as an important place to stop and refuel for planes headed to the South Pacific.

What remained after the bombing is now a bonanza for shipwreck divers from around the world—50 fascinating ships to explore and even a submarine. Most lie at depths down to 200 feet. Many of these sunken warships and freighters were garlanded with wonderful corals and amazing sea creatures. Danny showed up soon after the site was opened to divers.

"It was exciting going through the ships and seeing so many pristine objects—skeletons, Zero fighter planes, tanks, Jeeps, exotic corals, and all kind of marine life, including some aggressive sharks."

The more Danny dove, the more experience he gained in the tricky business of going deep and being safe. With more experience, he became more confident and extended himself in ways that he might have passed on a few years before. But he always tried to stay on the sane side of recklessness.

Narcosis

In the 1970s, 1980s, and through much of the 1990s, virtually all divers were using tanks filled with compressed air. Air worked fine, especially at the more shallow depths. But as divers began to go ever deeper, the problem of nitrogen narcosis took on greater importance.

When a diver goes down, the pressure of the water steadily increases on the body. At 33 feet, the pressure is twice as much as it is at sea level in the open air. It is the reason you feel the pressure in your ears when you dive to the bottom of the pool. At 99 feet, the pressure is four times what it would be at the surface. And so it goes.

What happens inside the body to the blood is similar to what happens when the Dr. Pepper people carbonate their beverages. When the liquid is exposed to gas under high pressure, a certain percentage of that gas dissolves in the liquid. If the pressure increases, so does the amount of gas that is dissolved.

So you have a diver breathing air. The pressure increases as he sinks lower. This pressure causes the air—which is 78 percent nitrogen and about 21 percent oxygen—to be dissolved into the blood.

The impact on the brain of this nitrogen-saturated blood is much the same as swilling booze at the local bar. In fact, the impact has been described in terms of martinis. The comparison goes that for every 50 feet a diver goes down, he is impaired to about the same degree as if he had drunk one martini, or about four ounces of alcohol. To descend 200 feet is about equal to drinking four martinis.

Like drinking alcoholic beverages, the affect varies from individual to individual, and much depends on their personal circumstances, physical conditioning, state of fatigue, level of happiness, and so on. To some degree, all divers lose their inhibitions, which can be dangerous. They are more liable to take risks they should not. For everyone, the range of focus—already limited by the dive mask—narrows further, making them less aware of their surroundings. This can be a killer for a diver exploring the innards of a sunken ship filled with broken pipes and hanging cables. Suffering narcosis, they also have greater difficulty making rational decisions and solving problems.

By comparison, a drinker juiced on four martinis—a snoot full for anyone—would be comparatively safer trying to drive home from the bar than a diver trying to navigate through a wreck where visibility is only about three feet and it's colder than the devil's heart.

Stories have even gone around of narced up divers who offered their regulators to a passing fish so it could take a breath.

Experienced divers say they eventually learn to cope with these impairments. But certainly divers like Danny, who were consistently going deep, had to be especially careful.

Danny Gets Cool

As time went on, Danny became more and more a diving pro. People ooh-ed and ahh-ed at his underwater exploits. His job at Ford was satisfying. He now had extra dollars just for fun. And he actually had a social life.

Then came a strange and wonderful discovery. Suddenly Danny found that he was becoming cool. In fact, he was about as cool as he had ever been in his life.

He let his hair grow long. He wore a beard. His self-confidence rose. And when he went to school reunions, he had something to talk about.

"People would say, 'Oh, you dive.' And 'You really go to those depths?' At the reunions," he said, "I could talk about how I'd done something with my life, too. I was doing something neat. I wasn't just the ordinary Danny."

Indeed, Danny was finding that he had become a somebody. He liked that feeling, and—like the rest of us—he wanted it to go on and on. And to even get bigger. And it would. Danny now was headed to the big show for divers.

By the mid-1980s, he set out to dive the *Andrea Doria*, the so-called Mount Everest of diving. Sunk in the roiling waters of the North Atlantic, the *Andrea Doria* was deep and big and it already had a reputation as a give-no-quarter assassin of divers. Danny dove the *Andrea Doria* not on one occasion, but on two—in 1986 and again in 1987. In those days, divers were still going down with the tanks filled with compressed air rather than the less dizzying gas mixtures that would come later.

When the *Andrea Doria* shoved off for its maiden voyage in 1953, it was a wonder to behold—a glorious symbol of Italy's post-war return to the seas. The *Doria* stood 10 stories above the water level. It was 637 feet long (more than two football fields) and one of the world's fastest ships. It could whoosh along at more than 26 knots, carrying a capacity of 1,200 champagne-sipping, caviar-dipping passengers and about 500 crew.

On July 25, 1956, this sleek Italian luxury liner collided with another ship, the *Stockholm*, and went down off Nantucket Island. On

By the 1970s, Danny Fader was no longer just another face in the crowd.
He was cool. He was a crack diver, having dived on wrecks around
the world, had a good job, and was having fun on weekends and vacations.

this last trip, the *Doria* was carrying 218 passengers in first class, 320 in cabin class, and 703 in tourist class.

The sinking of the *Andrea Doria* was one of the biggest news stories that summer. Newspapers were filled with aerial photos of the wounded ship, of panicked passengers, and of rescues. Television networks hired helicopters to fly their photographers out to shoot aerials of the sinking ship. Then, the film—no video in those days—had to be carried back to be developed in the studios.

Of those onboard during the accident, 1,651 were rescued and 51 died by the time the *Andrea Doria* sank 250 feet to the bottom.

Since this is a story about wreck divers, it's interesting to note that even though scuba had only been invented in the previous decade, two divers went down on the *Andrea Doria* just 28 hours after it sank.

Peter Gimbel, heir to the Gimbel's department store fortune, and Joseph Fox swam down 160 feet to the topmost part of the wreck to shoot photos for *Life* magazine.

As years passed, the *Andrea Doria* became a subaquatic icon for divers. The macho guys bubbled down, penetrated the wreck, and came back bearing wonderful souvenirs. Among the most prized were jewelry, signs, luggage, silver forks, knives and spoons, and fine Italian china dishes marked with the Italia logo.

To get into the first-class section for whatever goodies might be there, Gimbel torched a rectangular hole in the side of the ship in 1981. But cutting an entrance was only the first of the divers' problems. Once inside, they had to descend 90 very scary feet in pitch blackness.

In 1985, Bill Nagle and a team of five divers took the 10-hour ride from New York City out to the wreck aboard the dive boat *Seeker*, a 35-foot Maine Coaster. When they came back, they brought one of the greatest prizes to be taken off a sunken ship, its bell. They also managed to bring back a statue of Andrea Doria, the famed sixteenth-century Italian admiral for whom the ship was named. In order to free up the statue so it could be hoisted to the surface, the divers had to cut it off at the ankles.

The comparison of diving the *Andrea Doria* to climbing Mount Everest may be questionable. The *Andrea Doria* certainly is not the deepest wreck while Everest is the tallest mountain. Although extremely difficult to dive, it is arguably *not* the most difficult. Nor do climbers consider Everest to be the most difficult mountain to climb in the Himalayas.

But like Mount Everest, the *Andrea Doria* can be deadly. In just the last 20 years, a dozen divers have died while trying to probe the luxury liner.

The problem is that the *Andrea Doria* is very deep and dark. Since it is lying on its side, internal passageways easily confuse the divers. Strong currents steadily hammer the ship. Silt swirls everywhere. What is more, the ship is draped in huge fishing nets and everywhere are monofilament fishing lines. These lines are impossible to see and constantly threaten to entangle the divers and their gear.

Danny first arrived to dive on the ship in 1986, just one year after Nagle had pulled the bell. Now he was with the A-team of the Atlantic. Among those who signed his dive book for that charter were Gary Gentile, the renowned diver and writer, and Captain Steve Bielenda of the dive boat *Wahoo*.

It was one of those brave occasions that turned out miserably. Preparing to go, Danny upgraded all his equipment—a new Scuba Pro buoyancy compensator backpack that held two 72-cubic-foot tanks and could be inflated and deflated to adjust for proper buoyancy underwater; two new Scuba Pro regulators; and a new-style bottom timer that would tell how long he was at a particular depth. The timer was in a plastic housing that also included a depth gauge and a compass. Other equipment included a new pony bottle that could hold 15 cubic feet of air to be used in case of emergency, a special handline rope harness to hold 300 feet of nylon rope for emergency ascents, and an extra dive light, a knife, and a new dive suit liner, which is actually what keeps the diver warm.

Finally—and most expensively—Danny bought a new, top-of-the-line dry suit. The zipper on his old one had broken. As it turned out, on some practice dives before the trip, he discovered that the new super dry suit was less than advertised. In fact, it was a sieve. Instead of hermetically sealing him from the water, Danny found that wearing his new suit meant that he was constantly soaked "as though I'd been walking in a downpour." And then as an insult to the watery injury, one of the wrist seals broke open, allowing water to flood up his arm.

The dive shop where he'd bought the suit sent it off to be repaired and gave Danny a less-expensive suit for the trip. As it turned out, cheaper was better. No leaks at all.

Now properly outfitted, Danny showed up at the *Wahoo* for an extended weekend in July. Once onboard, he found himself in a muscle-flexing swirl of rampant machismo, "lots of swashbuckling guys who could carry two tanks with one hand. They all were going down on compressed air. And they had come to rape and plunder." After all, the *Andrea Doria* was in international waters. They could take anything they could jam into their goodie bags.

The *Wahoo* left New York harbor at 5 p.m. and headed out into the Atlantic where the wind was tearing off the tops of the white caps. It was a time of high anxiety. Waves were running six to eight feet. No one onboard slept. Danny could not help but think of the *Andrea Doria*'s reputation. He knew divers had died in its tar-dark passageways. He prayed the Rosary on the way out.

Prone to seasickness, Danny's stomach was doing double-flips and one-and-a-half gainers. On that first dive day, he had hardly gotten into the water when he threw up in his regulator.

He and a diver named Tom Christman slipped down the mooring line together. And then at the wreck, as often happens with deep wreck divers, each went his own way.

At 170 feet, Danny started looking around the promenade deck. He approached Gimbel's hole, looked in but decided it was too dark and dangerous for this trip. He was justifiably afraid that he might get lost.

In the process, his underwater light got tangled up in monofilament fishing line. It was an anxious moment, but he cut himself loose.

After that, Danny never dove without two diving knives—one on his leg, one at his hip.

After 15 minutes, Danny started to rise toward the surface to do his 45 minutes of decompression stops to allow his body to eliminate the nitrogen in his system. If going down had been bad, going up was worse.

At his last stops, he had to wait in the water first at 20 feet below the surface and then at 10 feet. This would not be a problem in smooth water. But that day, the North Atlantic was scratching at the sky. The waves were running 10 to 12 feet. It was all Danny could do to not be flung off the mooring line, much less keep his body at a constant depth. The current was running so strong near the surface, he said, that "I felt like a flag being flown on a flagpole."

Into the Toilet

As if that trip was not enough, Danny could not resist the idea of going back the next year. Again, he went out on the *Wahoo*. This time, the ocean proved more accommodating. On the first day, a fog enveloped the *Wahoo* cushioning it like speck inside a pearl. The waters lay out as smooth as raveled silk. And then the sun emerged. Danny found he could relax a bit.

Danny made three dives on the *Andrea Doria* on this second outing. This time he swam in through Gimbel's hole and then down the long descent. Ahead of him—or rather far, far below him—was his dive partner Jim Stewart, who knew the ship. They were guided in their descent by the ship's lines of cables and pipes. The trick was not to get snarled in them.

Down, down they went, deep into the innards of the *Andrea Doria*, where it was not just dark, but pitch black. Since the ship was laying on her side, they were following a hallway until it opened into a vast dining room. There they turned around and headed back, picking up booty as they went—glasses, bottles, broken dishes. Their plan was to meet at the end of the hallway and ascend together. But somehow, Stewart glided off while Danny was picking up glassware. When Danny looked up, Stewart was nowhere in sight.

And so Danny waited. And waited. And soon he began to worry. Had Stewart left him? He was a man whom he had met for the first time just the day before when he boarded the dive boat. Finally, Danny decided that he'd waited long enough. It was freezing cold in the guts of this ship. Too dark to see more than a few feet. And the waiting seemed interminable.

He finally caved into the realization that he would have to get out of the ship by himself. Even though he could not see it, even though he was not sure exactly where it was, he would have to swim up to the opening. And escape.

It took only a short time for Danny to discover his solo escape plan had backfired. In just minutes, he found himself not snaking his way toward the surface and its heavenly light, but he had hit a dead end inside one of the ship's bathrooms. Not only was it a shock, but this porcelain cul-de-sac struck him as unnervingly surrealistic with the toilet dangling in what might be described as midair, held aloft by just the water pipe.

Now he had no other choice but to retreat. To somehow find his way back to his starting point. Fully discouraged, he started to swim back when he saw what must have seemed like an angel's glow. It was the flicker of Stewart's dive light. Relief flooded through Danny's entire body.

But the *Andrea Doria* was not quite through with Danny. On the way back up, following Stewart, Danny ran into a skein of monofilament fishing line that tangled up in his dive light. He was stopped cold by invisible bonds. Stewart had to cut him loose.

Once back on deck, Danny spilled his story to Stewart. He cried out his sense of being lost and then found again. And Stewart, while a bit startled, stayed cool and matter of fact.

"Well, you know, Danny, I never would have left you down there."

It may have been obvious to Stewart but not to Danny.

So now in the mid-1980s Danny was hitting the big time. He was diving with the big boys where it was deep and dangerous. He had dived the *Andrea Doria*. And now, perhaps most important of all, Danny had been invited to join the famous Dave Trotter team. It would become his joy, his passion, and, ultimately, his undoing.

CHAPTER 4

The *Detroit* and The Captain

Even before they found the strongbox, David Trotter, Danny, and the rest of the team were goggle-eyed to be exploring the *Detroit*. It stood upright, almost as if it had sailed to the bottom. And almost everything was as it had been before its sinking. It was simply a wreck diver's dream.

One of the team, Jeff Moore said, "It's the best wreck I've ever been on."

But at first the divers did not know which ship they had found. That would take some detective work, which also led to the old steamer's fascinating backstory.

The tale included the ship's builder, E.B. Ward, son of a lighthouse keeper, who in an Horatio Alger rise to wealth became Detroit's first multimillionaire.

Diving the Detroit

In the world of movies, divers such as James Bond bubble down to a sunken ship and see the whole thing spread out before them. The water is so clear it could be used in an Aquafina commercial. They swim through inside passageways with plenty of light. Silt never rises from the bottom. Debris, knocked loose by the divers' bubbles, never falls from above. And in this liquid paradise, they rarely seem worried about anything except the occasional bad-tempered shark or bad guys with spear guns.

The hero is bare chested and the heroine wears a barely adequate bikini, her mermaid hair flowing. One tank of air is all they need to stay down for what seems like hours. And the water is always warm, warm enough that divers' teeth never chatter, warm enough to think about sex. "Ahh, 007 … " followed bubbles and more bubbles.

Get that picture out of your mind. Real life wreck diving—at least in the Great Lakes—is nothing like that.

Real divers go down in dry suits that make them look like they've joined a Gumby group. The men look like Gumby, the women look like Gumby. You might fear for the continuation of the human race if we all dressed like that. Who could tell which sex was which? Not to mention that any Gumby suit pretty much hermetically seals away anything that might help perpetuate the species.

And when it comes to seeing a sunken ship, things get even more complicated. Not to repeat, but underwater it's very cold and very dark at 200 feet.

And the silt can rise and swirl like a Gobi Desert storm. Because of some biological changes—notably the arrival of zebra mussels that filter the water—underwater visibility in the Great Lakes has improved since 1994. But in that year, Trotter's divers were never able to actually see the *Detroit* as a whole. In fact, it was hard to even get a distinct picture of individual parts.

Typical visibility was 3 to 4 feet in the mid-1990s. On good days, it might get to 6 feet. In 2006, Trotter went back to take a look when the lake waters were much clearer. He could see 20, even 25 feet thanks to the water-filtering zebra mussels that had hitchhiked in from the Atlantic.

"So that's what it looks like," Trotter said. "In 1994, I was never able to see the whole radius of even one of the paddle wheels." That radius was about 6 feet.

In 1994 the divers could not get an overview. They had to examine the ship up close and through the narrow scope of their diving masks. It might be compared to trying to describe the proverbial camel, while staring from six inches with one eye, through a toilet-paper tube.

So here's the side-wheel steamer *Detroit*. It is 157 feet long and over 23 feet wide. It is full of detail—engine, boiler, a collapsed smokestack, cabins, anchors, dishes, pilot's wheel, and so on. As a result, the divers could not just slide down the mooring line, take a swim along the deck, and be done with it. To really examine this wreck, they had to go down again and again, each time for only 15 or 20 minutes, to find what could be found and learn what they could learn about some small aspect of the ship.

One by one, Danny and the other divers brought back droplets of information. A walking beam on top. Two anchors hang here on the bow. The boiler is in perfect condition. Davits—frames to hang lifeboats on—are at the stern. They checked under the hatches. Lumped coal under the front hatch. Mush, probably a cargo of wheat, under the second.

Diver Rudy Whitworth, the methodical engineer, interviewed each diver as he came up. Whitworth was experienced at this; he had got-

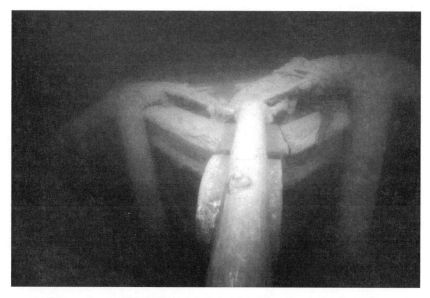

Two anchors still hanging on either side of the steering pole on the
steamer *Detroit* in 1994. Photo courtesy of David Trotter Collection.

ten his technique down cold. Like quizzing someone about last night's
dream, Whitworth did it as soon as they got out of the water, before
they forgot the details. And then he made drawings of their reports
on a big sheet of plastic. The divers were essentially surveyors sent
down to map a ship.

Here are the locations of the davits, they reported. The smokestack. The debris on deck. He noted that the promenade deck was
supported by round posts. They were 15 feet apart. Everything was
penned onto the ever-more-detailed map. The covers had fallen off
the paddle wheels. The bow had a steering pole with a ball on the end,
sticking up from the bow so the captain could line up navigational
points on land. The team was amazed that a fragile extension like the
steering pole could still be attached after almost a century and a half.

They also brought back information on what was scattered alongside the ship. Crockery and dishes off the starboard bow. A steel
bucket off the starboard bow, too. A rusted handcart.

This mapping not only added to their knowledge, but also to their
safety. Over time, the divers would get an ever-more clear sense of
what they could expect to find on the bottom. Most importantly, they
discovered where the ship had been bashed on the starboard side,
just in front of the paddlewheel. Clearly that was the cause of the
sinking.

In May 1854, the steamer *Detroit* was upbound, headed north on Lake Huron from Detroit to Sault Ste. Marie where locks were being built to join the lower lakes to Lake Superior. The *Detroit* was steaming its way across the mouth of Saginaw Bay in a slumgullion fog when the bark *Nucleus*, sailing blind, rammed into it.

Ship collisions were fairly common in those days. No radar. No GPS. And no established separation of shipping lanes. The captains all followed the same narrow path—the shortest distance between two ports—whether upbound or downbound. Time was money, so they were in a hurry to snag the greatest profit possible.

In the very early days of the nineteenth century, a single shipping lane presented few problems. But once the Erie Canal opened in 1825, the numbers of ships grew exponentially on the lakes, and with the increased numbers came the increased possibility of mid-water crashes.

Imagine, for a moment, a single-lane road where semis are rolling in both directions, all of them with tight schedules to meet. No flagman stands out there with a SLOW sign to direct which truck should stay in the lane and which should divert a bit. The only way one driver can avoid another is if he sees him in time to swerve. And he has to hope that the other driver does not swerve in the same direction. Now factor in a dense fog where sounds and distances are distorted. The crews of the *Nucleus* and *Detroit* never realized they were on a collision course until the final seconds. By then it was too late.

The crash left the *Nucleus* largely unharmed. On the *Detroit*, it was a different matter. One man's leg was broken. As it turned out, the *Detroit* was towing a second ship laden with cargo, a so-called consort. So the *Detroit*'s crew and passengers were able to transfer to the consort, which could be sailed in a pinch. Meanwhile, Lake Huron's dark waters rushed past the caved in boards of the *Detroit*'s bow. Nothing could staunch it. Within an hour, the side-wheel steamer tilted nose-down into the water and then slipped below the surface.

Of course, the Trotter team initially did not know what ship they had found. All they could do was report whatever clues they could find. A crushed section was in the starboard bow, that was a clue. So was the ship's bell.

The bell was made of nickel alloy, as shiny as the day it was cast. Jeff Moore clambered back onboard the *Obsession* to announce that the clapper still moved. He actually rang the bell underwater. What's more, he discovered some raised letters on the surface: "New York 1844." And for a while, the team thought that "New York" was the name of their mystery ship.

It's not easy to identify a camel while looking through a toilet-paper tube. They later learned that no ship named "New York" had been lost in that area.

Then on one dive Werner Wahl, known as the Doc, peered around the back side of the bell. He found two words: "Novelty Works." But when the Doc clambered back on deck, nobody believed him.

"Come on, Doc," they teased. "You must have been narced out of your mind. Novelty? I don't think so. It must have said Nautical."

A later dive proved the Doc was right.

Wahl had an in-law in New York City, and he asked the New Yorker to do some checking at the public library. His relative reported that the bell must have been cast at the Novelty Iron Works, which had been located at the foot of 12th Street on the East River.

The company, which sounded like it ought to be in the carnival business, in fact took its name from America's first-ever coal-burning river steamer. The company had built the boilers and engines for the *Novelty* in 1836.

Oddly—and Trotter's crew is often a little stunned by such coincidences—the *Novelty* also sank after a collision in 1854. In May, it was rammed by a steamer called the *Canadian* in Lake Ontario.

Even with these details, the team seemed no closer to identifying the wreck.

At the same time, Trotter sent details about the ship to his long-time friend Charles Feltner, one of the most eminent marine historians of the Great Lakes. Just as Trotter had turned the finding of ships into an art form, Feltner—an avid researcher—had done the same with identifying them.

Feltner, who has learned to tap into literally thousands of resources, relies heavily on newspaper accounts and especially on records of enrollment—that is, the official ship documentation. Over time, he has transcribed the key information from some 29,000 of these documents. So now his knowledge is both extensive and detailed about almost every ship that plied the lakes during the latter three-quarters of the nineteenth century.

Feltner said he examined the details of the *Detroit* and was able to work out the kind of construction, the type of propulsion, that it was in the steamer lane of Lake Huron, and its approximate age. With these aspects in hand, he narrowed the list down to six steamers that fit the identifying characteristics.

"It's almost a Sherlock Holmes kind of game," Feltner said. "You have to know an enormous number of details." At that point, he proceeded to research each of these six finalists in detail.

A solid clue to the identity of the steamer *Detroit* came from this image on a plate found at the wreck. Photo courtesy of David Trotter Collection.

At that point, Trotter still had not told Feltner the exact location of the ship.

When the two men spoke again, Feltner said, "To me it is obvious. It must be the *Detroit*." And then, with a certain Holmesian elan, Feltner gave Trotter the loran numbers for the *Detroit*'s location.

"Jesus Christ," Trotter said, "you came within half a mile."

Confirming Feltner's conclusions, the divers went on to discover further evidence that their pretty little steamer was, in fact, the *Detroit*. Lying in the mud near the bow, they found what appeared to be the captain's dishes. A give-away clue was painted on them.

Each dish had a picture of a side-wheel steamer that looked very much like the one they were exploring. Below the picture were the words "E.B. & S. Ward's Steamers," but no ship name. On the bottom of the plates were more words: "Imported by Jenness & Mather, Detroit;" and on others: "Mayer's Real Ironstone, Office, Pearl Street, New York, Prize Medal, August 1851." The puzzle-solving clue was "E.B. & S. Ward's Steamers."

With the help of some friendly researchers, they reconfirmed Feltner's conclusion that in 1854 a side-wheel steamer owned by E.B. Ward did go down in Saginaw Bay. The damage near the bow lined up exactly with reports of the ramming accident. It was the *Detroit*.

Documents vary as to when the ship was actually built, either in 1844 or 1846, but no question remains as to the year it went down—1854.

Captain Ward

Eber Brock Ward looked like his name. Solid, square-jawed, and sturdy enough to have been chopped out of one of the thousands of white pine trees he eventually owned.

As solid as he was, Ward was a man of great passion, strong opinions, a memorable temper, and almost prescient business sense. Newspapers described him as "the most eminent business man in the Northwest" (now considered the upper Midwest).

Everyone called him Captain. Even the newspapers referred to him as "Captain Ward." It was not some unearned honorary title like, say, Kentucky Colonel. He had spent many years as a captain on the steamboats of the Great Lakes.

Volatile as nitro, nervous energy seemed to bubble out of his body, often in surprising ways. New acquaintances were startled to discover that he had a peculiar tic where his eyes would squint alternately: left, right, left, right. And almost unconsciously while in the midst of a conversation, Ward would reach into his pocket, pull out a handful of silver coins, and start pouring them back and forth from one palm to the other making little, tinkling waterfalls.

Another oddity was that Ward was no conventional churchgoer. He was a spiritualist. He believed in consulting mediums. Like everything else in his life, he was proud of it and more than willing to talk about making connections with the spirit world. In fact, Ward said that he frequently sought clairvoyant guidance on business transactions.

Newspapers reported that Ward did not "chew, smoke, drink, or gamble." He was a Republican in the Abraham Lincoln–sense of the term and unflinchingly attacked the institution of slavery. In 1860 Ward, who by this time was big into iron mining and steel mills, offered to put his entire iron supply at the government's disposal.

"Rather than to have the constitution altered to favor slavery and corruption," he wrote, "I would make my iron an unconditional contribution to the cause of freedom."

Ward started as the son of a lighthouse keeper. At the age of 13, when most kids today are in the eighth grade, he hired on as a cabin boy. His uncle Samuel, a prominent businessman in Newport, Michigan (later renamed Marine City), soon recognized the lad's high energy and intelligence and hired him as a clerk for his company that built sailing schooners.

Eber Ward was the owner and builder of the steamship *Detroit* that was lost in Lake Huron. Starting as a cabin boy and quickly working his way up to ship captain, he soon was a shipbuilder and entrepreneur in steel making and lumber mills, becoming Detroit's first multimillionaire. Courtesy of the Burton Historical Collection, Detroit Public Library.

Of the ships Samuel built, perhaps the most famous was the *St. Clair*, which was launched in 1824. The next year, the 30-ton schooner would be the first to travel from the Great Lakes through the Erie Canal and all the way to the Atlantic Ocean.

The opening of the Erie Canal in 1825 marked the beginning of the Golden Age of ships in the Great Lakes that would last into the next century. Roads were rough and slow. Snow drifted over them in winter and they were knee-deep in muddy ruts in spring and fall. They were plagued by mosquitoes in summer as well as highwaymen and, sometimes, marauding Indians in any season. Railroad lines were still being built.

The best and easiest way to get from the East Coast to the burgeoning Midwest and West was by water. European immigrants arriving in New York caught ships headed toward promised lands. They came by the thousands—Irish escaping the famine, German farmers, Welsh miners, British adventurers, Swedes, Finns, Norwegians, and Icelanders looking for cheap lands to farm and good solid pay in lumber mills or copper mines. The famous editor Horace Greeley said, "Go West, young man." And they did. Often the first leg of a trip west was through the Great Lakes.

Lakeside hamlets and villages grew up to be cities like Cleveland, Buffalo, Detroit, Milwaukee, and Chicago. In-between places grew, too. Islands became stopping points for the steamships, where locals made big profits selling lumber to fuel the engines and meting out food and beverage to passengers.

If people were migrating west, the fruits of the western lands were moving back east. No deadheading or loss of profits for ship owners. On return trips, the ships carried wheat, corn, barley, iron ore, limestone, copper, and fresh lake trout and white fish back to the eastern markets.

Cruise ships plied the Great Lakes, especially in summer when the cities stank of garbage and pestilence. The clean, bracing air of the lakes drew people from the East and all of the Midwest. In the later part of the century, hotels and vacation homes sprouted all along the lakes. The still-famous Grand Hotel was built on Mackinac Island. Regal gentlemen with ladies in platter-sized hats lolled around the fancy restaurants and swimming pool at the Hotel Victory at Put-In-Bay on Lake Erie's South Bass Island. On Lake Michigan, summer people came to spend a week or even months everywhere up the eastern shore—from the Indiana border to Harbor Springs and on the western shore, especially on Wisconsin's Door Peninsula.

On a single day, a person could stand at Point Aux Barques at the tip of Michigan's thumb of land that points up into Lake Huron or perhaps by the lighthouse on Lake Michigan's South Manitou Island and watch while 100 or more ships passed by.

Energetic and smart, young Ward rose quickly through the ranks. By 1833 he and his uncle were building boats together as partners. Their company was E.B. & S. Ward's Steamers and their home base Marine City, which would for a time become one of the important shipbuilding centers on the Great Lakes.

Ward soon convinced his uncle that the future lay not in wind-powered schooners but in side-wheel steamers. With the opening of the Erie Canal and the Great Lakes experiencing huge growth in shipping, the steamers could not only go against the wind but they were extremely maneuverable in the small, crowded ports. The schooners were not.

In the spring of 1840, Samuel Ward's company built the *Huron*, its first steamship. Eber Ward was the captain. At age of 29, he'd also invested $1,000 of his own money in the ship. He had ambition. The young Ward eventually would captain several boats.

Uncle and nephew were at the right place with the right product at the right time. Shipping was booming. On the Great Lakes, ships could hardly be built and launched fast enough. As builders of ships, the Wards made themselves millionaires.

Among the ships they constructed were the *General Harrison*, the *Champion*, the *Samuel Ward*, the *Pearl*, the *Atlantic*, the *B.F. Wade*, the *Montgomery*, the *Pacific Ocean*, the *Caspian*, the *Planet*, the *Arctic*, and, of course, the *Detroit*. All these, plus a number of smaller ships.

Later, ships and shipbuilding would change. Within a few decades, steamships would be passing into history and iron-sided, propeller-driven ships—actually called propellers at the time—would be the latest, best thing. With the Kirby brothers, Ward also built iron ships including the *E.B. Ward, Jr.*, the *Sport*, and the *Queen of the Lakes*.

It comes as little surprise that newspapers of the era dubbed him "The King of the Lakes." You can almost hear the waterfall of Ward's coins, splashing from one palm to the other.

Of course, as the wreck divers now confirm every year, the business of sailing ships on the Great Lakes could be very dicey. Ships ran chockablock and the shipping lanes were jammed.

No shipping regulations existed in those days. Ships collided. They went down in foul weather. Constantly pressed to move more people and more goods faster, the captains—who often had no formal training—took dangerous chances. They sailed into storms, did not hesitate in fogs, and pressed the sailing season as far into winter as was sensible—and then pushed it further.

At the docks, profit-hungry shipowners and captains often overloaded cargo and did not properly tie down the loads. In heavy waves, ships would just tip over and sink. And fire was a huge danger, especially on wooden ships. As a result, quite a number of Eber Ward's ships went to the bottom.

An enterprising reporter for the *Detroit Tribune* in 1860 gathered a list of Eber Ward's shipping and cargo losses. They included the *Gazelle* in Lake Superior (1860, $40,000); the *Arctic* in Lake Superior (1860, $16,000); the schooner *Wyandotte* ashore (1856, $10,000); the *Detroit* in Lake Huron ($10,000); the *E.K. Collins* in the Detroit River (1854, $100,000 and the loss of 21 lives); the *St. Louis* in Lake Erie (1852, $15,000); the *Caspian* at Cleveland (1852, $80,000); and the *Atlantic* in Lake Erie (1852, $75,000).

To get a sense of those losses, you can figure that the value of an 1860 American dollar was worth about 23 times today's dollar in buying power. So the loss of the *Atlantic*, for example, would have been about $1,725,000.

Blink, blink, you can almost see Ward's eyes. Blink, blink. Left, right, left, right.

Like the steamer *Detroit*, another rather significant Ward ship went down in Saginaw Bay, Michigan, in 1873. It was the *Ocean*, a side-wheel steamer originally constructed in 1850. Twelve years later, it was converted into a barge. This ship rates a footnote in history because its walking beam was made from the first iron bar ever to be smelted (February 10, 1848) from ore culled from the Upper Peninsula.

Unfortunately, Ward was self-insured on all of these ships. So he took a financial beating. As it turned out, Ward was not busy in just the shipping business. By 1850, he already was investing in land, mostly timberland, as well as a mill, docks, a warehouse, and store in Forestville, Michigan. But he also bought forestland at Ludington and elsewhere in Michigan's Upper and Lower Peninsulas

Along the way, Ward married the niece of Uncle Samuel's wife Betsey. Her name was Mary McQueen. They had eight children—five sons and three daughters. This marriage turned out to be a financial dividend for Eber Ward. When Samuel died in 1855, Ward was able, through the will, to first manage and then grab up much of his uncle's property. But that was just the beginning for Eber Ward. Over the next 20 years, he would start to make really big money.

Just as he had predicted the coming of the steamships, he recognized when their era was over. Propeller ships were taking over. But more important, the railroads (not ships) were the next big thing. So he largely bailed out of shipping, grabbed up his profits, and moved to Detroit in 1855 where he built a mansion on some five acres of ground at Fort and 18th streets.

For locals, one fascinating aspect of Ward's realm on Fort Street was that he had a dozen greenhouses where he raised grapes. And not just any grapes—he had 60 varieties of grapes. He often made gifts of grapes to Detroit's poor. One can only imagine a scene on the street. "Oh Captain, you gotta dime?" "No, but here, have some of these nice grapes."

In time, Ward seemed to have a finger in every financially profitable pie. Since railroads were the big new thing in transportation, he became head of the Burlington & Iowa Railroad. And of the Burlington & Southwestern Railroad. And president of the Flint & Marquette Railroad. He owned iron mines and rolling mills in North Chicago, Illinois; Wyandotte, Michigan; and Bay View, Wisconsin. It was an Eber Brock Ward mill that turned out the first Bessemer steel ever produced in the United States. He had an iron works in Milwaukee with 4,000 employees.

His pinelands at Marathon, Wisconsin, totaled 15,000 acres. And he had a corundum mine in North Carolina, a product used for polishing glass. When silver was discovered on tiny Silver Islet in Lake Superior at Thunder Bay, Ontario, he bought the island. Just about everything he touched turned to gold except for a few mining operations out west—copper in the Arizona Territory, silver in Utah, and lead in Missouri.

Along the way, his wife Mary divorced him. He soon married Catherine Lyon, whom newspapers described as a great beauty with "yellow hair and limpid eyes." They had two children—Clara and Eber Brock Ward Jr.

The captain died suddenly on January 2, 1875. Newspapers reported that he was in his office by Detroit's waterfront when he got a summons to be a witness in a diamond drill suit in Superior Court. He pulled on his heavy coat, wrapped a scarf around his neck, and walked downtown. As was his style, he strode along at a purposeful pace. But then, in front of E.K. Robert's banking office on the west side of Griswold near Jefferson Avenue, he suddenly threw up his hands and fell to the pavement. Three minutes later, he was dead. The coroner ruled it was apoplexy, or a stroke.

Estimates of his fortune when he died ranged from $10 to $30 million, or as much as $5.1 billion in today's dollars. Most of it would go to Catherine and their two children, E.B. Jr. and Clara. The children, he said in his will, should get "liberal support and education."

At that point, the Ward name might have dropped from the public's consciousness and the newspaper pages. But daughter Clara, a blonde beauty like her mother, quickly proved to be front-page grist for the gossip mongers.

Backed by her immense inheritance, Clara moved to Europe and there she cut a libertine swath scandalizing newspaper readers on two continents.

Starting soon after she graduated from a convent high school in England, Clara—almost on a whim—married a Belgian count. But the Michigan heiress soon dropped him for a Hungarian gypsy violin player. This dalliance lasted for several years until she traded in the gypsy for a good-looking Italian station master. Last, she set up house with an Italian orchestra director. On each, she lavished money and gifts.

Newspapers had a field day from Detroit to New York and from London and Paris to Cairo.

Once again, one can almost imagine the old captain—a man who had started as a cabin boy at age 13—blinking madly in frustration. Left eye, right eye, left eye, right eye.

CHAPTER 5

Lord of the Wreck Hunters

In 1983, just about the time that Danny Fader was coming into his own as a deep wreck diver, David Trotter was hitting full stride as a premier wreck hunter. He had been finding virgin wrecks left and right going back to the late 1970s.

If the likes of John Steele, Paul Ehorn, and Kent Bellrichard were the pioneers in the Great Lakes, Trotter had turned wreck finding into a fine art. In those early days when he motored out onto Lake Huron with his side-scan sonar grinding out paper prints, he literally expected to discover a new wreck almost every weekend. It almost seemed like the long-silent underwater wrecks were just waiting for Trotter so they could step out onto the stage of his side-scan sonar. The lakes had seen nothing like him.

So when Trotter asked Danny to join his team, the younger diver knew he had arrived. Now Danny would be playing in the majors. He had dived the *Andrea Doria* three times, the so-called Everest of wreck dives, and now he was going to be part of one of the best wreck-hunting, wreck-diving teams in the Great Lakes.

Other divers may still have to hire charter boats and dive on wrecks where hundreds of divers had preceded them. But not Danny. Not anymore. Now he would be a true wreck hunter, not just another diver but a discoverer of maritime history. When long-lost ships were found, he would be among the first to actually see and touch them. Yes, joining Dave Trotter's team was a big deal.

When Danny arrived in 1986, David Trotter was a lanky 6-foot-2, 45 year old with a thick crop of brown hair and an engagingly shy grin. His was not a looming presence, but one of quiet assurance. That's the way he wanted it. He would have liked to be thought of as easygoing, as laidback. But even a casual acquaintance could recognize that Trotter had too many thought trains sizzling around on his brain tracks to be called easygoing.

Quietly measured might be a better description. He never seemed to be ruffled. His style was one of supreme, but not showy confidence. I remember several trips where his dive boat was being banged about by three-, four-, and five-foot waves. Everyone onboard was grabbing at something to hold onto. Trotter just stood on the aft deck, quietly talking, with his hands in his pockets. His was a voice that never blared. And just as he might double-check a row of finance numbers, he was careful with his actions—every spoken sentence, every word, every move.

He could be just one of the guys. He could slap backs, tell jokes, josh with his dive buddies. They could get close to David, just not too close. He was careful whom he invited onboard. He picked divers whom he considered genuinely good people, with an eye for who would blend with the group. Who would get along. Who had the diving skills.

Some on his team called Trotter "the old man," even though he was not that old. He was in many ways a father figure. Certainly he had financed the operation. He owned the boat, was its captain. He had put up tens of thousands of dollars to buy the side-scan sonar and other equipment.

The way finances worked on the *Obsession* was that all the divers, including Trotter himself, equally divided the expenses for gas and oil for the boat and for the compressed air, oxygen, and helium gases they used in diving. For the team it was an inexpensive way to do a lot of wreck diving. Trotter shouldered the rest of the expenses himself.

But it was more than just dollars. The team deferred to Trotter out of respect. They trusted him. They knew he had earned his chevrons as a diver and wreck hunter.

Also they respected the fact that Trotter was his own man. He followed his personal dream. It was a dream of discovery that they came to share. If other people didn't understand it, then let them sit on shore.

The Hat

For all his soft-spoken, conservative ways, if one element of his attire bespoke a sense of go-to-hell flamboyance, it was his hat. Almost every wreck diver in the Great Lakes who could tell a capstan cover from a dead eye knew about Trotter's hat.

It was a black Greek fisherman's hat with a snappy short brim and a little woven braid on the band. He started wearing it in the mid-1990s. To Trotter's mind, it bespoke history and ships and the inland seas. It became his signature. A tattoo could hardly have seemed more permanent. He wore it all the time and absolutely everywhere. On the boat, he'd jam it down tight so it would not blow off into the lake. But he also wore it where the nearest water simply ran through pipes—in local libraries at his video presentations about wreck discoveries, in the mall, in the grocery store, and sitting around the house reading the newspaper or watching television. He has, however, denied sleeping in it.

Deep wreck diving does have real dangers. And to be sure, Trotter has been in and out of some dicey underwater situations. Outside observers might disagree, but he denies being a risk-taker and says he never has been one. Even as a child he said, "I was probably more risk averse."

While no cowboy, Trotter does exude a strong sense of adventure, an enthusiasm for discovery. His sense of personal independence and his keen eye of social interplay—the sense that makes his team jell—also began quite early.

Like Danny Fader, Trotter's family suffered the lingering poverty brought on by the Great Depression.

"We were kind of poor," he said. "But then everybody else was, too."

His dad, Bill, was a loan officer who moved often with his company. So, like gypsies, he, his wife, Nona, young David, and his younger daughter Terrie seemed to pack up and move every few years. David was brought up like an army brat, just without the military trappings. And like an army brat, he learned to adapt.

Trotter was born in Ottumwa, Iowa. The family stayed there for five years and then moved to New Orleans; then when he was about age 12 they shuffled off to Toledo and then two years after that to Bloomington, Minnesota. And then, with just a year left in high school, the family moved to Decatur, Georgia. Trotter finished his senior year there.

Of necessity, kids who are moved constantly learn some special skills and how to harden their sensibilities. Suddenly they find that the familiar is gone. School, classes, teachers, friends, the local soda shop, movie theater, everything—gone.

Now, with a catch in the throat, they must face a new school, strange teachers, kids who may or may not be friends, learning what these kids think is cool and what isn't, even adopting new speech patterns. In Minnesota, no one said "Y'all," and in Georgia no one ever called a drinking fountain a "bubbler." In high school, it's all about fitting in. So gypsy kids learn to fit in, knowing if they do not, they will be left out.

They adapt in other ways. As much as they yearn for a sense of permanence, they come to distrust it. Deep down, they know another move always lies ahead. And then another and another. They learn to stand back a bit from emotional investment in friends and others. It's just too painful to lose very close friends.

On the other hand, many learn to be independent at an early age. The new and different do not intimidate them. They have learned to handle it. Some even come to crave it. They look forward to new beginnings and new discoveries and, yes, new adventures.

Like most boys, Trotter loved the outdoors, and that love never left him. As a boy in New Orleans, he and his buddies would go down to the canals to catch crawdads. "We'd put bacon in a net or maybe old fish heads. And when the crawdads crawled in, we'd yank up the net."

He remembered doing a lot of fishing later in the Mississippi River. "Not that I was adept at it. I'd catch carp and catfish." As a teenager, he would go out with his dad into the Minnesota fields with a 16-gauge shotgun to hunt pheasant.

Trotter said that of his two parents, "I connected best with my dad." In fact, his relationship with his father was in some ways similar to Danny's. Both fathers worked hard, lived decently, and the boys respected them. But at home, these men were often either missing or emotionally distant.

"We were not very close," Trotter has said, struggling a bit to show the deep respect he still held for his father. "He always had to work hard and watch a penny very carefully. But he grew up in hard times. I am not sure he had a good father-figure to work with," Trotter said, describing his grandfather who drank too much and died when his dad was only nine.

"He always had something for us for Christmas. We always had a tree. And it always had to be very, very beautiful."

If Trotter had moved a lot as a child, once he left high school he started caroming like a pool ball on a multi-bank shot. He was the Ricochet Kid while working his way through college for his undergraduate degree between 1959 and 1966, and then afterward. He bounced from place to place, but along the way picked up ever-more responsible jobs. Starting with jobs like truck driving for the Atlanta water works and selling cookware door-to-door, he moved up to being a loan officer. For a period of seven years, Trotter moved so often he could barely stock his refrigerator before repacking his stuff. In some places, he stayed only for a matter of months; settling in for a year or two was a rarity.

In Georgia, he went from the town of Young Harris to Atlanta to Athens (where he completed his college degree) to Albany to Atlanta again to Rome and back to Atlanta again, and then on to Baton Rouge,

Louisiana. Then, at age 25, he hired on with Ford Credit, a subsidiary of Ford Motor Company, which sent him to Fayetteville, North Carolina. Soon thereafter, he transferred to Ford headquarters outside Detroit. That's where he finally stuck, eventually reaching the level of supervisor of risk management. Along the way two important things happened.

Wedding Bells and Bubbles

Some time after Trotter turned 19, a friend hooked him up with a blind date for a hayride. The girl was a dark-eyed charmer with a saucy smile and an appealing goodness about her. Her name was Ann Michele Grayson, but everyone called her Mickey. They connected. But anything else would have to wait. She was only 16 and still in high school. And Mickey's parents had plans for her future that did not include David Trotter.

So David and Mickey waited three and a half interminable years. And then, that was enough. She had turned 19. They got married in 1963, despite protests from her parents and relatives. She went on to become a grade school teacher and helped support Trotter's diving jones both with money and, occasionally, as a crew member. Trotter, the gypsy, had finally found a true friend who would stay with him forever.

The second important thing in Trotter's early life came a year after the wedding. While the couple was living in a second-story flat in Rome, Georgia, Trotter signed up for his first scuba course. Years earlier, he had read Jacques Cousteau's *The Silent World* and was intrigued.

Before too many classes passed, he fell in love with diving. It's unlikely that either he or Mickey recognized it at the time, but this handful of classes would change his life forever.

Scuba, in those days, was considered quite daring. It had been invented less than 20 years before. And the course, Trotter remembered, was set up for machos. This was no surprise. The hugely popular TV series *Sea Hunt* had been on the air only a few years before, with Lloyd Bridges playing hero Mike Nelson with a knife strapped to his leg. The class was all guys, Trotter remembered. And after only four classes, the instructor said, "Let's go dive."

"We went down to Morrison Springs [near Dothan], Alabama, and got in late on Saturday evening," he remembered. At the time, Trotter was working five and a half days a week. He had to squeeze in that dive trip.

David and Mickey Trotter at the Bay Area Divers Shipwrecks and Scuba convention in Sandusky, Ohio, in 2005. Courtesy of the David Trotter Collection.

At the springs, he vividly recalled, "There was this sign. It said: 'Dive Safely!' And it gave the number of divers who had died in that spring."

"I remember thinking, 'This is not good.'" And to make it even scarier, they learned that the two local divers were preparing to go after a fellow diver who had not come back. "Definitely not a good situation."

But they dove on Sunday anyway. Thrilled, they bubbled down to about 50 feet (which seemed plenty deep for the beginners) and probed into the opening for a spring. They even ducked inside an underwater chasm. Trotter was captivated. Then, before he could complete the course, Trotter got a job offer in Atlanta and had to leave town. He never did finish the basic scuba course. Nor did he get his C card, the certification that allows divers to get compressed air for their tanks. But ever of an independent mind, that did not stop Trotter from diving.

For many years afterward, if anyone asked for a C card, which was needed to get air for his tanks or to buy equipment, he would just show Mickey's card. She had taken the full course a couple of years later. Ten years would pass before Trotter actually bothered to get a C card.

No worries. His approach—one that he carries to this day—is: Just figure out how to do something and then go out and do it. A piece of paper and a whole bunch of rules don't necessarily make it safer. Or better. Or smarter.

Years later, he would use that same learn-it-and-do-it approach when he began using the mixed gases for deep diving. Mixed gases were initially something that almost every dive instructor and dive magazine decried as an invitation to death. But Trotter and a small number of others simply went ahead. Trotter might be called a self-made underwater man.

That said, he did value diver training courses. The reason he finally picked up his C card was so that he could then take the course to qualify as a dive instructor. For more than a decade, he taught scores of new divers who were members of the Ford Seahorses, the company's dive club.

As for diving wrecks, Trotter started diving on wrecks the way most divers do in the Great Lakes. He went on charters and with friends. His first wreck dive was on the *Cedarville*, a huge freighter that went down in the Mackinac Straits. It was here he was jolted by his first lesson in not blabbing about his discoveries.

It was not long before he had bought a boat of his own. In 1976, he bought a 22-foot Chieftain made by Starcraft. It had a large cabin and a 140-horsepower inboard engine.

Solo Sensibility

Earlier that same year, Trotter motored out in a 19-foot open boat owned by Larry Coplin, a fellow diver. At that time, they would often do two dives in a day. A small air compressor hung off the back of the boat so they could refill their scuba tanks. The plan was to dive on the *Viator*, a Norwegian steamer that went down off Alpena, Michigan, in 1935.

"We were out there, just the two of us," Trotter remembered with a grin and a shake of his head. "And naïve me, I was thinking: 'How are both of us going to make this dive together?' Of course, I had been steeped in the idea of diving buddies."

At that moment, Coplin turned to him and said, "We want someone in the boat at all times. So I'll dive first and then you dive."

"That," said Trotter, "was when I found out about solo diving. The idea caught me by surprise. The *Viator* was deep—at 160 or 170 feet—and the visibility was lousy. Psychologically, that first solo dive was very unnerving at first."

The dive community still abhors the idea of going down without a dive buddy. It is just not done. Safety-conscious divers might compare it to jumping out of an airplane without a reserve parachute.

Over the years Trotter and many veteran wreck divers, while not totally disregarding the idea of dive buddies, have developed some strong alternative beliefs. They are wary of a certain laxness in thinking that comes when diving with buddies. Also, buddy diving presents some real hazards of its own.

About the mental laxness, Trotter believes that a diver tends be less careful if he thinks someone is always there to back him up. Maybe he won't be as diligent checking his gear. Maybe he does not fix or replace gear that has failed. Maybe he does not take a backup tank and regulator when he should. Maybe he'll take risks he should not.

When you dive alone, you have a more rigorous mentality, Trotter contends. You must because no one will be there to save you.

Also, when going deep, divers have long decompression times. A dive on a ship might last only 15 or 20 minutes, but the time hanging from the mooring line while the nitrogen dissipates could be up to an hour or more. Trying to buddy-breathe or share air from a single tank and regulator might kill both divers. Especially if they are breathing hard because of exertion or the panic in an emergency situation.

Too Near Death

Trotter distinctly remembers trying to save a young dive buddy while they were exploring the bow section of a ship called the *Morrell*, which Trotter and Coplin had discovered in 1979. The young man was Rick Boelsler, son of Walter Boelsler who was a longtime friend of Trotter's and a fellow officer in the Ford Seahorses Dive Club.

The two divers slipped down 165 feet of mooring line to the *Morrell*'s deck and then made a 250-foot long swim to where the ship had broken in two. Trotter took some pictures. By this time, 15 minutes had passed. So he started looking for Rick only to discover the young diver well below him, about halfway down the side of the ship at 180 feet. Just as he spotted Rick, the diver—who had been lagging—drew a gloved finger across his throat. He was out of air.

Trotter kicked hard and swam down to Rick with his mind screaming, "God! I can't let Walt's son die."

Following standard procedure, Trotter grabbed Rick's harness, pulled the diver around so he faced him, and then, using Trotter's small air bottle, jammed a regulator into Rick's mouth.

In the midst of this flurry of adrenalin-pumping excitement, the level of nitrogen narcosis was jumping up by the second.

Trotter started to pull Rick toward the surface. It was a struggle, more than it should have been. Even though the diver could now breathe, he was not helping, not even kicking his feet. For Trotter it was like trying to haul up a bag of rocks. Anxiety stacked on anxiety in Trotter's nitrogen-addled mind. Could they make it up? Would they have enough air for the decompression stops? Both divers were burning through their air supplies.

At 50 feet, Trotter was shocked to see the diver draw his hand across his throat. He was out of air. Again. It seemed impossible.

Now Trotter realized with a jolt, "There is no fucking way I can buddy breathe with him."

"There was only one thing to do. Keep going up. People do not drown on the surface."

Trotter's flippers thrashed below them and the two divers rose to the open air. They had come up from 180 feet in less than three minutes. Too fast. Far too fast after 15 minutes on the bottom. This was more than a flirtation with the bends. It was likely to kill them or leave them paralyzed for life.

When they hit the surface, Trotter looked closely at Rick and saw that his head had lolled back, his eyes were closed, and blood was seeping out of his nose into the mask.

"Goddamn, he's embolized," Trotter thought.

To embolize is when a diver makes a too-quick return to the surface while holding his breath. The lungs over expand and rip, the released air rushing into the blood stream. Then all-too quickly these air bubbles move throughout the body and to the brain. With no blood flow to the brain, life stops.

Trotter now had to make a hard decision. The boat had only one bottle of pure oxygen, the one thing that might curtail the effects of the bends. Trotter decided that Rick should get it. A third diver, John Dulzo, who was on the boat, hauled the young man onboard.

Trotter was left with one option—stay in the water and hope that he did not end up a paraplegic. For the next two and a half hours, he lay floating in the water, trying not to move at all. If you move, he said, the blood starts to bubble. It's like shaking a can of pop. Bubbles form and disaster follows. So he lay there, face down, breathing into his regulator as calmly as he could until the air supply ran out. And then he continued to float, now using a snorkel.

"We both got away with it," he said.

Later, Trotter analyzed that dive. The young diver, he said, "had an enormous amount of trust and confidence in me. When he dropped down to 160 feet, he had gotten overweighted and had not neutralized his buoyancy adequately." In other words, he had not adjusted the air inside his suit properly so it could give him the proper buoyancy to hover at a given depth. Without this adjustment, the diver quickly exhausted himself by trying not only to keep up with Trotter on the 250-foot swim alongside the wreck, but keeping himself from sinking even deeper into the lake.

"He went through a set of doubles [compressed air tanks] in 15 minutes. That's extraordinary," Trotter said.

This lack of neutral buoyancy also was the reason Trotter had such trouble hauling Rick to the surface.

"And the problem was he depended on me so much that he did not look after himself—after his own care. The experience scared the hell out of me. It scared us both. After that, it reaffirmed in my mind that I wanted to dive independently.

"By the way," he added, "we went diving the next day, Sunday. But we both went solo."

Dead Man Onboard

Very little time passed before Trotter realized that he did not want to just dive on wrecks, he wanted to find them.

In 1975, he bought his first dive boat—a 22-foot aluminum Starcraft. He would use that for the next 12 years until he got a bigger boat, a used 28-foot Marinette. It was aluminum, lighter than fiberglass, strong enough to handle the beatings that the Great Lakes hand out, and easily towed behind his van. He named it *Obsession*. Perhaps no boat has been better named. Then, in 1994, he replaced the original *Obsession* with a still larger boat. Once again it was a Marinette, but it was 32 feet long. This one he named *Obsession Too*.

And so it happened that every warm weekend from there on out, Trotter would be on the water—and under it.

Given his hundreds of shipwreck dives, people often ask Trotter if he has ever found dead bodies. For the most part, the answer is no. But in 1978, still rather early in his wreck diving career, he did find one.

He, along with the famed wreck hunter John Steele and several others, went to Isle Royale in Lake Superior to dive on a ship called the *Kamloops*. It had been discovered just the year before. The *Kamloops* was a 260-foot steel freighter that went down during a nasty storm on December 7, 1927. None of the 22-member crew survived.

The ship foundered in very deep water, 250 feet deep, and the uppermost part of the ship was no higher than 175 feet. So only the best and most confident divers dared to probe into this ship. Today, the U.S. National Park Service—Isle Royale is a national park—recommends that no one dive the *Kamloops*.

But these divers went down on air, dared to penetrate the dark stillness inside the ship, and for the first time swam into the engine room.

To Trotter's surprise, he found a body floating inside. Usually bodies do not last long underwater. Fish feed on them; currents carry them off. Apparently this one man's remains survived for 51 years protected inside the engine room.

"The body was translucent," Trotter remembered. "Sort of like tissue. If you took a bunch of tissue and you put it in water, it had that sort of look. I think if I had touched it, it would all have come apart."

Trotter called him "the engineer who was still on duty."

In a conversation in the summer of 2006, John Steele also remembered that same engineer on duty. "He saved my life," Steele said.

Steele had swum down into the engine room but, at that depth and in the silty darkness, was narced and became disoriented. "The ship was big," he remembered.

Trying to find his way out, Steele said, "I was shining my light around and it eventually hit him. He showed me the way out."

Now I Know Where We Are

With his new used boat, Trotter determined to outfit it with enough technology to make it one of the best wreck hunting boats on the Great Lakes.

In 1978, Trotter bought a $2,500 loran-C unit. He was only one of two civilians to own one at that time on Lake Huron. The other was owned by his friend and fellow diver Charles Feltner. The U.S. Coast Guard had two. The unit relied on broadcast towers—one in Florida, one in Wisconsin, and one in New England. The loran-C was a precursor to the GPS, which fixes its locations using satellites.

Now with loran-C, Trotter could tell exactly where he was in the lake. This had been impossible before, using just a map and compass. For wreck hunters, it was a major breakthrough. Previously, hunters could sometimes locate a sunken ship because fishermen had snagged their nets on it, or they used some early version of sonar or even a fish finder.

But the question was: Could they find it again? Often the answer was no.

A wreck they dived on one year might be unfindable the following year. Loran-C changed all that. Five years later, in 1983, Trotter made another financial commitment—one that separates the true hunters from the dilettantes. He and two other divers pitched in to buy a $48,000 side-scan sonar unit. This was basically a watery equivalent of radar.

The side-scan works this way. A long cable is run off the back of the search boat. Attached to the cable is a metal "fish" running deep below the surface. Typically it runs below the thermocline, which can distort readings. The silvery fish, which looks a bit like an old Flash Gordon rocket ship with a pointed nose and fins, is the sonar's eyes. Or more exactly, it is the sonar's ears. As the fish is towed along, it works something like radar. But instead of sending out electromagnetic pulses, the sonar sends out sound signals.

These sound pulses are sent in a wide, angular pattern down to the bottom and the echoes bounce back in fractions of a second. Each pulse reveals a narrow strip showing the bottom that is running below and to the sides of the fish. As the fish moves forward, it sends out another pulse, and another, and another. Onboard, these sound patterns create a series of lines similar to what you see on an old TV set when you sit very close. Put them all together and they create a picture.

With side-scan sonar, very solid objects on the bottom reflect more sound energy, causing a darker signal image. Soft objects do not reflect as much, so they show up lighter. And the complete absence of sound, say in the shadow behind a sunken ship, shows up the lightest of all, and is called the shadow.

Interestingly, while an oak ship shows up extremely well on the side-scan readout, a ship made of pine is almost invisible because pine wood has the same density as water.

The trick to finding sunken ships is then being able to decipher the markings on the side-scan's paper readout. This is a skill that is really more art than science, and the very best side-scan readers have had years of practice. Over time, Trotter got to be one of the best.

Fellow divers can only shrug and admit that David can look at a readout and see a schooner while the rest of them see only a smudge.

Others soon took notice of Trotter's skills. Among them was a group in Canada and a Lake Michigan dive group.

In Canada, Save Ontario's Shipwrecks (SOS) hired Trotter, starting in 1989, for a week each year for three years running to find wrecks off Point Pelee in Lake Erie. In that time, he located 16 ships. Remarkably enough, in one three-hour span he managed to find four separate vessels. Point Pelee Provincial Park now boasts 22 wrecks, most of them found by Trotter.

One of the more interesting Trotter finds off Point Pelee was the steamer *George Stone*, which ran onto a reef in October of 1909. The *George Stone*, it turns out, had one uniquely embarrassing moment in her history.

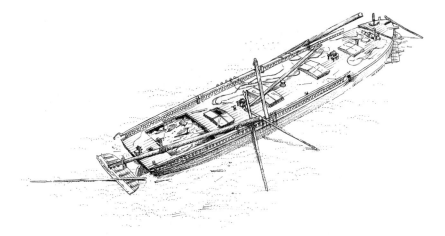

The schooner *S.H. Kimball*, which was found by David Trotter on the bottom of Lake Huron, was being towed by a ship called the *George Stone* when the line broke in 1895. The *Stone* turned so the line could be retied and somehow managed to ram the *Kimball* and send her to the bottom. Trotter thinks it may be the only instance where a ship sank a second ship that it was towing. Illustration by Robert McGreevy.

Caught in a thick fog in 1895, the *George Stone* was towing a second ship, or consort, called the *S.H. Kimball* across Lake Huron when the tow line broke. Turning around to fix a new line, the captain of the *Stone* misjudged his distance from the *Kimball*, smashed into it, and sank her on the spot. Trotter, who also found the *Kimball*, believes it is the only instance in the lakes where a ship actually sank its own consort.

Also, Trotter has been hired to look for lost ships for a week each summer by the Michigan Shipwreck Research Associates (MSRA) based in Muskegon. In 2006 he found the 208-foot steamer *Hennepin*, built in 1888, that plunged to the bottom in a storm on August 18, 1927.

More importantly, Trotter—with a keen eye that spotted what looked like a smudge on the side-scan readout—discovered the S.S. *Michigan*.

On February 9, 1885, the steel-hulled *Michigan* set out from Grand Haven with a crew of 29 to rescue the crew of a second ship, the *Oneida*, which had gotten stranded by the winter ice.

As it turned out, the elegantly equipped, four-year-old *Michigan* itself became hopelessly trapped in the ice pack. After 40 days, the crew finally had to abandon the ship, just before it was crushed by the ice and sank. It took the crew two days to walk to shore over the ice. All survived.

Ironically, the ship that the *Michigan* had hoped to rescue somehow worked itself free and sailed toward a safe port on the very day that the *Michigan* set out.

While Trotter sometimes earns a few dollars doing side-scan contract work, that is not his true interest. He simply loves finding virgin shipwrecks and then diving on them. He loves the historical detective work of figuring out where a sunken ship might be or which ship it is that his team has happened upon.

"Ships are much like people," Trotter has said. "They have a story to tell and it's very fascinating and exciting." He loves the process of putting together his video productions that let the world see what he has found—even if he never tells them exactly where it is. In part, it is his way of protecting the ship from recreational divers and artifact hounds who might disturb it. He also says his finds certainly are not the only sunken ships in the Great Lakes, and these waters are open to anyone who wants to spend the time and money to look for these relics of the past.

Half a Boat

Trotter's first major find came in 1979, using a far more primitive sonar than the side-scans of his later hunts. This early sonar, a Wesmar 160, was the kind used during World War II. While helpful, the machine—the ears of which were located in a dome underneath the boat—was difficult to operate and often gave erratic readings because of weather conditions and the sudden temperature change in the thermocline that can distort the signal.

Trotter went out into Lake Huron with Larry Coplin, each in his own boat. And what they were the first to discover was not a sunken ship—but half of a sunken ship.

On November, 28, 1966, the 600-foot ore boat *Daniel J. Morrell* was pounding its way north in a dangerously worsening storm with 29 men aboard. November is the month renowned as the ship killer in the Great Lakes. This was very late in November, but the press of business took precedence over good sense. Captain Arthur Crawley of the *Morrell* got the order to extend the ship's sailing season with one final run.

By 8:30 p.m., the *Morrell*'s crew watched as three-foot waves grew to eight feet and the winds notched up to 30 knots. By midnight, the storm really went on the muscle. As the *Morrell* was crossing Saginaw Bay, gale-force winds filled with snow barreled in from the north,

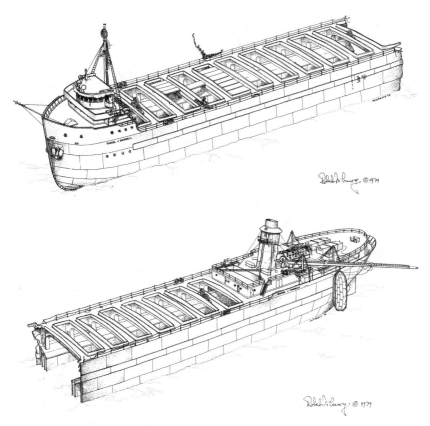

The *Daniel J. Morrell* was David Trotter's first big find. The ship, a 600-foot ore carrier, broke in half during a November storm in 1966. All but one of the 29 crew members died. The Coast Guard located the stern soon after the accident. But then the location was basically lost until 1979 when David Trotter—in one day—refound the stern and then located the bow that had been missing since the accident. The bow and stern were five miles apart. Illustration by Robert McGreevy, based on 1979 discovery information. As the wreck was explored, the divers determined that the break was one cargo hatch different.

hitting with a velocity of 60 knots. Waves began cresting as high as 25 feet, slashing across the ship's steel hatch covers.

The *Morrell* was big, the length of two football fields, but at age 60 it was too old to withstand the storm's beating. As the waves tore and twisted the ship, the crew saw a huge gash suddenly open on the *Morrell*'s starboard side and then, like a bad earthquake movie, the hole became a rip, tearing its way across the deck. The ship arched her back. And then, in what seemed like seconds, the *Morrell* broke in two, almost as a woodsman might snap a branch across his knee.

Only one crewman managed to survive, Dennis Hale. He awoke just before 2 a.m. to the banging sound of the ship's huge anchors pounding against the hull. Slogging through slushy ice in the dark, he managed to pull on a peacoat and join 11 others in an open raft just before the ship split into two pieces.

Curiously the stern, its engines still running and lights aglow, continued to motor on. The bow sank like a boulder. The wave created by the sinking bow threw all 11 men out into the freezing water. Only Hale and three others managed to get to a lifeboat.

Help would never arrive. Electrical cables in the pilothouse had been torn loose, and the ship's SOS signal was lost.

The Coast Guard did not find Hale until late in the afternoon of the day after the accident. The lifeboat had washed up near Harbor Beach, Michigan. Three of the four men had died of exposure. Hale, his feet frostbitten and body temperature down to 94 degrees, was the last one breathing. He was flown to the hospital at Harbor Beach. He alone was left to tell the story.

The Coast Guard, after several failed attempts, managed to find the *Morrell*'s stern the following January. It was sitting upright in 218 feet of water north of Port Austin, Michigan. Divers probed the wreck and brought up a section of steel from the break, which was analyzed. The steel proved to be typical of pre-1948 manufacture. It had turned brittle from old age and cold waters.

At the time, the Coast Guard marked the location of the *Morrell*'s stern with a large marker buoy. Unfortunately, the chain that held the buoy to the ship was heavier than the buoy itself, causing the buoy to sink 90 feet below the surface. Trotter and his group later found it floating above the stern.

With the position for the *Morrell*'s stern no longer marked, it and the bow would remain missing for the next 13 years, until Trotter and the others set out to find it.

On Sunday, May 18, 1979, Trotter, Coplin, and others, in two boats, were the first to relocate the *Morrell*'s stern. Using the still new and somewhat primitive loran-C positioning unit, Trotter put together a set of intricate calculations with the help of Charles Feltner who had gotten the loran-C location on a previous visit.

It was a matter of marking a compass course of 31 degrees true from the lighthouse that the Coast Guard had determined on its initial discovery, then coupling it with an estimate of 14 miles and then figuring where that location would crop up on the loran-C charts.

And yes, the stern turned out to be just where Trotter figured it would be. Just to be sure, divers went down from the boats to clap eyes on it for a positive identification.

By now it was 5 p.m. on that Sunday. Because the sky still held some light, they decided to at least make a pass at finding the bow.

They motored five miles to the northeast and turned on the sonar. Not much more than 15 minutes had passed when an image popped up. It looked like a mountain sticking up from the lake bed. It lay in 205 feet of water. Could it possibly be the *Morrell's* bow?

The divers came back several days later, using the loran-C to get to the exact spot. Down they went. The water was silty and visibility was less than a few feet. But they were able to determine that the wreck, in fact, was a bow section. It was sitting upright and intact and written on a name board above the pilothouse were the words *Daniel J. Morrell*.

It was a remarkable find since the stern lay a full five miles from the bow. It could have been anywhere in a 16-mile radius or more, and Trotter went right to it. The *Morrell's* stern had motored and drifted that far. As for how he found it, Trotter still has no clear explanation. Trotter's sense was that the bow somehow wanted to be found.

This was a day of firsts for Trotter. He had managed to find two ships—that is, two halves of one ship—in a single day. Halves that were five miles apart. This was his first big find. And it was the first time loran-C was used to locate a lost ship in Lake Huron. On that day, Trotter changed from being a wreck-hunting enthusiast to a full-fledged addict.

More importantly, he began to fashion his role as a Great Lakes shipwreck historian, one with swim fins. With this wreck exploration—and with many to follow—Trotter found he could clarify and add to the historical record. Analyzing the wrecks, he found that misperceptions would be cast aside. Factual holes could be filled. And a once forgotten history could be revived.

Trotter used the vehicle of his audio-visual presentations to spin out this maritime history. Over the years, he has given hundreds of presentations, not only to dive groups but to many civic groups as well. Add to this his many publications in various magazines and descriptions of his work in newspapers.

Trotter and the other divers made some 300 dives on the two halves of the *Morrell*. The result was a number of findings that helped clarify the historical record.

Dennis Hale—the man in the peacoat who was the lone survivor—vividly described how the front and back halves of the *Morrell* had banged against each other as the ship split apart. The divers, however, could find no evidence of this banging. They did reconfirm the metallurgical study for the Coast Guard, which described brittle metal in the hull.

The divers also learned that the stern—of which Hale had quickly lost sight—floundered on the surface some three hours after the bow sank. They found clocks in both sections. The clock in the bow read 1:55; the one in the stern had stopped at 5:15.

Inside the stern section of the *Morrell*, divers found sad remnants of life onboard and the sudden last-minute struggle for survival— dishes still sat in their racks in the galley, a pack of cigarettes lay on the table, a pair of binoculars was found on deck, and a phone was hanging out of a broken window in the wheelhouse. And they found evidence of panic. The doors to the life jacket storage cabinet were twisted and bent, perhaps by sailors in a last, desperate attempt to find something to keep them afloat.

As a postscript, Trotter tells of the *Morrell*'s sister ship, the *Edward Y. Townsend*, a duplicate built in the same year. On the night that the *Morrell* sank, the *Townsend* was three hours behind and managed to survive. But when it pulled into the St. Mary's River at Sault Ste. Marie, an inspection found a nasty stress crack in the hull. It was very like the one that caused the *Morrell* to sink.

The *Townsend* was sold to a European scrap market. While it was being towed across the Atlantic, the *Townsend* broke in two and sank. Eerily, like the *Morrell*, the bow sank immediately and the stern floated on the surface for several hours.

Shipwreck Alley and the White Hurricane

With the discovery and exploration of the *Morrell*, David Trotter now was in the thrall of his obsession. Over time he would turn the U.S. side of Lake Huron into his own wreck-hunting backyard. This was prime territory for lost ships. The line stretching from the Mackinac Straits down to Port Huron was one of the most heavily trafficked in the Great Lakes.

All of the ships in the nineteenth century and early twentieth century followed the same north-south path across Lake Huron, a path that loosely followed the Michigan shoreline. This route was basically the shortest distance between the north end of the lake and Mackinac Straits and the locks at Sault Ste. Marie and the south end, which connected to Detroit, the ports on Lake Erie, and beyond. This route also afforded a bit of protection from the winds that typically blew in from the west.

Because this shipping lane was popular did not mean it was safe. Lake Huron was a ship killer with a rap sheet that stretched for pages. The waters off Thunder Bay at Alpena claimed a score of ships, but perhaps the most dangerous of all was Saginaw Bay, where the westerly winds picked up speed and power as they crossed the open water.

Saginaw Bay was a shipwreck alley if there ever was one. And not surprisingly, it became Trotter's principal hunting preserve.

Shipwrecks happened on a regular basis during the nineteenth and early twentieth centuries. But the single worst time was during the Great Storm of 1913 or, as it was called, "The White Hurricane."

Over the weekend of November 7–10, a confluence of two storm fronts smashed into the Great Lakes—one sweeping down from western Ontario and a second with warm, moist air came up from the Gulf of Mexico. Snow-filled winds were clocked at 90 miles per hour and waves crested at 35 to 50 feet. On shore, barns were flattened, trees blown down, electricity was knocked out, and snow drifted 6 to 10 feet high, blocking roads for days.

Out on the water, a total of 19 ships went down in Lakes Superior, Michigan, Huron, and Erie. Another 19 ran aground. Some 256 crew were killed. The property and cargo loss was estimated at $100 million.

The storm vented most of its wrath on Lake Huron. The monster waves swallowed eight ships and killed 199 of their crewmen. Wreckage and dead bodies washed up on the lake's shores for weeks. Sadly, ghoulish pickpockets found some of the dead before officials. As a result, identification in some cases was nearly impossible.

In 1985, 72 years after the Great Storm, Trotter was the first to find the *John A. McGean,* one of the ships lost in the Great Storm. It was a 432-foot steel freighter headed north with a load of coal when it foundered off the Thumb of Michigan, dropping 180 feet to the bottom where it lay mostly upside down. All 28 crew members died, including the captain with the fanciful name of "Dancin'" Chauncy Nye.

The Trotter team, which now included Danny Fader, began diving the *McGean* the following year in 1986. In exploring the freighter, Trotter's team found that one blade was missing from the propeller and another was damaged. And more, the rudder shaft itself was twisted and bent, lying at a 90-degree angle to the hull. Their conclusion was that the ship bottomed out in the 30-foot waves, perhaps near shore off Port Hope, Michigan. Certainly loss of rudder control would have doomed the wave-battered ship.

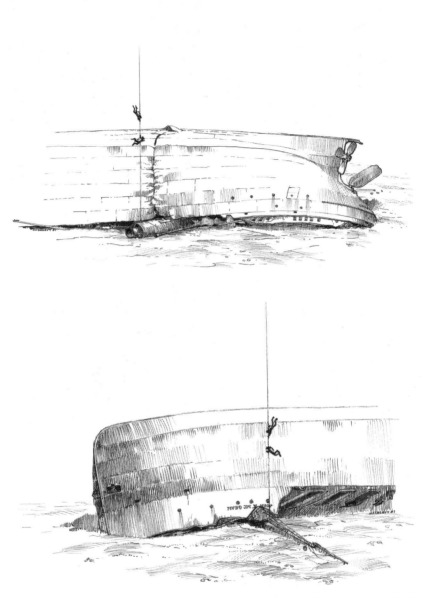

The *John A. McGean*, a 432-foot freighter loaded with coal, foundered with all 28 crew members during the Great Storm of 1913. Trotter and his team found the two pieces of the *McGean* in 1985. Illustration by Robert McGreevy.

After smacking the bottom, the ship probably then rolled over, spilled its cargo of coal, and floated (much like the stern of the *Morrell*) several miles before sinking 10 miles offshore.

For years following the accident, the *McGean's* coal left on the lake bottom was washed ashore after storms. The people of Port Hope would clamber down onto the waterline and collect that coal in five-gallon buckets, then trundle it home for heat during the long Michigan winters. In a way, that coal was a last gift from Captain Nye to his neighbors. He had been born and raised in Port Hope.

Not all the ships lost in the Great Storm of 1913 have been found. To this day, Trotter has on his search list one as-yet unfound ship that lies somewhere in Lake Huron. It is the freighter *Hydrus*. It went down with all hands somewhere off Lexington, Michigan. On the Canadian side of the border, the Great Storm also sank the steamer *James Carruthers*, which was carrying a load of wheat. All hands were lost. It is thought to lie somewhere north of Goderich, Ontario.

No wreck diver—at least not those diving to the depths of Trotter's team—can avoid mishaps. And Trotter had one of his own on the *McGean*.

Out with just Mickey onboard, Trotter descended alone on the *McGean*. Earlier he had found a large running light near the bow. It was something that might be stolen. So he decided to move it away from the ship so it would not be spotted, much like the team would later move the strongbox on the steamer *Detroit*.

Once on the ship, Trotter located the light and began to drag it away through the silty darkness. It was heavy, heavier than he expected. He struggled to pull it along with his right arm while unreeling a safety line with his left hand. The safety line would be the only way for him to find his way back to the ship.

Despite a harsh strain on his right arm, Trotter was able to move the light 40 or 50 feet away from the ship.

Breathing hard, he swam back to the ship, following the line and retrieving it as he went. Trotter then rose to 20 feet below the surface only to find that his right shoulder—the one that had been lugging the light—was mind-numbingly painful. It was the bends. He dropped down to 30 feet below the surface where the pressure was greater. The pain eased somewhat, but he could not stay there long. He was running out of air. So he rose again, making decompression stops at 20 and 10 feet.

By the time he was on the surface, he said the shoulder was screaming. Mickey helped him onto the boat, unhooked the mooring line, and headed for shore. Trotter immediately started breathing pure oxygen, the one thing onboard that might help. It did not. His shoulder was almost completely immobilized.

Trotter decided not to go to a recompression chamber. In fact, one was not nearby. He would ride it out. After several sleepless nights, lots of aspirin and fluids, the pain backed off. But he says, this was his "worst hit" of the bends, and the shoulder problem continues to plague him to this day.

Mowing the Lawn

Each spring for what was to become decades, Trotter and his team set out to search for lost ships, usually beginning in late April when spray off the bow still might turn to ice on your sleeve.

They would spend the next three or four months of weekends "mowing the lawn." They would pick an area based on a ship for which they were looking and then would follow straight-line courses. Up and back, up and back. Each line just overlapped the last line enough to ensure complete coverage, just like someone would mow the grass.

As years passed and their searches consistently turned up new finds, they became more and more serious. In the beginning, a weekend of searching usually meant going out for eight or so hours to search on Saturday and then again on Sunday. Later they saw no reason they could not search at night. After all, night or day, it made no difference to the side-scan. Hunting became a marathon, stretching from Saturday morning, all through Saturday night, and well into Sunday. If it was a long holiday weekend, they might search Monday, too. The only thing that could stop them was foul weather.

The team worked in shifts. Two guys were on for two hours—one driving the boat, the second watching the side-scan readout. Everybody on the team stood watch. No exceptions.

For some of the young hotshots, the months of searching were a mind-numbing bore. After a few hours, they ran out of conversation. So they watched videos or read dive magazines and paperback books. Or they slept. On one hand, this boring routine ran against their very natures. After all, they had gotten into wreck diving for the adventure and the excitement, not to sit for hours in a cramped cabin watching a roll of paper unreel itself.

At the same time, they understood that these were necessary dues. If they wanted to dive on virgin wrecks, first they had to find them. After that, you could play *Sea Hunt*.

Typically a Trotter search began with background study, checking old documents and newspapers. Yes, this ship would be interesting to find. It was historically important. It had a great story.

Where did it go down? The captain was quoted as saying this in the *Detroit Free Press* or the *Milwaukee Sentinel*. Or a crewman from a passing ship had spotted the ship itself, or perhaps bits of flotsam from the wreck.

But whatever was said or written, the divers took it with a heavy dose of salt. Trotter, his team, and every experienced ship hunter in the lakes knew one thing for certain: A sunken ship is never where they said it was.

It's understandable crewmen would get it wrong. After all, they had almost no tools to figure out where they were. Certainly no loran or GPS. They had a compass. They might remember the last sighting of land. But in a storm or a fog, hours could slip away after the last glimpse of shore. If they abandoned ship in one place and the craft still had not sunk, it could—like the *Morrell*—continue to float for hours or even days, constantly being moved by the wind.

Sometimes, as Trotter was mowing the lawn for a specific ship, it might be the first ship he'd find. But more often than not, he'd turn up "targets" on the side-scan that he had never anticipated. Serendipitous finds. Good ships, ships worth diving on.

So year after year, Trotter and his team continued to map the bottom of Lake Huron. And soon—not that there was any real competition—Trotter became a sort of Rand McNally of the Huron lake bottom. No one knew it better.

Team members might search some weekends but not others. Trotter was almost always there. His hours on the water became almost uncountable. Between diving and searching, Trotter has likely spent more time on the lakes than any charter or pleasure boat owner.

By 2006—after more than 25 years of searching—he mapped more than 2,000 square miles of the Lake Huron bottom.

The side-scan searches paid off in a couple of ways. Obviously they located lots of sunken ships. Almost as importantly, the team learned where ships were not. So when they were looking for a particular steamer or propeller-driven ship, they did not have to re-search an area to find it.

Virgins in the Lake

By the time Danny had joined the team in 1986, the Trotter team had found a number of historically famous ships.

Of course, there was the *Daniel J. Morrell* and the *John A. McGean*. Earlier had come the *Rocket*, a 143-foot two-masted schooner that got rammed by the bark *Ocean Wave* just as the Civil War was starting in 1860, and the *Emma L. Nielson*.

The *Nielson*, a 98-foot three-masted schooner, was sunk after being rammed by the *Wyandotte*, a steel ship almost three times its size. They collided in a fog off Michigan's Thumb, with the *Wyandotte* ripping into the *Nielson*'s port bow.

Trotter and Coplin might never have determined the name of the *Nielson* except the two forward hatches each carried a six-digit number—135665. With that, they were able to track down the name.

Mickey Trotter tells of a scary moment when her husband was diving on the *Nielson* before she knew much about handling the dive boat. That day just the two of them were onboard. The winds were calm, and sunlight was skipping off the water. Trotter went down and Mickey stayed onboard.

She had been scanning the horizon, watching a huge steamer approach. Even seen from a distance, it seemed right on course to hit them. At first she thought, well, the big ship will turn. But it didn't. It just came at her, relentless, a thick moustache of white water tearing away from the bow. Getting anxious, she tried to radio the freighter. No answer. Another passing cargo ship picked up her call and tried to contact the freighter. Still no answer. It seemed impossible that a freighter could be churning up the lake, apparently on autopilot, with no one on watch and no one to answer the marine radio.

She and the tiny boat sat within minutes of being crushed.

So even though Trotter was still underwater, Mickey had no choice. She had to move the boat alone, a boat that she had never driven before. This meant starting the engine, unhooking from the mooring line, and not getting it tangled in the propeller. Fortunately, she had asked Trotter how to start it before he started his dive.

She invoked her lesson, revved the engine, and deftly moved it out of the way. A mouse escaping the footfall of a dinosaur. Down below, Trotter heard the bellowing engines of the freighter and dropped down to 50 feet while the behemoth steamed over him. With the freighter's passing, Mickey got back to the mooring line to pick up her husband when he came up.

After that near disaster, Trotter said Mickey got a full course in boat handling.

Perhaps Trotter's most important find in the early years was the *Goliath*, which was a mess for divers but historically very significant.

The 131-foot freighter, launched in 1846, was one of the very first propeller-driven boats on the Great Lakes. It boasted two screw

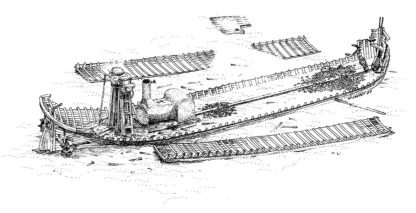

The *Goliath* was one of the very first propeller-driven ships in the Great Lakes. The 131-foot freighter, carrying a load of bricks and gunpowder, exploded off the Michigan Thumb in Lake Huron in 1848. Trotter and his team found it in 1986. Trotter contends it is the oldest, intact propeller ship found in the lakes. Illustration by Robert McGreevy.

propellers that were powered by two separate steam engines. These propeller-driven ships were a major advance over the steam-powered side-wheelers.

John Ericsson was one of the first to patent a propeller design in 1840. His propellers were shaped like short tubes with the blades on the outside. Ericsson was the same man who later designed the famed Civil War ironclad ship the *Monitor*.

The *Goliath*, with a crew of 18, ran into big trouble in September 1848, two years after she had been built. Her cargo, destined for Lake Superior mining companies, was 20,000 bricks, 40 tons of hay, 2,000 barrels of provisions, and, most significantly, 200 kegs of black powder and a supply of lucifer matches.

Just as the ship was nearing Point Aux Barques at the tip of the Michigan Thumb, a fire broke out and the gunpowder exploded. The explosion blew off the entire upper deck along with some of the sides. Eight miles away people on shore could see the smoke. Weighed down by the load of bricks, the *Goliath* immediately plunged to the bottom. The entire crew died.

When the Trotter team dove down onto the *Goliath*, they discovered that much of the old ship was gone. But what remained was hugely significant—the hull, the two steam engines, and the two propellers.

The *Goliath* was the fifth steam-powered propeller ship to be built to the Ericsson design. The first was the *Vadalia*. But all the earlier propeller ships are now gone. Trotter contends that the *Goliath* is now the only complete ship built to the early Ericsson design.

While all was moving briskly ahead with his underwater explorations, Trotter's personal life took a tragic turn in 1988.

His daughter, Kelly, who had been chronically depressed, committed suicide at the age of 16. Kelly, a bright and pretty girl, was on the school honor roll, worked part-time at the public library, and wanted to become a doctor. But Kelly's depressive states were getting worse. Over the years, despite the constant love and support of her family, she admitted having considered killing herself, underwent psychiatric counseling, and, as she worsened, was facing hospitalization to get at the root causes. Additionally, she had been taking prescription drugs, mood-elevators, and they seemed to be helping. Then, in what would turn out to be her final days, her doctor turned thumbs-down on hospitalization and took her off the drugs. It was the worst decision possible. Her life ended with a gun shot in the family bathroom.

The death shattered the lives of David, Mickey, and their two sons, Jay and Ross. Trotter said suddenly their lives seemed hardly worth living. And in a prolonging of their agony, there followed a civil suit against the doctor and later criminal charges filed against him. The Trotters won the civil suit. The doctor was charged with perjury and convicted of altering medical records. Statistically with child suicides, the majority of the parents' marriages soon end in divorce. In contrast, David and Mickey found strength and reassurance in each other and their need to care for their sons. If anything, their marriage grew stronger.

Of course, like Mickey, Trotter could never fully escape the weeping emotional wound of Kelly's death. However, he was able to find some degree of relief aboard the *Obsession* with its technical routines, its mind-absorbing adventures, and its physical separation from his painful world ashore.

So he threw himself into his explorations with even greater passion. Here, too, the searches could prove frustrating.

But Where Is the Minnedosa?

If some sunken ships seemed to almost announce themselves to Trotter, others played Greta Garbo, who famously said, "I vant to be alone." For Trotter, the *Minnedosa* became a personal holy grail.

This was a ship designed for superlatives. Called "The Pride of Canada," it was the biggest schooner ever built in Canada and, in

The legendary *Minnedosa*—David Trotter searched for this ship for 15 years
before discovering it in Lake Huron in 1993. With a length of 250 feet and
four masts as high as 150 feet, the *Minnedosa* was the largest sailing
ship ever built in Canada. The ship went down in a storm in 1905.
Courtesy of the David Trotter Collection.

terms of tonnage, was the largest Canadian sailing vessel ever to sail
the Great Lakes. It was 250 feet long—almost the length of a football
field—had four masts instead of the usual two or three, and could rip
along at 17 knots.

The *Minnedosa* went down in a Lake Huron storm in 1905, fifteen
years after she was first launched at Kingston, Ontario.

People thought they knew where the *Minnedosa* had foundered.
Newspapers of the day reported it. They also thought they knew
exactly how deep it lay. But Trotter, the best wreck finder in the lakes,
could not find it.

One year of searching passed. And another and another. Still the
Minnedosa sat at the top of Trotter's list. After years of survey work,
frustration began to eat into his confidence. He began to wonder if
somehow in all his careful searching, he had missed it. He even began
to doubt that it might ever be found.

CHAPTER 6

Divers, Hunters, and Ships: From the *Griffon* ...

Perhaps before but certainly since the 1960s, men and women have gone down with scuba gear to look for sunken ships in the Great Lakes.

Lots of submerged vessels are there to be found. An estimated 6,000 ships have gone missing in the freshwater seas; some say as many as 10,000 ships.

So far, 1,000 or so have been discovered, and more are being found all the time, at about the rate of 10 or so a year.

To be sure, not every newly discovered shipwreck holds interest for divers or anybody else for that matter. These wrecks are so dismantled that they are little more than a mess of wooden boards, random nails, and bits of hardware. They offer little to see or explore. Also many ships, especially the old wooden ones, suffered fires and burned to the water line.

But divers do find other sunken ships that are virtually complete from rudder to figurehead, almost as pristine as the day they dropped out of sight. Like the *Detroit*, many actually seem to have sailed to the bottom and are found sitting right side up. Like jetliners at Chicago's O'Hare International, these ships seem to have landed rather than crashed.

And so they sit, frozen in time by the big lakes' cold, fresh waters. They are time capsules hidden not in cornerstone cement, but in a great aquatic refrigerator.

Divers in recent years have found ships—some 150 years old or older—with wire rigging still dangling from the masts, caulking between the boards, even a cigarette package still sitting on a table as though a smoker had just stepped out for some air. Of course, the big steel freighters and ore carriers are even less prone to decay than the earlier wooden ships.

The fine preservation of these ships in the fresh waters of the Great Lakes might be compared to the famed *Andrea Doria* in the

John Steele, the wreck-diving pioneer of the Great Lakes, wearing a
wet suit in the early days. Like most divers in the big lakes,
he soon switched to wearing a dry suit that was much warmer.

Atlantic, which eats wrecks alive. After just fifty-plus years in the salt
water, this grand dame of the seas already is collapsing in on itself.

For Great Lakes hunters, the last several decades have proved to
be a golden age of wreck finding. They have pinged upon some of the
big lakes' most legendary sunken ships. With these discoveries the
wreck hunters have revived the ships' fame and garnered some for
themselves.

It would be nigh impossible to name all the wreck hunters who
have plumbed the Great Lakes, especially since their numbers have
blossomed in recent years. But John Steele, Paul Ehorn, Kent Bellrichard, Harry Zych, and Dick Race have to be listed among the early
pioneers. Out in their dive boats every warm weekend throughout
the 1970s and 1980s, they were among the earliest to discover virgin
shipwrecks in the Great Lakes. For the most part, they explored Lake
Michigan and Lake Superior, but they also probed the waters of Lake
Huron and even Lake Erie to find ships.

For them, Lake Ontario was far away, and its extremely deep U-shaped bottom made many of the wrecks too deep for scuba gear, especially when divers were breathing only compressed air.

Charles Feltner, the Great Lakes marine historian, generally divides Great Lakes wreck hunting into three time periods, which we might describe as early, middle, and recent.

Steele and his kindred spirits were in the early period. They were the frontiersmen. For the most part, these early hunters "did little research," Feltner said. "They simply went out in their boats, wandered around, and turned on their search gear. They might be using a fish finder and perhaps a magnetometer." Their style might be called the Columbus System: Find it and land on it—no matter what it is.

On the heels of the early-period hunters came a more research-oriented group of searchers with much-improved equipment—loran locating systems, sophisticated side-scan sonar, and the like.

Feltner puts himself, David Trotter, and some others in this category. And importantly, these wreck hunters built their searches on a strong foundation of research. They spent many hours in libraries culling through old ship records and newspapers on microfiche.

Feltner, speaking of his more academic style of wreck hunting in the middle period, said, "I would never go out and just mow the lawn. After extensive research, I can usually find what I am looking for in a day or two."

Tom Farnquist of Sault Ste. Marie, Michigan, might fit in this middle group. He found or helped to find perhaps a dozen lost ships in Lake Superior and became a major force behind the development of the Great Lakes Shipwreck Museum at Whitefish Point, one of the state's—probably one of the country's—finest small museums. Farnquist is now its director. He also has contributed to and been a part of most of the serious studies of the *Edmund Fitzgerald*, some of which led to controversy involving relatives of the lost crew.

Of course, it should be realized that these periods of wreck hunting were not pure; one typically morphed into another. The likes of Steele and Ehorn quickly adopted side-scan sonar and loran; Steele, certainly, dedicated himself to a lot of library research.

The third group in the most recent period are those who started hunting in the last 10 or 15 years or so.

"They've had it easy," Feltner says. "They benefit from all of the research and experience of their predecessors, plus they can get first-rate equipment at relatively low cost."

Certainly this is true in the case of GPS, which is replacing loran. Anyone can buy a GPS unit for as little as a few hundred dollars.

Feltner came to his fascination with marine history honestly. As a boy, he grew up on the coast of the Carolinas.

"When I was in high school," he said, "I was stepping on marine history at Cape Hatteras," where the powerful Atlantic had splattered scores of ships.

Professionally, he went on to get a Ph.D. in mechanical engineering and was hired by Ford Motor Company. In the meantime, he and his wife, Jeri, took up scuba diving, first after a resort course in the Caribbean (which he describes as a "suicide course") and later they signed up with the Ford Seahorses for an official PADI course. As it turned out, Trotter was their instructor.

While other divers grooved on the thrills of the deep, Feltner was most fascinated by the history. He did buy his own boat and discovered six virgin ships in the Mackinac Straits including the *Sandusky*, the *Eber Ward*, and the *Northwest*.

His most important contribution to wreck hunting and diving came in his precise mapping and naming the ships that were found, often correcting mistakes.

Early on he went out to search for a ship west of the Mackinac Bridge that divers were calling the *Northwest*. He too wanted to dive it. When he got a blip in his fish finder, he dove down and found a ship.

As it turned out, the ship he dove—which no one had previously discovered—was the actual *Northwest*, a schooner. Feltner was able to verify that the ship everyone else had been calling the *Northwest* was in fact not even a schooner, but a bark called the *Maitland*.

Feltner did virtually all the sunken ship identification work for the Thunder Bay National Marine Sanctuary at Alpena, Michigan, and for the Straits of Mackinac Underwater Preserve. His book, written with Jeri, *Shipwrecks of the Straits of Mackinac*, is a definitive survey of that area's wrecks and history.

Feltner also taught a course and published a book that gave away the secrets of how to research the history of Great Lakes shipping. Now unfortunately no longer in print, it is *Great Lakes Maritime History: Bibliography and Sources of Information*. He is particularly proud of the *Bibliography and Sources* book because it put research techniques into the hands of both divers and the general public. Before, such techniques had been the exclusive province of professional academics.

Feltner, who was diving in the 1970s when most divers were pulling artifacts off ships, quickly came to realize that if this wreck plundering kept up "nothing would be left to look at." For almost 40 years Feltner has made his mark as a stout preservationist. In 1981, he helped to pass a Michigan state law that would make it illegal to take artifacts from shipwrecks. They are considered a nonrenewable resource. In 2006, he was awarded the prestigious Award for Historic Preservation by the Association for Great Lakes Maritime History.

While it is impossible to detail all the stories of the important lost ships and the people who hunt for and dive on them, a handful of significant ones deserve a close look.

Any discussion of lost ships in the Great Lakes should begin with the *Griffon*. This is the true holy grail for wreck hunters. The tiny two-masted ship, built by the French explorer La Salle, was lost in 1679, almost a century before the U.S. Revolutionary War. It was the first European ship with sails to ever enter the upper lakes of Erie, Huron, and Michigan, and the first one to disappear.

Now a wreck hunter-diver—one in a long list of *Griffon* searchers—thinks he may have found the *Griffon*.

While the *Griffon* may seem like an obscure lost ship, the *Edmund Fitzgerald* will not. Famed in a popular song by Gordon Lightfoot and many books, the big ore carrier went down in 1975 with its 29 crew members. Despite the many books and newspaper articles, one amazing story has largely been left untold.

In the mid-1990s, two young men dove the *Fitzgerald* in nothing more than scuba gear. They put gloved hands on the rail, the only ones ever to do so since it sank. This was no mean feat. The *Fitzgerald* sits down 530 feet below the surface of Lake Superior, making their dive the deepest wreck dive in the Great Lakes and one of the deepest wreck dives in the world.

Wreck hunter John Steele, of course, was the most eminent of the pioneer wreck hunters. One of his discoveries ended up in the Smithsonian Institution. Paul Ehorn set legal precedents on who does and does not own a shipwreck. More recently Clive Cussler, the famous novelist, put his heft behind a search, not for a ship but for a Northwest Airliner that went down in Lake Michigan in 1950. The Christmas Tree Ship, found by Kent Bellrichard, was a piece of Chicago's holiday history. And there is Garry Kozak, the side-scan whiz who took years to find what he hoped would be the most profitable ship ever salvaged.

Here are their stories.

The Griffon

If only one lost ship truly deserves the name "Holy Grail of the Great Lakes," it is the *Griffon*.

Commissioned by the famous French explorer La Salle, the little two-masted ship was built at the Niagara River and was the first ever to sail in the upper lakes.

No one really knows what happened to the *Griffon*. Was it sunk in a storm? Did it burn? Was it stolen for its cargo? A small, two-masted ship, it simply vanished off the lakes just a few months after it was launched in 1679.

It also might be said that no lost ship in the Great Lakes has ever been "discovered" more times than the *Griffon*. Every decade or two, someone shouts "Eureka!" The only problem is that once academics and scientists take a close look, every *Griffon* discovery has proved to be bogus. At least so far.

Steve Libert, a veteran Great Lakes diver with a flair for publicity, has been the latest to claim a real possibility of having found the *Griffon*. In 2001, while diving in the silty waters off Poverty Island in Northern Lake Michigan, he made what he hopes was a remarkable discovery. It was a wooden pole, perhaps a ship's bowsprit.

Libert sliced a small sliver from the wood pole and sent it off for carbon dating. The tests, while far from precise, seemed to reveal that the wood has a one-in-three chance of coming from the right time period.

Since then, all investigations have stalled. Libert has gotten snarled in legal battles with the state of Michigan over who actually has the right to study and salvage his find. The state says Libert's discovery lies in Michigan waters, thus it holds dominion. But dominion over what? And where? Libert refuses to tell the location.

The state says it has a right to preserve its history. If it's a matter of history, Libert counters Chicago's Field Museum is interested and is helping him write a research grant.

What's more, he says, the *Griffon* was not a Michigan ship but a French ship. Because of France's original ownership, Libert says, he was able to convince the French government to assert a claim, giving him salvage rights.

Progress in this case was, at this writing, as stuck in the sand as the wooden pole Libert found. But Libert is only the most recent of *Griffon* hunters. Others preceded him. Lots of them. Research science undid them all.

For many years, people believed pieces of the *Griffon* and even skeletons of two crew members had been found at the west end of Manitoulin Island in northern Lake Huron. Also in Lake Huron, another likely *Griffon* find cropped up near Tobermory, on Russell Island off the tip of Ontario's Bruce Peninsula. This find seemed particularly promising because the remains showed a boat that was approximately the right size and made with materials that seemed typical of the era. And there were at least 10 other *Griffon* "discoveries" reported, going back to 1848.

Studies of the so-called *Griffon* on Manitoulin demonstrated that the wooden remains were from a much larger ship than the *Griffon*. As for the find on Russell Island, it turned out to be a variation of a Mackinac boat from the mid-1800s.

The list of oops-oh-never-mind goes on. A *Griffon* discovery in 1805 at Hamburg, New York, on Lake Erie turned out to be the remains of a British man-of-war wrecked in 1786. One found on Birch Island in Les Cheneaux Islands near Hessel, Michigan, was measured at 120 feet, twice the length of the *Griffon*. When researchers looked at another supposed *Griffon* at Fitzwilliam Island in Lake Huron's Georgian Bay, they figured out that it was the *Alice Hackett*, a schooner wrecked in 1828.

And to much embarrassment, a presumptive *Griffon* near Southampton, Ontario, proved to be not a ship at all. Instead, it was a bridge abutment.

And so, like Anastasias of the northern waters, ersatz *Griffon*s have appeared again and again only to be revealed as pretenders.

The story of the *Griffon*—sometimes spelled *Griffin* or *Gryphon*—must necessarily begin in the mid-1670s with Rene Robert Cavalier Sieur de La Salle. La Salle was most famous in high school history books as the dauntless explorer who traveled down the Mississippi River to its mouth and claimed all the adjacent land for France. Despite his long French name and title and the reverence in history books, in fact, La Salle was a much more flawed human being than is typically recorded.

La Salle, it turns out, was a failed priest who washed out because of, in his own words, "moral weakness." While he certainly proved to be a man of great personal courage, it also might be said that La Salle was a liar, a scamp, and a self-absorbed bully. One study has suggested that he was possibly a paranoid schizophrenic.

After arriving in Montreal, his first venture was to look for the passage to China. He got as far as Lake Erie. It took little time for his traveling companions to realize that La Salle was absolutely incompetent. They later wrote that he could not speak either Algonquin or Iroquoian and "was in a daze, more or less not knowing where he was going." Later La Salle claimed on that same Lake Erie trip that he discovered the Mississippi River before Marquette and Joliet.

A few years later, he went back to France, bribed some officials, and was given exclusive rights to explore the area between Mexico and Florida—and to build forts along the way. For this project, he had the *Griffon* built at Cayuga Creek above Niagara Falls. To give you a sense of how early this was in the era of exploration, his group became the first Europeans ever to see Niagara Falls.

The small, two-masted ship, listed as 45 tons, was loaded with tools and other gear to build a second ship that would explore the Mississippi. Also, because the relations between the settlers and the Native Americans were unsettled, it was outfitted like a man-of-war, with seven small cannons and some muskets. On the bow, they placed a carved griffon—a mythical monster that is half-lion and half-eagle. The *Griffon* set sail on August 7, 1679.

The tiny ship crossed Lake Erie, went up the Detroit River, and on August 11 passed through what La Salle named Lake St. Clair. Continuing on, the *Griffon* got smacked around by a nasty storm on Lake Huron, but arrived safely at Fort Michilimackinac at the northernmost tip of what is today lower Michigan. From there, the *Griffon* sailed on to what is now called Washington Island at Green Bay, Wisconsin. At the island's protected Detroit Harbor, the crew loaded on 12,000 pounds of furs that Native Americans had brought for trade.

Since La Salle was deeply in debt, he decided to send the *Griffon* back to Niagara with a small crew to pay off some of his creditors. The idea was that the ship would quickly return so they could continue their venture to the Mississippi. While the *Griffon* was making this round trip, La Salle and most of his group would canoe south toward what is now Chicago.

On September 12, the pilot, Luc—who apparently detested La Salle—and five sailors pulled the anchor and headed north with a cargo that was estimated at $12,000. The plan was to stop along the way at Fort Michilimackinac. The *Griffon* never showed up at the fort.

As for the fate of the *Griffon*, theories at the time ranged widely. Some believed that Indians—either Ottawas or Pottawatomies—boarded and burned her. Others think her own crew scuttled her. Still others believe the *Griffon* went down in a storm.

La Salle himself was convinced the pilot and crew grabbed the furs and sank the *Griffon*. Apparently La Salle said he had been in contact with an Indian who said a white man, who apparently looked like Luc the pilot, was being held as a prisoner by a tribe west of the Mississippi River. He and four others had been captured in canoes laden with goods. They killed the four other men, the Indian told La Salle.

In contrast, Father Hennepin, who was part of La Salle's group, wrote that Indians later told him that the *Griffon* "came to anchor at the mouth of Lake Illinois [Michigan], where it was seen by savages, who told us that they advised our men to sail along the coast, and not toward the middle of the lake ... [but our pilot said he] would steer as he pleased ... the ship was hardly a league from the coast when it was tossed up by a violent storm in such a manner that our men were never heard from since."

So are the pieces of wood discovered by Steve Libert part of the remains of a storm-ravaged *Griffon*? Or, if and when scientists get a good look, will this *Griffon* prove to be just another on the ever lengthening list of wannabe "discoveries."

The Christmas Tree Ship

Other lost ships are more famous. On other ships, more lives were lost or the ships were loaded with more valuable cargo. But almost no other ship carried the sentimental value of the *Rouse Simmons*, at least not for Chicagoans. The *Rouse Simmons* was the Christmas Tree Ship.

The *Rouse Simmons* was a three-masted schooner built in 1868. For most of the next 54 years, the 125-foot *Simmons* went from one Great Lakes port to another as a tramp, picking up whatever cargo needed to be carried—at first loads of wheat and later timber and other cargo.

The ship probably would have sailed all its days as just another of the hundreds of anonymous schooners in the big lakes. But in 1910, the ship, which had changed owners several times, was bought by Captain Herman Schuenemann.

It seems that in the early 1890s, Captain August Schuenemann, Herman's brother, discovered that he could extend the sailing season and make a tidy little profit by carrying Christmas trees to Chicago from Michigan's Upper Peninsula. Just as Thanksgiving marks the beginning of the Christmas season today, in the early 1900s its arrival was marked by the docking of the Christmas Tree Ship.

Hundreds of people and countless children would crowd the harbor to watch the ship come in. The ship was a virtual Chia Pet of evergreens. Trees seemed to sprout out of it everywhere. They not only filled the hold, but were tied to the masts and hung from the rigging—50,000 trees, all freshly cut and redolent with the smell of the north woods. With the holiday season pressing, everyone wanted to be among the first onboard to pick out a prime tree.

Captain August, who started it all, became known as Christmas Tree Schuenemann. Sadly, he died when his ship the *Thai* went down off Glencoe, Illinois, in the fall of 1893.

Then his brother Herman picked up the Christmas tree run and his daughter Elsie soon began making extra dollars by weaving wreaths out of evergreen branches.

In November 1910, after Captain Herman acquired an interest in the *Rouse Simmons*, this vagabond freighter made its first run as the Christmas Tree Ship. And again the next year.

Two years later, in the fall of 1912, once again the *Rouse Simmons* headed north for the annual Christmas Tree run. Coming from Chicago, it tied up at Manistique, Michigan. From the docks, Captain Herman and his crew and woodcutters set out to find and cut the very best trees. By the time a tug was pulling the *Rouse Simmons* out of the harbor on November 22, a forest of green trees filled the ship from stern to bow.

As it turned out, November 22 was a bad day to start. A storm was brewing. Winds grew bitter and then fierce, and then were bashing the *Simmons* sails at gale force. Temperatures plummeted below freezing, and a thick, angry snow began to flail at Lake Michigan.

The next day, the crew on shore at the Kewaunee Coast Guard station spotted a ship in distress. They called the nearby Two Rivers rescue team, which sent out a 34-foot power boat.

The Coast Guard crew onboard spotted the *Simmons*. It was in bad shape. They reported later that its hull was coated with ice and the wind had shredded its sails.

But then, as the rescuers were nearing the wounded ship, a snow squall swept in. It was a whiteout on the water. Almost within shouting distance, the *Simmons* suddenly vanished in the whirling snow. It was never seen again.

Not long afterward, a well-corked bottle with a note inside washed up on shore near Sheboygan, Wisconsin. Inside was a note from Captain Herman:

> *Everybody good-by. I guess we are thru.*
> *Leaking bad. Endwald and Steve fell*
> *overboard. God help us.*

For the next 25 years, people along the Wisconsin shore would find Christmas trees—stalks with barren branches—tossed up among the coastal rocks and tangled in fishermen's nets. But nothing was found of the ship itself.

Then, 59 years after she was sunk, on November 30, 1971, Kent Bellrichard—a colleague of John Steele, who was using his boat—got a dark outline on his sonar screen.

He had been looking for another ship, the *Vernon,* when an image of the *Simmons* showed up on his screen. It lay at 160 feet.

On his first dive that day, Bellrichard dropped down into the swirling silt and could not determine which ship he had found. Then on later dives with Steele, they found the quarterboard with the *Rouse Simmons* name.

The ship was still chock-a-block with trees. None had their needles any longer. Even so, the divers brought up two.

The next Christmas season, one of the trees was set up in the lobby of Marine National Exchange Bank in Milwaukee, along with a painting of the ship. It was a brief revival of the Christmas spirit of 1912.

The Mystery of Flight 2501

Sometimes the most interesting thing resting on the bottom of the Great Lakes is not a ship at all. In this case, it's an airplane.

In addition to the sheer tragedy when a Northwest Airlines plane crashed into Lake Michigan, a mystery remains. Why did it go down? Some suggested an errant spark or vicious winds. Or, thought others, perhaps it was brought down by some more unearthly force.

And it is that mystery that captured the attention of one of America's most famous authors and finders of lost ships—Clive Cussler.

The day of the plane's disappearance began normally enough. At 7:30 p.m. on Friday, June 23, 1950, Northwest Airlines Flight 2501 took off from La Guardia Airport in New York City and headed west for Minneapolis. From there, it was scheduled to fly to Seattle.

The skies were clear over New York and the flight went smoothly under the firm hand of Captain Robert C. Lind. Onboard the DC-4 propeller-powered plane were Lind, copilot Verne Wolfe, a single flight attendant, Bonnie Ann Feldman, and 55 passengers who included 22 men, 27 women, and 6 children.

At 10:49 p.m., Flight 2501 passed Cleveland. By that time, the passengers had eaten dinner and most had tilted their seats back and were trying to sleep.

At 11:51 p.m., still on Eastern Standard Time, Captain Lind radioed to traffic control in Chicago that he was over Battle Creek, Michigan, and estimated he would reach Milwaukee at 11:37 p.m. Central Standard Time.

Just as the plane came to the Michigan shore, Lind once again contacted traffic control. He knew a storm was firing up over the lake.

He requested a drop of his altitude from 3,500 feet to 2,500 feet. Traffic control said no.

That was the last contact anyone ever had with Flight 2501.

Just prior to midnight Central Standard Time, Northwest Airlines staff at Milwaukee radioed New York, Chicago, and Milwaukee that Flight 2501 was overdue.

At that point in history, it was the world's worst commercial aviation disaster.

Search teams headed out onto Lake Michigan at 5:30 a.m. the next morning. Response teams came from the U.S. Navy, the U.S. Coast Guard, and the state police from Michigan, Illinois, Wisconsin, and Indiana.

By that evening, a Coast Guard cutter found an oil slick, debris, and an airline logbook floating on the surface offshore between the towns of Glenn and South Haven, Michigan.

Later four Coast Guard cutters on the scene began picking up small bits of debris—seat cushions, clothing, blankets, luggage, and fragmented body parts that were no bigger than a man's hand. Before long this ghoulish detritus of tiny, shredded body parts began to wash ashore.

The city of South Haven closed its most popular swimming beach for nine days following the crash because each set of waves seemed to bring in new body parts. The beach did not reopen until the day before the July 4 holiday.

What happened to Flight 2501? So far, even five and a half decades after the crash, no one is quite sure.

Earlier reports speculated that the plane exploded in the air. A Berrien (Michigan) County prosecutor and the Coast Guard speculated that high winds twisted the plane, causing a spark that then set off an explosion in the fuel tanks.

The prosecutor, Louis Kerlikowski, said, "It must have been a terrific explosion to disintegrate the bodies so badly."

An investigator for Douglas Aircraft, the company that built the plane, thought maybe the high winds flipped Flight 2501 upside down, sending it into a fatal dive. He said that on occasions in the past when winds flipped this model of plane over, the pilots still managed to save the day if the plane had been flying above 6,000 feet. Unfortunately, Flight 2501's altitude above Lake Michigan was 3,500 feet. To save it at that altitude would have taken a magician, not a pilot.

Then from the village of Glenn, Michigan, came some very eerie versions of the crash from eyewitnesses. William Bowie, who owned a gas station/restaurant in Glenn, told reporters he saw it all happen as he was sitting out in front of his station at 12:15 a.m. with 10 other people.

He and the group concurred that the engines seemed to be running roughly. One of the group, as a sort of joke, yelled out as though to the pilot, "Bring that plane down here, buddy. We'll fix it for you."

Bowie said that as the plane veered out over the lake, the engine sounded "like a stock car with a blown gasket." He then added—and this is where it starts to get weird—that there was this funny yellow light trailing behind the wing.

Bowie's wife agreed, saying, "All of a sudden there was this flash. It was a funny light. It looked like the sun when it goes down. It only lasted a second. And then it was gone."

And that was not the only light seen over Lake Michigan that night. On the Wisconsin side of the lake, people reported seeing a bright light over the water some two hours after the crash.

A UFO? To this day, web sites that traffic in such extraterrestrial things list the crash of Flight 2501 as one of the unexplained phenomena. The answers are yet to be found.

But one group, the Michigan Shipwreck Research Associates (the same group that annually hires David Trotter to search for sunken ships in Lake Michigan) has been searching several years for this long-missing airplane.

Valerie Van Heest, the group's leader and spokesperson who also is writing a book about Flight 2501, thinks that even though the plane probably disintegrated, a real possibility exists of finding the four Pratt & Whitney, R2000 "Wasp" piston engines. Investigators would find no black boxes. They did not exist in those days. But maybe the engines would give up a clue or two.

As Van Heest tells it, Clive Cussler telephoned out of the blue and asked, "Do you want help finding the airplane?"

"We were floored," she said but immediately accepted the offer.

Cussler offered the assistance of the man who does his side-scan work, Ralph Wilbanks, one of the country's best. They agreed that Wilbanks would spend some time in May of 2004, 2005, 2006, and 2007 helping them look. As of this writing, no luck.

Wilbanks also has been helping Cussler search in the North Sea for the remains of the famed *Bonhomme Richard*, John Paul Jones's ship that was lost in 1779 during the U.S. Revolutionary War.

In the heat of the battle, the captain of the British ship *Serapis* asked if Jones would surrender. To which—as the history books report—the American captain replied, "I have not yet begun to fight."

Jones indeed won the battle, but lost his ship. The search goes on for the *Bonhomme Richard*.

Cussler, now in his mid-seventies, authored some dozen Dirk Pitt adventure books. But he also has written *The Sea Hunters*, a non-fiction book, and searched the world over for lost ships and other drowned mysteries. Having formed the nonprofit National Underwater Marine Agency, the Cussler group has found some 60 historically significant ships. Two important finds were the CSS *Hunley*, a Civil War submarine that was the first to sink a ship in battle, and U-20, the submarine that sank the *Lusitania*.

Now if they could just get a fix on Flight 2501.

John Steele: King of the Lakes

In the 1970s and early 1980s, he would arrive at annual wreck-diver meetings awkward, angular, and as shy as an Ichabod Crane. Peering through his thick glasses, he seemed oblivious that his shirt never seemed to match his tie, and his presentations—in contrast to many of the slick videos—typically showed blurry underwater snippets shot with an old 16 mm camera. Any single sequence in a Steele show ran no more than three minutes. That's all the film his camera could hold. Photographic technique, it appeared, had as little interest for him as his style of dress. But none of that mattered to the rapt audiences of divers.

They recognized they were in the presence of the famous John Steele, "King of the Lakes," who was busy finding lost ships when most of his audience had yet to put on a pair of flippers.

"He was a legend," said Valerie Van Heest, recalling the day she first met and dove with Steele. "I felt timid in his presence. But he was nice. Sort of fatherly. He explained things."

By the time he quit diving at age 73, Steele had found and dived on some 40 previously undiscovered wrecks. They were scattered through all the Great Lakes except Ontario, which he felt was too long a drive to reach.

Others of the wreck-hunting originals—such as Paul Ehorn and Kent Bellrichard—were Steele's diving partners.

Steele had a dive boat, originally an old diesel fishing tug called the *RV Hunter*. He had among the earliest versions of sonar. And, importantly, after spending hours in the library doing research, he regularly found lost ships.

And so come the weekends—or maybe starting on Friday or even Thursday—these early wreck hunters would head out to find and dive on lost ships. When hunting in Lake Superior, they would leave Wisconsin in the late afternoon and take turns driving all night just so they could get in two full days of diving.

A student of history, Steele loved swimming down into an unsullied past. He told a reporter that every time he enters an old wreck it is almost the same as opening a door on the main street of a town, walking into a business, and finding that time has stood still. Everything, he said, is the same as it was in the past.

Steele came by his passion for the Great Lakes honestly. Growing up on the shores of Lake Michigan in Waukegan, Illinois, he said, "I always liked to swim." His father was a recreational sailor and used to enter his sailboat in the annual race from Chicago to Mackinac Island. And then, in World War II, Steele joined the Navy.

When Steele tested near the top in intelligence, the Navy sent him to electronics school and made him a radar technician. In the process, he learned quite a bit about sonar. That knowledge would serve him well in his later diving years.

His career path in business had been long established, in much the same way that careers are set for direct descendants of reigning monarchs. He would become the chairman of the First National Bank of Waukegan. The family had owned the bank for a century. His great-grandfather founded the bank in 1852. Subsequently, the chairmanship fell to his grandfather, his father, and then to John.

"There's an advantage to being chairman," said Steele when we talked in the summer of 2006. "You can always sneak away."

Paul Ehorn, with whom he dove for a dozen years, described Steele as not only a passionate diver, but something of an eccentric.

Clearly, as a bank chairman, he had plenty of money. But he had no interest whatsoever in any sort of display of wealth. At one point after the divorce from his first wife, Ehorn said, Steele moved into an abandoned gas station in Waukegan. Inside was a 10,000 BTU furnace, piles of the *Wall Street Journal*, and his diving tanks. What passed for room dividers were bookcases. Outside, he parked his dive boat. He lived there for at least eight years.

"He was a millionaire, but he lived like a homeless person," Ehorn said.

Ehorn remembered an occasion when Steele gave his old Volkswagen van to his daughter who was living up in some rough-and-tumble area of Michigan's Upper Peninsula with lots of dirt roads. In turn, she gave her dad the fancy car she had been driving. Ehorn thought it was a BMW. Steele, it seemed, had no idea that he was driving around in a prestige automobile until someone at the bank mentioned it. At that point, he put the Beemer in a garage and refused to drive it.

"He didn't need fancy things," Ehorn said.

However, Steele would put money where his love lay—and that was diving. He managed to get some of the early sonar equipment. These included an early Elac sonar (sort of a glorified fish finder) and also a 3,500-pound unit from government surplus that may, according to Ehorn, have originally been on a submarine. It had a five-mile range and used to make a pinging sound, just like in the old World War II submarine movies.

At times, Ehorn said, Steele's lack of concern for money left him open to being cheated by those close to him. Part of the deal of diving with Steele, as it is with Trotter, was to help pay for the fuel. Ehorn said, "I always paid," but many divers on his boat just walked away after a diving trip and never offered a dime.

Describing his office at the bank, Ehorn said, Steele had a huge desk covered with papers. The papers were lined up in 12 rows, one for each month of the year.

"But when people would call for him on Monday or Tuesday, his secretary often might tell them, 'Sorry, he's out swimming.' If they called on Thursday or Friday, she was likely to say, 'Oh, he's out diving.'

"But," Ehorn said, "he was always there on Wednesdays."

Steele, who has now settled into a comfortable old age with his wife in a well-appointed condominium, grins about his old cut-and-run-off-to-dive days, when he and Ehorn would leave Waukegan in the late afternoon on a Thursday, drive 10 hours in the darkness to arrive bleary-eyed at 3 or 4 a.m., but ready for a full day of diving off Whitefish Point in Lake Superior.

He dove a lot. And he admitted that at times it could be dangerous.

Steele always dove using compressed air, never moving on to trimix, a combination of helium, oxygen, and nitrogen that reduces narcosis. He has said that he'd usually get one real scare a year.

"I was blinded a couple of times," he said. "I got bubbles in the blood. I always carried a small tank of pure oxygen on the boat," he said, to counteract the effects of nitrogen in the blood.

"At 200 feet," he told a reporter, "you have no sense of direction, no sense of up or down. And you are very careful about entering a ship because you may not be able to find your way out once you get in."

Throughout his diving career, Steele found many historical treasures, but never the sort of thing that might be called riches. Nor did he even come close.

On board the dive boat *Obsession*, David Trotter takes notes while watching the side-scan printout. Rocky Arsenault drives the boat. Photo courtesy of David Trotter Collection.

Pioneer Great Lakes wreck hunter Paul Ehorn in an underwater search.

Garry Kozak, one of the country's best side-scan experts, getting ready to make a hard-hat dive down to the *Dean Richmond*—what he thought would be a treasure ship. He had searched for nine years in Lake Erie. The actual treasure proved elusive.

A compass still in its box found aboard the 38-foot tug *G.F. Becker*. Photo courtesy of David Trotter Collection.

Danny Fader just floating and smiling and floating and smiling and floating after a successful dive on the *John A. McGean*. Photo courtesy of David Trotter Collection.

Danny Fader, Rudy Whitworth, and Rod Soja *(left to right)* aboard the *Obsession* studying side-scan images of a recently discovered wreck. Photo courtesy of David Trotter Collection.

Historic photo of the *Hunter Savidge* docked in Alpena *(top)*.
The name board of the *Hunter Savidge*, found by
David Trotter off to the side of the sunken ship in 1988.

Rudy Whitworth struggles to keep Danny Fader (in dark glasses and hat) alive on the deck of the *Obsession* in 1994. Photo courtesy of David Trotter Collection.

Rocky Arsenault helps a Coast Guardsman get aboard the *Obsession* after he has been lowered from a helicopter in response to the emergency call about Danny Fader's accident while diving on the steamship *Detroit* in 1994. Photo courtesy of David Trotter Collection.

Danny Fader being raised in a basket to the Coast Guard helicopter
following his diving accident on the *Detroit* in 1994.
Photo courtesy of David Trotter Collection.

Werner Wahl, "The Doc," studying the walking beam engine on the
steamer *Detroit* in 1994. Photo courtesy of David Trotter Collection.

The name plate of the *Daniel J. Morrell* on the pilot house. David Trotter refound the stern and was the first to discover the bow in 1979.
Photo courtesy of David Trotter Collection.

Inside the stern and next to the engine room of the *Daniel J. Morrell*. Tools still hang in their places and jars holding small things like nails and screws hang from the ceiling by their lids. The *Morrell* split apart in a violent storm in 1966. The bow sank quickly and the stern only went down later after floating in the stormy seas for five miles.
Photo courtesy of David Trotter Collection.

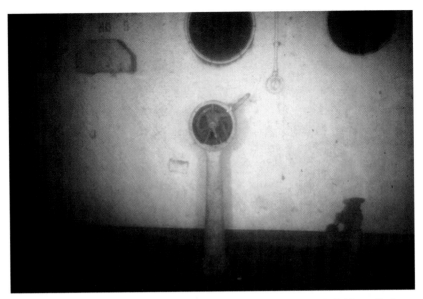

A stern telegraph with broken face plate found on the *Daniel J. Morrell*, the
600-foot ore carrier that had broken in two during a storm in 1966.
The telegraph is used by the captain or pilot to contact the engine room.
Photo courtesy of David Trotter Collection.

The *Minnedosa*, Canada's largest sailing ship at 250 feet with 150-foot masts,
sits dockside during the early years before it became a load-carrying consort
to be pulled along by another ship. The *Minnedosa* foundered in
Lake Huron in 1905. David Trotter and his team found it in 1993.
Photo courtesy of David Trotter Collection.

The port bow of the *Minnedosa*. M.T.C. stands for Montreal Transportation Company. Photo courtesy of David Trotter Collection.

A member of Dave Trotter's team examines the mast of the *Minnedosa* in 1993. Photo courtesy of David Trotter Collection.

John Steele, the original king of the Great Lakes wreck hunters. The photo was taken in 1978 by David Trotter while they were doing dives on the *Kamloops*, which went down off Isle Royale during a storm in December 1927.

Lifeboat onboard the *Kamloops* that went down off Isle Royale in Lake Superior on December 7, 1927. The 260-foot steel steamer sank extremely deep, to 250 feet. All 22 crew were lost. John Steele, Paul Ehorn, and David Trotter were among the first to explore the ship in 1978. It was in the engine room that Trotter found the remains of a crewman "still on duty." Photo courtesy of David Trotter Collection.

Rudy Whitworth, David Trotter, Danny Fader, and Werner Wahl *(left to right)* aboard the *Obsession* are examining the side-scan printout of the *Minnedosa* in 1993. Photo courtesy of David Trotter Collection.

David Trotter gets ready to make the first-ever dive on the *Minnedosa* in 1993. He had searched for this largest Canadian sailing ship for 15 years. In hand, he has the coiled mooring line and a float. Photo courtesy of David Trotter Collection.

David Trotter, the most proficient finder of lost ships in the Great Lakes, emerges from a successful wreck dive on the *Minnedosa*. Photo courtesy of David Trotter Collection.

This drawing portrays the *Frank H. Goodyear* during her final year on the Great Lakes. The crew of the *Goodyear* had no time to react on May 23, 1910, when the 534-foot *James B. Wood* came out of the night and rammed it. Loaded with iron ore, the eight-year-old *Goodyear* went down with 18 passengers and crew. Five survived. The *Goodyear* was especially distinguished because of the luxury railcar set on the deck for the owner's comfort. Trotter and his team discovered the *Goodyear* in 2002. Illustration by Robert McGreevy.

A coffee cup on the deck of the *Hunter Savidge* in 1988. Photo courtesy of David Trotter Collection.

The famed *Edmund Fitzgerald* as she rests now on the bottom of Lake Superior. The huge 729-foot ore boat went down in a brutal storm on November 10, 1975, with all 29 crew members. Its enduring fame was insured with a song by Canadian singer Gordon Lightfoot, "The Wreck of the Edmund Fitzgerald." Lying at 530 feet, two young divers in scuba outfits actually descended to its deck with the deepest wreck dive ever in the Great Lakes. Illustration by Robert McGreevy.

Down to the *Fitz*, the Great Lakes deepest wreck dive. The dive team that reached the famed ore carrier *Edmund Fitzgerald* down 530 feet in Lake Superior included *(left to right)* Ken Furman, Terrence Tysall, Mike Zlatopolsky, Randy Sullivan, and *(seated front)* Mauro Porcelli. They are pictured here in front of the *Fitzgerald* exhibit at the Great Lakes Shipwreck Museum at Whitefish Point, Michigan. Tysall and Zlatopolsky made the actual dive down to the deck of the *Fitzgerald* and laid a gloved hand on the rail in 1995. Until the publishing of this book, their daring exploit was little known outside the diving community. It was planned in secret and afterward the divers shunned national publicity.

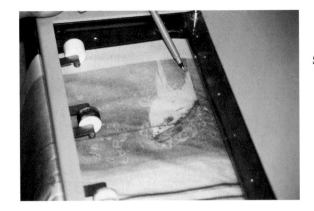

Side-scan image of the steamer *Detroit* on the day it was discovered in 1994. Photo courtesy of David Trotter Collection.

Danny Fader inspecting a dinner platter decorated with Asian designs on the deck of the steamer *Detroit* in 1994. Photo courtesy of David Trotter Collection.

The starboard paddle wheel on the steamer *Detroit*. Broken sections of the paddles were the result of the usual wear and tear, not from the accident that sank the boat. Photo courtesy of David Trotter Collection.

Rocky Arsenault shining his dive light on the mysterious strongbox inside the partially collapsed cabin on the side-wheel steamer *Detroit* in 1994.
Photo courtesy of David Trotter Collection.

Rocky Arsenault *(in blue)* and Jeff Moore *(in red)* on the day they pulled the strongbox up from the steamer *Detroit* in 1997.
Photo courtesy of David Trotter Collection.

Artifacts from the *Minnedosa*—a sumlog (the torpedo-looking device, which was towed behind a ship to determine its speed), two pitchers, and a glass flask set up for a photo shoot on the roof of the cabin structure. Photo courtesy of David Trotter Collection.

Werner Wahl checking out the engine with its walking beam aboard the side-wheel steamer *Detroit* in 1994. Photo courtesy of David Trotter Collection.

Steele did not discover the ship *Pewabic*. But he did dive it, with at least mild hopes of finding something of value on the steamer that, in 1865, dropped 160 feet to the bottom of Lake Huron near Alpena, Michigan. It reportedly went down with 300 tons of copper ingots, slabs, and mass copper, possibly $40,000 in the purser's safe, and, sadly, the 40 people onboard.

Steele came back with only one copper ingot. The safe, he said, was empty.

Because of its high value, nineteenth-century salvagers had found the *Pewabic* soon after it sank and pulled out major portions of the cargo with three separate operations.

The wreck *Pewabic*, it must also be said, was a killer. A man named Billy Pike drowned while trying to salvage the *Pewabic* in 1865. Two or three others died at the bottom during expeditions between 1880 and 1884. And in June 1897, newspapers reported that George M. Campbell and another diver drowned because the glass window broke in "the diving bell while at work on the wreck of steamer *Pewabic*."

Steele was the first to discover the steamer *Philadelphia* in 126 feet of water in Lake Huron off Pointe Aux Barques, Michigan. It went down with a load of coal, some merchandise, and 26 passengers and crew. The *Philadelphia* also had a safe. Hopes swelled. But when the divers pried it open they found neither gold nor jewels. Just $83 in change.

Steele also found a safe onboard the *Milwaukee*. The 325-foot car ferry was one of Steele's biggest finds. The *Milwaukee* was swamped and went down during a Lake Michigan storm on October 22, 1929. At 325 feet long, it was the second largest ship ever to go down in Lake Michigan.

The *Milwaukee* was a car ferry carrying railroad cars—17 of them. And in one of these big cars were other cars, a smaller kind—four brand new 1929 Nash automobiles.

The safe was another disappointment. When Steele brought it up, the only thing inside was four rolls of nickels.

In the early days of Great Lakes wreck diving, it was all about plunder. Divers—spirited on by a finders-keepers mentality—scrambled onto sunken ships largely to strip away anything of value, all to the distress of researchers and state historians.

These researchers rolled their eyes in horror to discover that diver swag included not only anything that was moveable, but also a whole lot that wasn't. Small items filled their goodie bags—cups, saucers, platters, dishes, oil lanterns, and tools. But in other cases, divers found ways to hoist out immense anchors. Portholes had been cut out of the side of ships. Marine compasses disappeared and so did ships' wheels, masts, spars, ornate figureheads, and even toilets and bidets.

In time a new, more conservation-minded ethic came into play. And divers such as Trotter and many others went down carrying cameras, disturbed very little, and usually returned to the surface carrying no more than those same cameras.

Like the others in the early days, Steele took his share of souvenirs. But he said that he quit after his first 13 years of diving. And, he said, virtually all of the artifacts he brought to the surface have ended up in museums.

Exhibits with Steele artifacts have been shown at the Milwaukee Public Library, Chicago's Shedd Aquarium, the Museum of Arts and History at Port Huron, Michigan, and the Valley Camp Museum at Sault Ste. Marie.

But it was the Smithsonian Institution in Washington, D.C., that turned one of Steele's shipwreck discoveries into his most famous.

The ship was the *Indiana*, one of the very first screw-propelled steamers in the Great Lakes.

The very first propeller-driven ship was launched in 1841. It was designed by John Ericsson, a Swede, who later designed the Civil War ironclad the *Monitor*.

Up until the early 1840s, side-wheel steam ships, like the *Detroit*, dominated Great Lakes transportation. But then the newly invented propeller-driven ships started appearing. The ships, in fact, were called "propellers."

The propellers were especially useful for carrying cargo in the Great Lakes because they were powerful and much narrower than the side-wheel steamers, so they could easily slip through the narrow locks and canals.

The *Indiana* was built in 1849. It should be said that this ship was not the earliest propeller-powered vessel ever to be found in the Great Lakes. David Trotter, in fact, found an older one—the *Goliath*.

On June 6, 1858, the *Indiana* was hauling a load of iron ore from the mining town of Marquette in Michigan's Upper Peninsula. As it motored east across Lake Superior toward the locks at Sault Ste. Marie, it developed a gushing leak in its stuffing box at the rear of the ship. The crew could not stanch the leak and the *Indiana* was soon sucked to the bottom not far from Crisp Point. All 17 crew members and 4 passengers managed to escape in lifeboats.

Historically, while the 146-foot *Indiana* was not the first propeller, it was the very first boat to sink in the Great Lakes with a load of iron ore. That's a big deal, because carrying iron ore has been and remains one of the mainstays of Great Lakes cargo carrying. Curiously, the *Indiana* settled in the lake just four miles from the final resting place of the *Edmund Fitzgerald*, another ore carrier, which famously went down with 29 men in November 1975.

Staff at the Smithsonian Institution soon heard of Steele's find and wanted it—or at least portions of it—for their collection in Washington, D.C.

In 1978, the *Indiana* was declared eligible for the National Register of Historic Places. The next year, divers for the Smithsonian—including Steele—pulled the ship's engine, boiler, rudder, related machinery, and its propeller.

The *Indiana*'s propeller was, according to *Michigan History Magazine*, "the style universally in vogue." It was patented by Richard F. Loper, of Philadelphia in 1844–45.

This propeller, it turns out, was a newer version of the propeller Trotter found on the *Goliath*, which was a copy of the original 1840 Ericsson design.

Steele was delighted to have pieces of his discovery in the Smithsonian. In fact, he was more than pleased to have almost all of the artifacts he collected in museums.

"When it's in a museum," Steele chuckled, "someone else has to do the dusting."

CHAPTER 7

Divers, Hunters, and Ships: ... to the *Edmund Fitzgerald*

Paul Ehorn: Devil or Don Quixote?

To put it bluntly, Paul Ehorn is the most controversial wreck diver in the Great Lakes.

To strict preservationists and state historians, Ehorn is a lake scourge—an unreconstructed wreck stripper. But to many wreck hunters and wreck divers—David Trotter included—Ehorn is a hero. He is a Don Quixote willing to fight "the unbeatable foe" of over-reaching government regulation.

No matter which view you take, it is undeniably true that Paul Ehorn has redefined wreck discovery and the discoverer's rights for the whole country. To meet him is a different matter; he in no way seems like a villain. Nor does he strike you as a man impractical enough to tilt at windmills.

In his early sixties, Ehorn is as lean and hard as a man half his age. He is one of those absolutely genuine guys you meet every now and then—no pretense, no guile. You trust him immediately. His smile captivates, his laugh is quick. More than anything, he exudes a sort of surging, almost uncontainable energy that seems to burst from his pores. You see Paul Ehorn today and you can easily see the 11-year-old Illinois farm boy who got the diving bug.

It wasn't because he'd heard of Jacques Cousteau, the reason thousands of Americans got into diving. Nor had he seen *Sea Hunt* on TV, another typical inspiration for divers. But he did have a buddy, Chuck Elliott, whose family had a swimming pool. It was a matter of opportunity breeding invention. Together, the two boys hatched an underwater diving experiment that today would give PADI the heebie-jeebies.

"We got an air hose from a gas station and glued it to an old face mask," he said, with a big grin, "and then we attached the hose to a shop air compressor.

95

"Well," he said, "it was good for the pool."

As the saying goes, one thing led to another. And what resulted was a pretty good picture of what diving was like in the early years. Four years later in 1960, after the 15 year old had earned his first paycheck with a summer job, he spent it all for a dive outfit.

"Tank, backpack, regulator. It cost $123. Top shelf. The best," Ehorn remembered.

He took a 10-week course with a local dive club. It was not PADI. Its certificates came from a local print shop. But he remembered the training as very physical and demanding.

"You had to swim so far with a 10-pound weight belt and then you had to tread water for so long. They would throw your mask and fins and dive gear to the bottom of the pool and you'd have to go down and clear the mask and put on the gear. It was a skill builder."

He eventually did get his official PADI certification.

Soon he was diving local wrecks. He remembered being cold. He was skinny as a kid, weighing only 130 pounds. First, he dove in just wearing a swim suit. Then he got a $27 wet suit that he had to cut to his size and then glue together.

"I was cold. Shivering," he said.

He started diving off Port Washington, Wisconsin, on the *Niagara*, a 245-foot luxury steamer that went down on November 24, 1856, with 60 people in about 50 feet of water. It was one of the greatest transportation disasters in the state's history. He also dove on the *Toledo*, another steamer that sank the same year, only this one was on October 22. The *Toledo* foundered just a thousand yards from Port Washington. More than 40 people died in the accident.

"I did hundreds of dives on the *Niagara*. There were lots of divers. It was promoted as a dive site," Ehorn said.

He and the other divers grabbed up whatever they could find on these old wrecks—hammers, saws, hinges, dishes, cups, silverware, flintlock rifles.

"It was fun. Look what I got. Anybody could do it. Nobody said, 'No.'"

Ehorn became a better and better diver. From Port Washington wrecks, he moved on, started diving on wrecks in other places in Lake Michigan and in the other Great Lakes. He bought his own dive boat, a 26-foot aluminum Marinette. "Dave (Trotter) got his because of mine."

Ehorn went on to become part of that early cadre of wreck divers—along with John Steele and Kent Bellrichard—who were finding and diving on Great Lakes wrecks when the rest of the world was wearing bell-bottom pants, sideburns, and thought "the swim" was a dance move.

Soon after the deep and dangerous *Kamloops* was discovered at Isle Royale, Ehorn was diving it. "I don't think anyone has dove *Kamloops* more than I have. I brought up a dead guy off the *Kamloops*."

The diver was down 267 feet. He had gone into a deep hole inside the bow. He had two lines. One went to the surface; the second did not. So instead of pulling himself to the surface, he went down. This was maybe the deepest body recovery ever made.

"He was 26," Ehorn remembered, speaking of the dead diver. He only had been diving for two years. Nobody should be diving a ship like the *Kamloops* with that little experience."

Soon Ehorn was finding his own lost ships. He continues to this day, having already found 13, three of them with John Steele. One of his most recent was the *Senator*, which he located in 2005.

During all this time, he continued to pick up mementos during his dives. And that's where trouble found him and eventually led him to court.

Ehorn was charged with pilfering objects from the shipwrecks. He was charged on three different occasions. One of these cases eventually ended up in federal court and yanked open the door for what recreation divers could—and could not—do on shipwrecks.

This case involved the *James R. Bentley*, a three-masted schooner, that sank on November 12, 1878, while carrying a load of rye from Chicago to Buffalo. Passing through the Mackinac Straits, the *Bentley* hit a reef. Lakewater rushed into the hold. The crew struggled to plug the leak, but could not. After three and a half hours, they gave up and abandoned ship. All made it to shore safely. As for the *Bentley*, it nosed down 150 feet to the lake bottom.

More than 100 years later, Ehorn and John Steele found the *James R. Bentley* not far from Cheboygan, Michigan, in 1984. Later that same year, Ehorn brought up the *Bentley*'s figurehead.

Figureheads were unusual in that period. Schooners were working ships that had little of refinement or artistry about them, but an artist had done some fine work on this figurehead. It was the carved image of a dragon with small wings, large scales, and a rope looped around the tail. Six years later, Ehorn decided the figurehead was too magnificent to keep, so he gave it to the Manitowoc Maritime Museum in Wisconsin.

"On behalf of the museum, I thank you for the extraordinary donation of the figurehead from the *James R. Bentley*," wrote the museum director Burt Logan in a letter to Ehorn.

Then, eight years after that and 14 years after he had brought the figurehead to the surface, Ehorn found himself under arrest in Michigan. The state attorney general's office charged him with theft. He was booked and fingerprinted. It rapidly became clear that the state would not be satisfied by giving him a slap on the wrist.

Ehorn was charged under the Aboriginal Records and Antiquities Act. If convicted, he would face a $5,000 fine and a two-year prison term for removing an artifact from a shipwreck. In addition, the state charged him with receiving and concealing stolen property. If the prosecution proved its case, he would face a possible $2,500 fine and a five-year prison term. Both charges were felonies. Clearly the state was out to make Ehorn the poster boy for bad divers.

Ehorn had no choice but to fight. If he was convicted of a felony, he could lose his job. Going to jail was simply unthinkable.

Speaking for preservationists, John Halsey, the Michigan state archeologist, said these wrecks belong to the state and they should remain untouched. He even dislikes that Trotter's crew will move items such as pitchers or ceramics in order to get better videotape pictures. The location of these items, he said, can have historical significance.

In response to the court action, Ehorn filed for ownership of the *Bentley*. The logic was simple, he said: "If you own the wreck, you cannot be charged with stealing from yourself."

Ehorn's case eventually worked its way up to federal district court in Detroit. There Judge Victoria Roberts issued a decision. The question is, she wrote, does the state of Michigan or Paul Ehorn have a right to the *Bentley* under the Abandoned Shipwreck Act of 1987?

The judge ruled for Ehorn. Under the Abandoned Shipwreck law she said, for the state to legally claim ownership, the ship must be embedded. Under the law, the term embedded means:

> … firmly affixed in a submerged land or in coralline formations such that the use of tools of excavation is required in order to move the bottom sediments to gain access to the shipwreck, its cargo, and any part thereof.

What exactly are tools of excavation? The law explains:

> Tools of excavation would include, but are not limited to, hydraulic, pneumatic, or mechanical dredges; explosives, propeller wash deflectors; air lifts; blowtorches; induction equipment; chemicals; and mechanical tools used to remove or displace bottom sediments or coralline formations to gain access to shipwrecks.

Judge Roberts continued by writing that, based on testimony, videotapes, and photos, it was clear that the *Bentley*, which was upright and 90 percent exposed, was not embedded.

With that judgment, Ehorn became the official owner of the *Bentley*. For preservationists—particularly state historians—it was a setback.

For wreck hunter David Trotter and others, it was a defining moment. The ruling proved that the state did not have carte blanche ownership of every underwater wreck.

Trotter points out that the decision is particularly significant in the Great Lakes because, with the exception of Lake Erie, the bottoms are largely mud and hard where the currents—unlike the ocean—do not tend to bury things. So most sunken ships in the Great Lakes—and Trotter has seen a lot of them—do not fall into the category of "embedded."

Also, wrecks can be protected by putting them on the historic registry. Many have been. That, of course, is difficult to do if the state does not know where the wreck is located. This case might apply to Steve Libert's find that might possibly be the *Griffon*. He certainly is not volunteering the GPS numbers.

Having finally won a long and expensive court battle for the *Bentley*, Ehorn then did go ahead and strip the ship.

It was a big win for Paul Ehorn. On the other hand, he took a financial beating. When counted up, his attorney fees were immense.

The 60-year-old Ehorn sees no retirement any year soon. "I figure," he said, "that I'll be paying them off for the rest of my life."

As for the *Bentley*, much of the old ship now resides on dry land at Ehorn's house. The huge anchor sits in his front yard. He has a lot of other artifacts off the ship, enough that—along with his other finds—the Ehorn home could serve as one of the finest maritime museums in the Great Lakes. In the meantime, Ehorn continued to dive and hunt for lost ships.

He did suffer a setback in 1986 while diving on the 138-foot *Cornelia B. Windiate*. It came not long after he and John Steele found the wreck in Lake Huron that same year.

The wreck was a diver's dream. Most of it was intact—even a yardarm was still standing on a mast.

The dive went fine that day, Ehorn remembered. But, once back on deck with his tanks off, Ehorn spent some time struggling with the starter rope on the engine that ran the on-board air compressor. He was pleased because the exercise of pulling on the rope warmed him up after the cold dive. As it turned out, all his efforts to crank that engine were a bad idea.

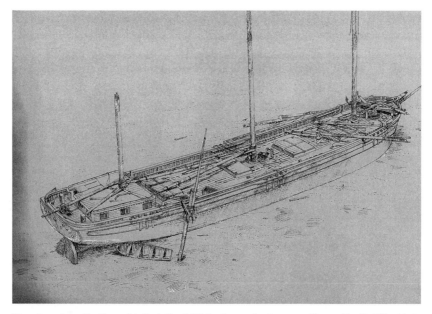

People originally thought that the 136-foot canal schooner *Cornelia B. Windiate* was lost in Lake Michigan during a November storm in 1876. Instead it was found in 1986 by wreck-hunting pioneers John Steele and Paul Ehorn in Lake Huron, lying on the bottom in near perfect condition. It was on the *Windiate* that Ehorn suffered a nasty hit of the bends. Illustration by Robert McGreevy through the courtesy of Thunder Bay Marine Sanctuary.

"The body is like a soda pop bottle," he explained. "It's fine unless you heat it or shake it up."

He shook his body and warmed it up during a time when his blood still had plenty of nitrogen from the dive. Soon he felt unusually tired. He took a pass on lunch. He just was not hungry.

"The symptoms were there," he said, "I just did not recognize them."

He took a second dive in the afternoon. That felt great. Of course, his body was under pressure again. In effect by diving, he had plunged himself into God's own recompression chamber. But when he came up, reality struck—the bends.

"It felt like the point of an ice pick in my back and chest. I went numb from the nipples on down." The pain was unimaginable.

He lay down on the deck and raised his feet, trying to calm his internal pop bottle. He sucked on pure oxygen from a small tank.

As soon as the divers landed, they rushed Ehorn to a recompression chamber in Alpena, Michigan. It did not seem to help much. He later went through four more so-called chamber rides in Milwaukee.

To this day, Ehorn suffers from that bout with the bends. He is still numb and feels tingling down his right thigh to his knee. Despite some real fears following his accident, Ehorn continues to dive and to search for lost ships.

In 2005 he discovered the *Senator,* a steel-hulled freighter that went down off Port Washington, Wisconsin, on Halloween, October 31, 1929. It was rammed by a second ship, the *Marquette.* Onboard the *Senator* were 250 brand-new Nash automobiles. Would Ehorn dive that ship?

"No," he said, explaining that the ship was down 500 feet.

"That's like driving a car at 500 m.p.h.," he told a newspaper reporter. "Could you do it? Well, theoretically, yeah. But what's the chance of killing yourself?

"Pretty damned great."

Garry Kozak: Side-Scan Wizard

The story goes that Garry Kozak started finding lost ships at the age of 16. He went out in a rowboat with nothing more than a depth sounder. Later, after two years of college at Detroit's Wayne State University, he became a commercial diver. It was during this period that he learned about the steamer *Dean Richmond.* Kozak determined if ever there was a Great Lakes treasure ship, the *Richmond* was it.

At the time of its sinking, newspapers reported that the 238-foot *Richmond* went down on Friday the 13th of October 1893, during a terrible storm on Lake Erie. The entire crew was lost.

But here was the part that captured Kozak's imagination. The *Richmond* reportedly was carrying 200 tons of lead ingots and 100 tons of zinc ingots. In addition, rumor had it that somewhere onboard was a load of gold bullion for Wells Fargo.

The cargo alone was valuable. But bullion—that would be a treasure on an epic scale. The question was: Where was the *Dean Richmond?*

Reportedly, the ship had been spotted near Erie, Pennsylvania, before it sank. But a few days later, bodies from the *Richmond* washed up 40 miles to the east, near Dunkirk, New York.

Kozak saw the *Richmond* as his ticket to big money. He quit his job as a commercial diver and started searching full-time in 1974, tracking over Lake Erie from April through September.

His edge was a first-rate Klein side-scan sonar. Scratching for money, he ran into a major piece of luck when he was hired by the sonar people, Klein Associates.

Still he searched and searched. Nine years passed. In that time, he spent $100,000, scanned almost 600 square miles of Erie's lake bottom, and found 28 shipwrecks. Not only had he turned himself into a premier wreck finder, but also one of the best in North America in the fine art of operating side-scans. But still no sight of the *Richmond*.

Then on June 15, 1983, a dark image showed up on his side-scan paper readout. He was searching in an area about 11 miles from Erie, Pennsylvania. It sure looked like the *Dean Richmond* on the readout. And in fact it was.

The ship—a twin-engine propeller—was lying in 110 feet of water. Unfortunately, it was upside down. Kozak then joined up with Massey Commercial Diving for the salvage operation. They had to cut a hole in the hull to get inside. They searched through the dark guts of the ship. The lead was there, so was the zinc. But they found no safe filled with gold bullion.

The lead and zinc, he thought, should surely be a moneymaker. But it turned out to be a good news, bad news story. Indeed they were pulling out ingots, about $4,000 worth every day. But as he told Trotter in a telephone conversation, "It's costing us $6,000 a day to do it."

After two weeks, he gave it up.

Edmund Fitzgerald: *The Deepest*

If asked about Great Lakes shipwrecks today, most people could probably name just one—the *Edmund Fitzgerald*. Without a doubt, it is the most famous.

Attacked by gale-force winds and 30-foot waves on November 10, 1975, the 729-foot *Fitzgerald*—one of the biggest ships in the Great Lakes—plunged to the bottom of Lake Superior, taking with it a full load of 26,116 tons of iron ore and all 29 crewmen.

The disaster was inked in headlines across the world. Since the sinking, at least a score of books have been written about the ship and its tragic sinking. Researchers have studied it. To this day, more than 30 years later, newspaper articles periodically pop up about the *Fitzgerald*.

And, of course, many still can recite lyrics from Gordon Lightfoot's haunting ballad "The Wreck of the Edmund Fitzgerald," which stayed on the pop charts for weeks in 1976:

> *The Lake, it is said, never gives up her*
> *dead when the skies of November turn*
> *gloomy.*

Given all that, one might guess that we know just about all there is to know about the *Edmund Fitzgerald*. Yet one astounding story has remained largely untold.

In a record-setting expedition, two young men—one a Florida dive instructor, the other a Russian expatriate—secretly came to Michigan's Upper Peninsula in 1995 and made the first and only scuba dive down to the *Edmund Fitzgerald*.

It was a feat of rare danger. The two went down an astounding 530 feet in 36-degree water and actually touched the rail with a gloved hand. At that moment, they set the record for the deepest wreck dive ever in the Great Lakes and one of the deepest in the world.

Other divers had gone to greater depths. But none to a wreck—or to any destination at all for that matter.

No one had ever actually touched the *Fitzgerald* with a human hand since she sank. Small submarines had gone down for a look. Remotely driven cameras have shot videos. A man outfitted in a pressurized, aluminum Newt suit—looking somewhat like the Michelin Man—had touched the ship with mechanically operated steel pincers. But never a human hand.

Furthermore, theirs was a dive—due to sheer danger, political complexity, and recent Canadian law—that will, in all likelihood, never be repeated.

The idea for the expedition was hatched in Florida, where the two young divers met for the first time in 1994 at a spring-fed cave-diving site near Ocala. Mike Zlatopolsky, better known as Mike Zee, had driven down from Chicago for some cave diving. At 36, he was a short, shaggy Russian immigrant with a dark beard, bushy hair, and a penchant for unreconstructed machismo.

He grew up in Russia where he learned to swim at age 3 and by his twenties was diving in the Mediterranean, the Black Sea, and Indian Ocean. Later, with his home base in Chicago, he started a small dive charter business guiding wreck dives in Lake Superior off Whitefish Point.

Wreck divers around the Great Lakes were vaguely aware of him. They would say, "Oh, I know about Mike Zee. He's the one who drives that Hummer."

Indeed, to this day Zlatopolsky drives the monster SUV, painted a sinister black. And just to show he means business, he installed an exhaust pipe that extends up above the roof. Why? So he can drive it underwater.

Zee, whom few know by any other name, of course knew about the *Edmund Fitzgerald*. And he wanted to dive it. Badly. He was a self-confessed danger junkie. "I don't dive anything under 200 feet," he said. And this dive would certainly hit the danger quotient.

Over time he had tried to lure other divers to join him for a *Fitzgerald* adventure, but all had begged off. Then in Florida, he met Terrence Tysall, who was an instructor at Forty Fathom Grotto. And they got to talking. As luck would have it, Zlatopolsky had, by chance, met one of the few people who could pull off this venture and, at the same time, keep him alive.

If Tysall was not Zlatopolsky's polar opposite, he was certainly far different. Where Zlatopolsky was darkly shaggy and foreign, Tysall was an all-American boy, clean cut as a Navy pilot. In fact, at 28, he had the good looks and enough cock-sure style to have played Tom Cruise's role in *Top Gun*. Like the character Maverick, Tysall was good. And he knew it.

Fast talking, funny, and charming, he had turned himself into one of the best technical divers in the country. His confidence was based on long and careful training and lots of experience.

Tysall said he started swimming late, at age 6, but by age 8 he was diving. By 28, when he hooked up with Zlatopolsky, he had a resumé that veterans twice his age could envy.

He had penetrated deep caves in Florida and Mexico; dropped down into the 400-foot deep Blue Hole off Belize; dove 25 times on the *Andrea Doria*, the so-called Everest of wreck dives; and trained the military divers who went down on the Civil War ironclad war ship the *Monitor*, of *Monitor* and *Merrimack* fame. On top of that, he had trained to be a Navy SEAL and only failed to graduate because of a knee injury that resulted in five operations.

He knew his stuff. He had done it all, or most of it. He had been deep and dangerous and knew the tricky business of exotic gas mixtures the way Dan Marino knew his playbook.

For the next year, Mike and Terrence trained separately. They planned out the details of this highly technical dive. Tysall did practice dives, going deeper and deeper in the Atlantic. At one point, he went down more than 400 feet.

"I am a big fan of training," Tysall said. "The idea is to get the depth out of the picture right away," meaning that once he was no longer distracted by the sheer depth, he could concentrate on other matters.

Zlatopolsky did dives down to 300 feet and made ice dives over the winter to prepare for the cold bottom temperatures of Lake Superior. They set Dive Day for the end of the summer of 1995.

"We kept it a secret," Tysall said, "because you never know when things might fall apart."

In the preceding summer, a flap over the *Fitzgerald* had arisen. Family members of the *Fitzgerald*'s crew were incensed to learn that photos had been taken of dead people on the sunken ship and were likely to be published. It was a scandal that hit the newspapers. But Tysall said the Michigan brouhaha was not the reason their team stayed quiet. He said he was unaware of it.

From the very beginning, the *Edmund Fitzgerald* was no ordinary ship. When it was first launched in the summer of 1957, the *Detroit News* described the *Fitzgerald* as "the biggest object ever dropped into fresh water in recorded history."

A crowd of 15,000 cheering people showed up for the official launch on June 7. Out on the Detroit River, tugboats tooted in its honor and 250 pleasure boaters shouted and waved.

The *Fitzgerald*, costing $8 million, stretched out to 729 feet in length (short enough to slide into Sault Ste. Marie's 730-foot-long locks, but just barely), 75 feet wide, and 39 feet deep.

At that size, the *Detroit News* reported, the ore boat was "three-fourths as long as the *United States* liner [and] longer than the Penobscot Building is high." At one time, Detroit's Penobscot Building was the tallest in the world—until it was dropped to second, after the building of the Empire State Building.

The ship's payload was 26,000 tons of iron ore—bigger than anything in the Great Lakes. But that did not mean the *Fitzgerald* was slow. For a ship its size, the *Fitz* could cruise at a remarkable 16 m.p.h.

In fact, the *Fitzgerald* set several speed records. It regularly buzzed from Lake Superior down to Toledo in only five days, a speed quick enough for her to be dubbed "The Toledo Express." The young team would be diving on what was not only a modern tragedy, but an important piece of Great Lakes history.

Despite the significance of their proposed dive, this was no highly financed expedition with endless amounts of time, money, and resources. Tysall's trip north from Florida was in an aging Toyota pickup along with two backup divers—Ken Furman and Mauro Porcelli. The compact truck was so small that only two people could sit in front. The third had to lie in back and try to sleep among the accumulation of dive tanks. Rotating drivers, the three drove straight through in 27 hours, to finally stop at Paradise, Michigan, just down the road from Whitefish Point.

At Paradise, they met Zlatopolsky and his business partner, Randy Sullivan of Sault Ste. Marie, Ontario, who was a diver and, more importantly for the venture, captain of their dive boat called *First One*, since it was the first dive boat that Sullivan had ever owned.

Sullivan had already scouted out the location, dropped a mooring line, and hooked onto a railing on the *Fitzgerald*'s bow. The line was marked with a buoy.

The *Fitzgerald* lies on the bottom in two pieces. The bow section stands upright, driven into the bottom. The aft section landed upside down.

Although later writings said that Sullivan had gotten a government permit for the dive, he allowed as how that was wrong. At the time, Sullivan said, no law or regulation had been set regarding the *Fitzgerald*, which lies in Canadian waters. No permission was needed.

In fact it would not be until 2006, more than 11 years later, that Canada passed a law specifically restricting access to the *Fitzgerald*, as well as two other historic ships in Lake Ontario.

On their first full day together the team did tune-up dives, bubbling down on the 178-foot wooden-screw steamer, the *John M. Osborn*, which went down after a collision in 1884.

Tysall, who had dived exclusively on sunken ships in the ocean, was amazed how Lake Superior's cold, clear water had maintained the *Osborn* in such pristine condition. The ship was down 180 feet—nothing even approaching the depth they were contemplating. But the team, including the two support divers, was able to practice in detail what would be a carefully timed, carefully choreographed dive.

The next day, Lake Superior turned nasty with 10-foot waves and 30-knot winds. Too much for the 32-foot, fiberglass *First One* dive boat. The team did a dry-land dry-run in their motel parking lot.

As Tysall said, he's big on training. And that was good, because while he could not have known it at the time, their dive would not be trouble-free.

"I knew that 29 people had died on the *Fitzgerald*," Tysall said. "I did not want us to be numbers 30 and 31."

On the third day, September 1, Lake Superior offered up a gift—blue skies, sunshine, and waves that topped out at about six inches. Perfect. But this would still be a dicey dive.

Tysall and Zlatopolsky would use several different gas mixtures to breathe. Tysall knew he carried the weight of responsibility because, "I was going down with a guy who had not made a lot of deep dives."

First they sent down an oil rig camera that was attached to a 750-foot Kevlar cable. Its light showed where they were going on the ship, and the cable would be their dive line.

The two divers were similarly outfitted with gear and tanks that weighed close to 300 pounds. Each had two large tanks on his back. Zlatopolsky had two 120-cubic-foot cylinders; Tysall had two 104-cubic-foot cylinders. These would carry the mixture they needed for the bottom, a tri-mix of 9.6 percent oxygen, 62 percent helium, and the remainder nitrogen. This mixture would allow them to breathe and dramatically reduce the effects of nitrogen narcosis.

If you have a mind for recalling numbers, you might remember that the amount of oxygen in air is 21 percent. The amount in the bottom mix is much lower, only 9.6 percent oxygen. On its face, this may not seem logical. After all, isn't oxygen the very stuff of life?

Well, yes. But in moderation. When the body is under pressure at depth, oxygen can be toxic. It is called nervous system toxicity or hyperoxia, and in even a short period of time, it can cause convulsions and knock a diver unconscious—then, of course, he drowns.

After some unfortunate experimenting with breathing pure oxygen, the famed Jacques Cousteau and other early divers discovered that while different divers reacted differently, a reasonable safety threshold to avoid oxygen toxicity was about 20 feet. These same toxic effects also occur when breathing compressed air, only at great depths.

The problem is the huge water pressure on the body and the gas itself. On the surface, when we are normally breathing air (21 percent oxygen and 79 percent nitrogen), we actually only use about 4 percent (all of it oxygen). The rest we exhale. At 33 feet, where the pressure is doubled, we take in twice as much gas because it is denser. Studies have found that when breathing compressed air, the same oxygen toxicity will hit at 218 feet below the surface that with pure oxygen hits at 20 feet.

Using tri-mix helps solve that problem. The amount of oxygen is reduced. Helium is added, which is easier to breathe and for regulators to manage. And helium has no narcotic effect, thus reducing the effects of nitrogen narcosis.

In each diver's third tank, strapped pyramid-style on the two larger bottom tanks, was a 120-cubic-foot cylinder of compressed air.

In addition, off the left hip, each carried a 45-cubic-foot cylinder with a so-called transitional mix. This gas mixture was designed to help them return to the surface. This also was a tri-mix, but in different proportions—16 percent oxygen, 35 percent helium, and the rest nitrogen. On the right side, Tysall brought along a back-up 80-cubic-foot cylinder of compressed air—just in case one of the three main cylinders failed.

And finally, in a pocket, each carried a small cylinder of argon. They would use this gas to inflate their dry suits. The inflation prevents "suit squeeze" from the extreme pressure in very deep water and it is also a much warmer insulation than air.

With their legs wobbling under the weight, the two stepped off the swim platform at the back of the boat into Lake Superior's frigid waters.

They descended looking at each other face mask to face mask, down along the camera cable.

A number of bad things can happen to divers in deep water. So this face-to-face technique was important, so each could watch the other for signs of something called high-pressure nervous syndrome (HPNS).

When divers go down quickly to great depths, HPNS symptoms can show up. They include dizziness, nausea, vomiting, tremors, muscle spasms, and stomach cramps.

It was not HPNS, but trouble hit them sooner than expected.

They had planned to descend 250 feet—less than halfway—using compressed air and then switching to the tri-mix for the bottom. But at 180 feet, Zlatopolsky's regulator suffered a free flow.

To nondivers, the term free flow might engender some very pretty images—free-flowing water or perhaps a pretty girl in the wind with free-flowing hair. For divers, it's a terrifying experience. It means the regulator has frozen in the open position and the gas inside the tank—the very stuff they are breathing—is gushing out in an uncontrolled, heart-stopping flurry of bubbles.

In this case, Tysall was able to quickly shut down the regulator and Zlatopolsky switched early to the bottom mix. The exchange, said Tysall, took 15 seconds. As it turned out, Tysall was able to reactivate the failed regulator later by turning it on and off several times.

At 250 feet, Tysall switched to the tri-mix on schedule. By that point, any glow of light from the sunlit surface was almost gone.

At 300 feet, it was pitch black. The visible world narrowed substantially—closed in by the sides of their masks, the water, and the reach of their dive lights.

At 490 feet, the two got their first sight of the *Fitzgerald*, a faint glimmering in Tysall's dive light and the glow of the light from the camera.

The broken half-ship lay in an underwater darkness like none Zlatopolsky had ever experienced.

"It was like no other wreck and no other place on the planet," he said. "It was like being in a black hole. The lights reach out and just disappear, eaten by the darkness."

Their plan had been to descend to the *Fitzgerald* in three to five minutes. But they had gone slower, arriving in about seven minutes.

They could see where the ship's bow had driven into the clay bottom, surrounding the craft with large clay chunks "the size of chairs."

As they came to the rail, Tysall remembered it as an emotionally powerful moment.

"For the first time in almost 20 years, living hands were touching the *Edmund Fitzgerald*. I knew that people had died in this wreck. And that was what affected me most. In that moment, I wanted to send a message to those who had died: Hey, nobody has forgotten you."

They had been on the bow of the *Fitzgerald* for no more than six minutes. But now it was time to leave.

To avoid getting the bends that can leave a diver paralyzed or even dead, they would take a very long time decompressing as they rose to the surface. Because they were using helium in their dive mixes, they would have to further extend the time necessary to rid the nitrogen from their bodies. Time was short. The longer they stayed down, the longer the decompression process.

"Every extra minute on the wreck," Tysall said, "would be an additional 45 minutes of decompression."

At this point, a comparison might be made between this sort of extreme diving to mountain climbing expeditions in the Himalayas. Both this sort of dive and the mountain expeditions take months, even years of planning and preparation. Then there is the actual business of getting to the top—or in this case, to the bottom. In the minds of the uninitiated, the job seems to be done. After all, haven't they reached their goal?

But the job isn't done. Now both the climber and the deep diver need to get back. And this can be the most difficult and dangerous part. For example, more people have died on the descent from the top of Everest than in making the assault to the top.

Added together, their time for descent and on the *Fitzgerald* was less than 13 minutes. Their return to the surface would take three hours and 15 minutes—rising, then stopping and holding their position for a time, then rising again to the next stop—all the time letting nitrogen escape from their bodies.

They rose to 310 feet and at that point switched to their transitional-mix gas, which they carried on their left sides. They then rose slowly at a rate of 30 feet per minute to 210 feet, where they switched to air.

Next, at 180 feet, they were met by Ken Furman—one of the support divers. He brought down tanks with a different gas mixture, nitrox. This one had 40 percent oxygen and 60 percent nitrogen. The increase in oxygen helps purge the dangerous nitrogen from the system. But bad luck was not all behind them.

At 80 feet, Zlatopolsky's regulator froze. Furman, who had been floating on the surface with yet another bottle of nitrox, saw the problem, quickly descended, and speedily switched tanks. But the problems were not over.

Just as Furman was returning to the surface, Tysall's regulator froze and began to free flow. He temporarily solved the problem by first closing the tank's valve and then opening it periodically to inhale the escaping nitrox.

Regulators that free flow are not an unusual problem when the divers are in very cold water. The mechanisms literally freeze up.

Once again, Furman came down with a new tank. They had planned well enough to have four extra tanks onboard.

At 20 feet, Tysall and Zlatopolsky reached a pair of regulators that were hung on hoses off the dive boat. These, attached to tanks on the boat, supplied 100 percent oxygen. They stayed at this level for 25 minutes, occasionally taking breaths from the compressed air tanks to reduce the possibility of oxygen toxicity.

Once on the surface, Furman and Porcelli helped them take off their big tanks, trying to make sure that the divers had very little exertion. Exertion can aggravate the effects of nitrogen on the body. At that point, they just lay on the surface for another half hour breathing pure, nitrogen-cleansing oxygen. Then it was time for high fives back on deck.

"I felt so good," said Zlatopolsky, "totally invigorated."

Back on shore, they trooped over to the Great Lakes Shipwreck Museum at Whitefish Point and had their pictures taken standing in front of the *Fitzgerald* exhibit.

Later, word did leak out about the dramatic dive. Both Tysall and Zlatopolsky got calls from the family members of the *Fitzgerald* crew, who worried that the divers had defiled the grave site. The two said they explained that they meant no disrespect and the callers seemed satisfied.

Tysall also got a call from the sensationalist TV magazine *Hard Copy* to do the story, but he declined. Discussing the dive ten years after the event, Tysall commented.

"For me diving the *Fitzgerald* was a logistical challenge, same as the Blue Hole. But don't get me wrong," he said, "I'll stamp my name in the history book any time."

CHAPTER 8

Zebras

Starting in 1988, just two years after Danny Fader joined Trotter's team, the diving experience in the Great Lakes began changing in some upsetting and very visible ways.

Within less than a decade, everyone living by the lakes would notice how the apparently immutable water donned a new personality. But divers in particular—people who actually spent extended amounts of time in the water—would notice big differences in what they could see underwater and what they could *not* see. They soon recognized they would have to make some adjustments with their diving equipment.

The cause of all this change was—and continues to be—zebra mussels.

About the size of a fingernail, the brown-and-yellow mollusk is a native of Europe and in particular the Caspian Sea. In 1988, researchers were startled to discover colonies of these mussels along the edges of Lake St. Clair, a wide spot in the river that runs between Lakes Huron and Erie.

Not much time would pass before these little herringbone-striped mussels proved themselves to be the cockroaches of the Great Lakes. They drive people and marine life nuts, breed like black flies on Viagra, and are almost unkillable.

Scientists believe the mussels were brought to the big lakes in ballast water carried by European cargo vessels. Ballast water is water that is sucked up (in this case from the ocean or some faraway sea) and loaded into the bottom of a ship to keep it from tipping over when it has no cargo. When cargo is put aboard, the ballast water is no longer needed and crews simply dump it. Unfortunately, along with this alien water, the ships also have been dumping a number of alien hitchhikers like the zebra mussel.

In fact, this dumping of ballast water has been blamed for most of the invasive species that have entered the lakes in recent decades. As of this writing, the Great Lakes now are host to an astounding 183 of these foreign invaders. The number of new alien species is increasing at a rate of one every six and a half months.

Over the years, some of the worst have included lamprey eels, alewives, Eurasian ruffes (a forage fish whose voracious appetite has reduced stocks of yellow perch and walleye), round gobies (aggressive feeders that take over prime spawning grounds), and the tiny spiny and fishhook waterfleas (which foul fish lines and feed on tiny animal life, robbing it from native larval fish).

The zebra mussels have proved they can multiply with the speed of an IBM computer. Each female can produce about 100,000 eggs per year. They spawn twice a year. Their offspring are about the size and diameter of a human hair, so they are easily carried by currents and can drift for miles. Humans often transport them inadvertently.

These little ones can get into anything, anywhere—boat bilges, engine cooling systems, bait buckets, live wells—that a boat or fisherman can move from one body of water to another. The grownup zebra mussels attach themselves to anything solid, including boats and boat trailers—and thus they get transported.

Within 10 years of their arrival in 1988, zebra mussels had invaded all five of the Great Lakes plus Lake Champlain and the river basins of the Mississippi, Tennessee, Hudson, and Ohio rivers. In 1992, Michigan had just one inland lake with zebra mussels—now more than 100 lakes have mussel colonies.

Go almost anywhere around the edges of the Great Lakes and you'll find zebra mussels. They were swept in on beaches, where their sharp shells cut swimmers' feet. The adults, using adhesive strands called byssal fibers, attach themselves to almost anything solid where the current is not too strong. They are found clamped onto boats, docks, piers, rocky shores, plants, things made of rubber, plastic, glass, cloth—even onto slow moving creatures such as clams, crayfish, and turtles.

On boats, such as the huge ore carriers, a coating of zebra mussels can slow the boats' speed and increase costs of commercial shipping. In some cases zebra mussels, which can form in layers up to eight inches thick, have actually sunk marker buoys.

One of the most expensive problems created by the zebra mussels so far has been the clogging of intake pipes that feed water into power plants, golf courses, municipal water systems, and the like. At one point, water was cut off for three days to the city of Monroe, Michigan, because of zebra mussels. In coming years, the economic impact of the zebra mussels is expected to run into the billions of dollars.

For divers, the arrival of zebra mussels has meant good news and bad, but mostly bad.

The good news is clearer water. Almost anywhere in the lakes divers have been seeing astounding improvements in underwater visibility, or *viz*, as they call it.

Zebra mussels are filter feeders, that is, they take in water (about a liter a day for an adult) and filter out every microscopic plant or animal. The particles that they cannot use are wrapped in a kind of mucus and spit out. All the rest is consumed. When you consider that mussels can sometimes settle in clusters of 100,000 per square meter, that's a lot of filtering going on. Researchers estimate that zebra mussels now are filtering the entire volume of Lake Erie's western basin once a week—every week of every year.

With the loss of these microscopic plants and animals, the water is getting clearer and clearer by the month. In Lake Erie, water clarity has improved an amazing 600 percent. Divers there report where once they might be able to see just six inches in front of their masks, now they can see several feet. Some people insist that Lake Erie could use a good filtering, but this seems to be getting out of hand.

In 2006, Trotter's group went back to visit the steamer *Detroit*. During their first dives in 1994, the visibility was at best about 3 to 5 feet. In 2006, they had days of seeing up to 25 or 30 feet—all thanks to the zebra mussels. Trotter said for the first time he was able to see and videotape the entire paddle wheels and almost the width of the whole deck, something that he had not been able to do a dozen years before. That all sounds good. But then you must consider that the zebra mussels also are gluing themselves onto sunken ships.

Before the mussel arrival, divers would find sunken ships that were as pristine as the day they sank—name boards could be read, engines looked like they simply needed to be dried out before being fired up again, and on long-sunken compasses divers could read the letters N, E, S, and W and see the needle. No more. Now the aquanauts descend to find slatherings of zebra mussels inches thick, even on ships as deep as 200 feet or more. Zebra mussels have become freshwater barnacles.

As always—but now in a different way—wreck hunters must struggle to figure out exactly which virgin wreck they have happened upon. Now, instead of coping with silt-engendered myopia, they are spending time underwater scraping the mussels off the sides and various parts of the ships.

What's more, their equipment is taking a beating. The sharp-edged zebra mussel shells tear at the divers' equipment. Now they often must wear special gloves that resist being ripped by the mussels and take care not to rip holes in their dry suits. A leaky dry suit bodes extremely wet and extremely cold diving.

Trotter and every member of his team have repeated it again and again, "Given a choice between low viz or zebra mussels, I'd take low viz."

The damage, of course, extends far beyond an inconvenience to wreck divers. The zebra mussel filtering robs food from the larval stages of native fish. In Lake Erie, it is estimated that the microscopic plant life (the very basis of the food web) has been reduced by as much as 80 percent. It is still unclear what the mussels' impact will be on fish populations in the lakes. In particular, they could endanger salmon and walleye populations.

In addition, the greater water clarity has allowed light penetration to go deeper into the water. As a result, plants rooted on the bottom are growing in greater densities and depths. In addition, researchers have found that the mussels can even colonize on the shells of freshwater clams. In some areas, the mussels have wiped them out entirely.

As much as divers and everyone else around the Great Lakes would like to get rid of zebra mussels, little hope exists at the moment. Like the cockroaches of New York City, they are there—and there to stay it seems.

Businesses and municipalities with clogged intake pipes have found that certain filters work. They also go out and do the job that divers do on sunken ships—scrape the mussels off by hand.

Chlorine can kill them. But massive use of chlorine is out of the question. It would be like using a nuclear bomb to clear a village full of terrorists. The collateral damage to the lakes would be just too high.

Researchers have looked for biological solutions. Some animals actually feed on zebra mussels. They include migrating ducks and certain fish including yellow perch, freshwater drum, catfish, and all the sunfish. But this bird-and-fish snacking is not enough to have any significant impact. In fact, feeding by fish and birds has created an additional hazard.

Because of the huge amounts of water the mussels filter and because of their high body-fat content, zebra mussels accumulate 10 times more PCBs (polychlorinated biphenals) and other toxic contaminants than other similar mussels. These contaminants can cause skin and liver damage and possibly cancer. The contaminants are especially dangerous for pregnant mothers and small children. The birds and fish feeding on mussels now present a potentially serious danger of contaminant cycling for the big lakes.

Yes, divers would like to be rid of zebra mussels. So would everyone else. But no answers are in the offering. At least not for now.

CHAPTER 9

Mountains and Caves

It has been written that "A man's life is a matter of mountains and caves—mountains we must climb and caves where we hide when we cannot face the mountains." For Danny Fader and for everyone onboard, the *Obsession* was both.

The obvious mountain tops were, in fact, depths, depths to be dived and wrecks to be explored. It is important to point out that every man on the *Obsession* had other mountains in his life—marriage, family, work, the list goes on.

The dive boat also served as their cave. A place of safety and comfort. Certainly from the dangers of the cold darkness below. But also a place where men sat in the company of other men. Here they found freedom. They could relax. Life was simple and straightforward on the *Obsession*.

Man-to-man relationships are, by and large, uncomplicated. Certainly not as complex as, say, husband-and-wife relationships. If the men of the Trotter team dove well, pitched in, and helped and acted with decency, nothing else much mattered. They earned the kind of respect that does not need much explaining. If they could cook or understood the workings of a marine engine or had a sense of humor, so much the better.

Onboard, nothing much mattered except the diving. Food was largely an afterthought. Breakfast was instant oatmeal (one of Danny's innovations), cheap, filling, and didn't upset already wave-rocked stomachs. Lunch might be a cellophane-wrapped sandwich picked up at a gas station or, if the weather was bad, saltine crackers and Coca-Cola (which was supposed to calm the stomach). In this floating world, by and large without women, the men worried little about bathroom amenities. It was not just a matter of seat up or seat down. The *Obsession* had a phone-booth sized room with a chemical toilet. But they rarely bothered to even hook it up. The guys, being guys, just braced their knees against the gunnel and peed over the side.

In a less martial way, the men on the *Obsession* were like men in combat. They bonded in a dangerous singularity of purpose. The rest of life—that is, life on the shore—was never as potentially lethal. Nor was it as simple.

That fateful Sunday morning in October 1994, Danny sat in the aft section as the *Obsession* surged out toward the mooring line on the *Detroit*. As was his ritual, he quietly checked his dive gear.

To the east, a pale light was painting the horizon. But still the nighttime breeze bared its teeth. Its bite helped snap him awake. He needed it. For months, Danny had been running under a load of cumulative fatigue—pressures at home and on the job, the welcome exhaustion of overtime hours at work. While diving was his respite, the sheer logistics demanded much from his thinning thread of energy. Just getting from his home to dock was a three-hour drive, usually at some ungodly hour of the morning.

He tried to ignore the weariness, but it increasingly wore at him. The fatigue almost seemed to fog the periphery of his vision and weigh on his shoulders with a soft, yet leaden poundage. But never mind, now he had to concentrate. He unzipped each of his two three-foot-long duffle bags of dive gear.

From one, he pulled out his bright blue dive suit. It was his fourth. He had bought it the year before and he loved it the same way a man can love a BMW, a perfect piece of equipment that works flawlessly. Just looking at it made him smile. The one he'd owned before was the equivalent of an East German Trabant. It never worked right. It leaked at the shoulder, and no amount of special glue would seal it. At dive's end, he always rose to the surface shivering.

Before putting on the blue suit, he'd squirt some silicon spray on the inside of the neck and wrists. These fits were tight; the spray would ease sliding his head and hands through the openings.

He checked his buoyancy compensator pack, which served as the backpack for his tanks but also had a bladder that could be inflated or deflated with air so that he could maintain a certain level underwater.

He had weights, too—a 25-pound weight belt and 2½-pound weights that strapped around each ankle. Without them his legs might rise and turn him upside down.

One by one, he checked out his pieces of gear. That was in the front of his mind. Grumbling at the back of his head were other matters—matters he could not so easily check off or control.

Seventeen years before, Danny had met the woman who would give him the most joy he'd ever known. She was Jeanne Alcantara, a classic mixed-heritage American. Her mother was from Palermo, Italy, and her father from the Philippines. And she was from the Planet Laughter.

At the time, Danny was in his living-it-up stage. His first marriage was history. His life was careening between adventure and recklessness. He tried sky diving, was wreck diving in the summers, helping to teach a pool course in the off-season, skiing during the snowy months, and dating a lot in every season.

"I was fancy free. I loved to party. I loved to drink. And I loved to have fun," he said.

Danny first saw Jeanne in the fall of 1977. He had dropped by a dance put on by the Pendulum Club. The Ford singles club had rented a ballroom at the Ramada Inn across the interstate from Detroit's Metropolitan Airport. A DJ was spinning rock 'n' roll discs. Dancers shimmied and flailed their arms in the air and shouted as the room fairly shook with bass guitar drum thumps.

Danny, decked out in a brown-and-white striped shirt and dark slacks, immediately hit the dance floor. One dancing partner followed another. Not too much time passed before he spotted the girl with jet black hair in a pixie cut. Standing next to a girlfriend, Jeanne was wearing a black, red, and white A-line skirt, a black top, and low heels for dancing. She just loved to dance. The beat ignited every inch of her five-foot frame, so much so that if she wasn't dancing, she was bouncing in place to the music.

And suddenly, Danny was there, standing in front of her. "Would you like to dance?"

"He had a lot of curly hair. And this smile … he had this beautiful smile," Jeanne remembered. "He looked boyish and was so happy. He just radiated a happy spirit."

So they danced and laughed together and danced some more.

"Hey," he noticed, "you're copying some of my dance steps. That's neat."

They danced until the DJ called it quits and shut off his microphone. As they left, Jeanne gave him her phone number. A few days later, he called.

They met for dinner in Ferndale, a community just north of the Detroit city line, at Doug's Body Shop. It was a theme restaurant where the diners sat in antique cars instead of booths.

Again they laughed and talked. She was a bit surprised. Danny asked her lots of questions about herself. Most of the guys she had dated could only talk about themselves. Jeanne said that she too had been divorced and now was finishing a college degree at Oakland University. Danny talked about diving, of course. But he also told her about his two daughters with muscular dystrophy. He explained that he was a strong Catholic. As it turned out, so was Jeanne.

Danny and Jeanne Fader

Not too many days passed before Danny told his mother, "She may be the one for me. We have a lot in common."

He was delighted by Jeanne's openness, her bubbly nature, a sense that she could share his life. Jeanne told him that she wanted to go up north in the fall and collect leaves. Wow, he thought, she likes the outdoors.

Winter came and they went skiing together—his sport. She barely managed the bunny slope, but that was okay. He wanted her to take up diving—once again, his sport. They spent more and more time together. Later, they even took a white-water rafting trip—his kind of vacation—down the Colorado River. Both agreed it was the best vacation of their lives.

Danny's neighbors told him, "We always know when Jeanne is over. There's always so much laughing."

Jeanne soon met his two daughters. Danny recalled clearly how she hugged them and gave them a sense of being loved. For him, that clinched it.

As their lives began to blend, Jeanne realized something important. "We were best friends. He could tell me anything and I could tell him everything."

The relationship moved forward—not without some fractious bumps—but it led to marriage two years later on September 22, 1979, at the Oakland University chapel. One hundred and fifty people showed up, many of them divers.

The priest told the two he had confidence in their marriage. He called it a joining of faith and laughter.

After the reception, which featured lots of dancing to a live rock 'n' roll band at the VFW Hall, Danny and Jeanne took off in his 1975 red Mustang on a tour to see the fall colors in New England.

The Prince of Dives had whisked away the Princess of Laughter. But reality awaited their return.

Years passed. As life does, it brought changes. And hardships. Good things happened, but hardly a year went by without something awful besetting the couple. More than ever they were needing all those elements that had built their relationship—the laughter, the sharing, and their faith in God.

One by one their parents died. The two daughters moved in with the couple. Their medical needs were getting more demanding, more complicated. Although they were not her biological children, Jeanne shouldered the burden of their care.

Danny and Jeanne had wanted a child of their own, but for a long time Jeanne could not conceive. She tried fertility drugs and artificial insemination. Each frustration brought new sadness. Nothing seemed to work. Then after three operations, Jeanne got pregnant and young Dan was born two months premature. He survived and grew up healthy and became, in Jeanne's words, "the joy of my life."

Danny began working more and more overtime. He was delighted to get the extra money. Like his father, he understood the importance of being a good provider. Putting food on the table. Making a better life for his family. Eventually, he was able to afford a new house. It was a big, airy ranch-style house in open country far to the northwest of Detroit. The windows were large and the deck overlooked a small lake. It was a slice of suburban perfection. They put a statue of the Virgin Mary in the front yard.

But stress began taking its toll. Jeanne was not healthy. Danny was away from home a lot. Every other weekend, he put in overtime hours at the Ford plant. On the alternate weekends seven months a year, he was onboard the *Obsession*. It was his cave. He needed it as a stress reliever, to provide adventure and challenge. But Danny's time away to relax and enjoy life did nothing to relieve Jeanne's struggles at their house with two very needy daughters.

"I came to resent his diving," Jeanne said, "and the overtime work. He was constantly gone and there was no support at home."

She appreciated that he was a good provider, that he did not play around with other women, and that they lived in a beautiful home. But her anger grew at his constant absences and she became seriously depressed.

"Who cares about the damn money? You marry because of love, and you want communication."

The laughter was slipping away. In its place came arguments, loud vicious arguments. She had begun to see Danny as selfish.

"My God," she said, "can't he at least spend some time at home? He would see the girls. But it was always his call when he'd see them or how much time he'd spend with them. If it interfered with diving or work, no. He always put himself first. If it did not fit into *his* program, then forget it."

The time had arrived when Jeanne no longer wanted to follow Danny's dance steps.

Danny, for his part, felt like he was doing his best. He followed the example of his father, a man he respected. A man who earned respect by providing for his family. When his dad slept all day and was gone every night, no one asked him to spend more time with the kids. No one expected it.

Jeanne's anger left him a bit bewildered. Wasn't he working hard? Didn't he provide? More than provide, didn't his family live in a terrific house, better than anything he'd ever known as a child? Didn't he put in extra work hours to make that happen? Why wasn't *that* appreciated? Why wasn't *that* valued?

Couldn't she understand that he needed that time on the *Obsession* to recover? To recharge his badly worn batteries?

For the couple, bewilderment morphed into anger and the anger then boiled into the red zone—and stayed there.

The heart-to-heart talks were over. The couple, who had been best friends, who could tell each other anything, were at war. They no longer talked; they yelled at each other.

The more they argued, the less Danny liked staying at home. And the less time he stayed at home, the angrier Jeanne got—and the more depressed she became. By March 2, 1993, Jeanne had reached the end of her string.

"I was ready to go to divorce court," she said. "Danny was constantly gone. And I was at home with three kids and no support. This is it."

On a day when it looked like things could get no worse, they got worse—suddenly, horrifyingly worse.

Driving home on Michigan Highway 59, Jeanne suffered a head-on collision. She had been taking a new drug for depression. It blanked her out. Their daughter Barbara, who was in the car, survived unharmed. Jeanne was not so lucky.

Her head was bashed. Doctors called it a closed head injury. The steering wheel smashed her chest. A lung collapsed. Her heart stopped briefly. And the car door collapsed on her arm, crushing it. The emergency medical team had to use the jaws of life to get her out.

Jeanne slipped in and out of consciousness. "I really thought I was dead."

In the coming months, Jeanne would undergo five surgeries. Danny took off work for three months to look after things at home. Given the crisis, the two girls were placed in a group home.

During the time he was at home, Danny and Jeanne did start talking again. They achieved a bit of healing for their relationship. But at the end of three months, Danny went back to work.

Jeanne's suffering did not end. Physical therapy for her arm was brutally painful. She continued to have excruciating head pains. A strange uncontrollable itching feeling spread over her scalp. She went from one hospital to another; one antidepressant to another. It would take more than four years before Jeanne found any real sense of recovery.

Once back on the job, Danny's old habits quickly re-emerged. He began taking on lots of overtime assignments on weekends. By that summer, he was back onboard the *Obsession*.

Danny did try to do nice things for Jeanne, to make up for all the time he spent diving and working. Even though he was exhausted at the end of a work week, he often took her out to dinner before leaving for a weekend of underwater adventure.

Like many things in marriage, dinners out were not just dinners out. Yes, the meals were good. There was candlelight. And wine. But it was clear that these dinners also were bribes, payoffs so Danny could keep on doing what he wanted to do. And Jeanne knew it.

And so it was on a Friday night before Danny's ill-fated dive on the steamer *Detroit*. He had just turned 48 the week before. The two drove over to a nice restaurant called P.J. Putter's. The lights were dim. The steaks were prime; the wine was sweet. Danny tried to be charming and talkative. And loving. For him, it was a nice evening out. Jeanne remembered it somewhat differently.

"I was worried," she said, speaking of Danny's upcoming dives. "He was exhausted and was making only his fifth dive on mixed gas."

Danny tried to offer words of reassurance. "Nothing could ever happen to me, Jeanne."

The Doc's birthday. Werner Wahl's 64th birthday was celebrated on board
the *Obsession* in October 1994 with a cake and a 1986 swimsuit calendar.
The celebration would come just weeks before Danny Fader's accident
and the last time that Wahl would ever dive on a wreck.
Photo courtesy of the David Trotter Collection

Danny wanted his words to be a comfort, offering a sense that
he had everything under control. Jeanne wasn't buying it. Later she
described them as "arrogance."

Back on the *Obsession*, a shout went up. They had spotted the
marker buoy for the *Detroit*.

Danny would be diving with Werner Wahl, "The Doc," a frequent
dive partner. Wahl was older than the rest, having just turned 64. He
was overweight. His stomach stretched the fabric of his dive suit. But
he was a veteran wreck diver, having started with Trotter even before
Danny arrived on the scene. But they would not be the first pair to go
down.

Rocky Arsenault and Jeff Moore would go before them. The
two were the most recent additions to the team, but they were good
divers. To them fell the important mission of the day—to hide the
strongbox.

The plan was that they would go down to the deck of the *Detroit*,
attach a lift bag to the strongbox (so they could actually move it), get

the box off the side of the ship, and, once it was on the bottom, somehow move it 50 feet away.

With that, like subaquatic conjurers, the team would make their treasure box disappear.

Danny and the Doc would go down next to simply look around the *Detroit* one more time. Also, Danny wanted to pick up a reel and line that he had left on the ship the day before. The next to go down would be Trotter and Whitworth. They planned to continue shooting 35 mm slides for an upcoming program on the *Detroit*.

Danny, never thinking that plans might change, continued methodically checking his gear.

He eyed the neoprene hood that covered his entire head, only leaving a hole big enough for his mouth, nose, and eyes.

He would carry three tanks on his back. Two big ones, 72-cubic-foot steel cylinders; one would carry compressed air, the second with a tri-mix for the bottom—a blend of pure oxygen, helium, and nitrogen. Fastened to the two big tanks, like the top of a pyramid, was a smaller, third bottle. This pony bottle held 40 cubic feet of compressed air in case of an emergency.

Generally Danny did not worry much about running out of air. His pals on the boat said, "Danny breathes like a girl." It was a compliment. Because Danny was so calm and relaxed underwater, he used far less compressed air than the other guys.

He checked the valves on each tank. Then he checked his regulators, the piece that would go into his mouth so he could breathe. He had two new regulators. Those were attached to the big tanks. They operated fine.

He also had a third regulator for the pony bottle. This one he had been using for four years. The three would hang side-by-side in a bunch over his right shoulder.

One question did lurk in his mind. A month before, also on a dive on the *Detroit*, the older regulator on the pony bottle had failed. It had free flowed. The regulator jammed and the air from the tank rushed out in an uncontrolled flurry of bubbles. The free flow came after he had emptied his large tank of mixed gas, and he reached for a second regulator. Danny described it in his dive book:

"My pony regulator free flowed. I grabbed this regulator instead of the other one for the 72 c. bottle by mistake. I immediately ascended and changed regulators at 80 feet (My first decompression stop). The pony regulator stopped free flowing, but was out of air. (Two tanks are now at zero p.s.i. [pounds per square inch].

"I drained the third tank (of air) at 10 feet and used the oxygen regulator supplied from the boat to finish decompression."

To Danny, the incident hovered like a dark shadow in his memory. But he dismissed it. Oh well, the dive season's almost over, he thought. A new regulator will be expensive. This old one will probably do for one more dive. I'll get a new one for next year.

It would be one of the worst mistakes of his life.

CHAPTER 10

The Team

Out in Saginaw Bay, the dive boat *Obsession* had muttered to a stop. The sun had cleared the horizon. The divers on deck could see their wobbly shadows casting long across the water. The waves were short-topped and slap-slapped against the hull. Looking down the mooring line into the water, the divers could only see about 8 or 10 feet. But they knew that 200 feet down, wedged in the muddy darkness, was the side-wheel steamer *Detroit*.

On deck, the divers were making final preparation. The hatch was pushed open on the *Obsession*'s forward deck. Below sat an oxygen tank with two long hoses, regulators attached. These were dropped over the side and run down along the mooring line, with the regulators hanging at about 20 feet below the surface.

These regulators were a safety measure for divers in their final stages of decompression. If their own tanks ran dry, the oxygen waited for them. The oxygen also speeded up the decompression process, helping to rid the body of dangerous nitrogen.

All six men on the team knew the day's dive plan. Rocky Arsenault and Jeff Moore would drop down first. Arsenault had joined the year before; Moore joined in just that season. Both were young, aggressive, and strong. Both also had experience diving with mixed gases. And both had experience with deep dives.

The incalculable element was the pressure. This mission was important. Very important. The most important since they'd been brought into the Trotter fold.

According to the dive plan, Arsenault and Moore would descend to the deck of the *Detroit*, attach a lift bag to the 200-pound strongbox, and inflate the bag to lighten the load. Then they would slide the box off the deck and move it as far from the ship as possible, as much as 50 feet.

Time would be short. It always was on deep dives. The two divers would be limited to only 20 minutes to drop to the deck and do the job. After that, they would need an hour or so to decompress, slowly rising toward the surface making five timed stops along the way.

As one diver joked, deep wreck diving is like sex. After hours of effort and expense, all you get is 15 minutes of bottom time.

The two divers were almost ready. They had struggled into their neoprene dry suits and tugged on their two-and-a-half-foot-long flippers. Each in turn then sat on the stern while others on the team helped them put on the hefty backpacks with triple tanks, attach a back-up tank for inflating the lift bag, then handed them dive lights and weight belts and reels of line.

The morning was still cool, perhaps in the 50s. After this preparation, the divers, now fully sealed in the underwater equivalent of snowmobile suits, were already starting to sweat into their thermal underwear. They yearned for the relief of cold water. So at the very second everything was ready, each rose shakily to his feet and jumped, holding his mask to his face and spreading his legs like opening a pair of scissors.

Within minutes, they paddled around to the bow, grabbed the mooring line, and then they were gone, leaving behind only occasional wellings-up of bubbles.

At that point it was a matter of waiting. The team on deck would not see the two divers again for almost an hour and a half. They might as well relax, because whatever happened down there—good or bad—was out of their hands.

As Trotter had said many times, "If you are down 200 feet you might as well be 200 miles away for all that can be done for you."

For Danny, the routine was familiar, a rhythmic dance of wreck diving that was performed again and again almost every weekend for the nine seasons he had spent diving with Trotter's team. In that time, Danny had made the team his second family. He had watched it evolve.

The term *team*, as in Trotter's team, might give a sense of something fixed and immutable, a gathering of men whose faces never changed except perhaps for some wizened wrinkles at the corners of their eyes.

In fact, Trotter's group was more like a modern baseball team. Some divers came to the team, tested the waters for a time, and then moved on. Others like Danny, "Doc" Wahl, Rudy Whitworth, Rod Soja, and later Rocky Arsenault and Jeff Moore were more of the stable hard core. Their presence on deck became as much a fixture on the *Obsession* as, say, the radar screen or the loran guidance system.

One envious diver once described them as "Dave's goons." It was a singularly inapt description implying a certain thuggishness that was unthinkable, although it did rightly convey a sense of loyalty and permanence.

Each new member brought a new set of talents, sensibilities, and observations. All were guided by Trotter's steady hand.

Rudy

Danny and Rudy Whitworth came onboard full-time in the same year, 1986. Danny was an up-and-coming hotshot. He had dived the *Andrea Doria* that year and would do it again the next. He brought not only the courage of youth, but was open, enthusiastic, and quick to laugh.

Whitworth was of a different stripe. He was reserved, quiet to the point of dourness, and had a dry wit that made only cameo appearances. What he did show was an impatient intelligence and a bristling, uncompromised engineer's mind. He was a Ford engineer. He demanded a high level of quality and precision in all he did. As everyone onboard was quick to learn, he demanded an equally high quality level from everyone else.

Lean and often acerbic, he could be insensitive to others' feelings. But those close to him knew that Whitworth's often brusque nature was, in fact, a protective shell that covered a deeply sensitive and emotional core.

"He's very caring about a lot of people," said Rod Soja, who was his closest friend onboard. "He's the kind of guy if you need help, he'll be there." And Whitworth would more than prove that in the coming hours.

Although their relationship was cool at the outset, over time Danny and Whitworth warmed to each other as they came to recognize the special values of each other. Whitworth, because of his skills, intelligence, and willingness to work, quickly became what everyone onboard agreed was "Dave's right-hand man."

Over time Whitworth also made himself a first-rate photographer. His photos played an ever more prominent role in Trotter's presentations. And interestingly, Whitworth's photographic approach was a fine counterbalance to Trotter's own.

While Trotter tended to shoot bigger scenes and sweeping action, Whitworth loved to hone in on the detail and shoot most of the close-ups of scroll work and dishes and intricate machine parts. As years passed Whitworth's photos—especially those he shot later in the warm clear waters of the Caribbean and the Pacific—became regular winners of photo contests and were appearing in magazines and on calendars.

Whitworth really liked working on Trotter's slide and video presentations. He liked the historical research and strove to make the presentations as accurate as possible. While underwater on a wreck, he loved the vision-of-the-past thrill—of "swimming down a corridor or going into a room and knowing that the last person through that door was walking." Unlike divers who were adrenalin junkies, Whitworth's diving joys were more artistic and intellectual.

On deck, this engineer for Ford was constantly fixing and rewiring things so they could be used on the *Obsession*'s 12-volt system. He installed the radar system, a new radio, a depth finder, a microwave, and a TV and VCR for a bit of entertainment in the long hours of searching with the side-scan sonar.

He also brought important discipline to the Trotter exploration process. It must be remembered that these Great Lakes divers rarely if ever could see a whole ship, even a small one. At best, particularly in the early days before zebra mussels began clearing the waters, the divers' vision might extend only 3 to 5 feet. On a rare day, perhaps 7 to 10 feet. And once they were swimming around for awhile, they would kick up a haze of silt that made things even harder to see.

Basically they were Mr. Magoos with aqualungs. And on drugs (nitrogen narcosis). Like shortsighted men studying a camel, at least at the outset they would not know if it was a skinny elephant, a rather lumpy horse, or a Great Dane with a glandular problem.

To solve the Magoo dilemma, each diver was given a mission. You examine the bow. You, the forward deck. You, the starboard cabins. And so on. And then, in a program that Whitworth devised, when the divers resurfaced he debriefed them immediately. It had to be done right away because if the questions were delayed even a half hour, the narced-up divers typically forgot exactly what they had seen.

With each report, Whitworth took a big piece of plastic and proceeded to draw a detailed map of the ship. A mast had fallen here. The port cabins are collapsed here. Dishes were in this cabin. Two big anchors hang from the bow. He was the underwater map maker.

The systematic mapping did a couple of important things. Firstly, with Rudy's drawings, the divers had—over time—an ever clearer idea of what the ship looked like and where they were going. Chances were reduced of getting lost in the silty darkness. It was an important safety factor. Secondly, this gathering of details helped to identify the wreck—often not a very easy job.

A lot of the nineteenth-century ships looked alike, especially the schooners that were cranked out like Christmas cookies. These were working ships. In many cases, no ship's name was handily inscribed on the stern or on either side of the bow. As a result, the divers needed to gather telling details. The make of the engine. Inscriptions on dishes. The location of damage. Then it often took weeks of library research to make a confirmation.

In 1986, the first season that Danny and Whitworth had joined the team, their big discovery was the *John McGean*.

This was the wreck of a five-year-old, 432-foot freighter that went down with a load of coal. What put the *McGean* in the history books was that it was one of the ships sunk by the Great Storm of 1913—recorded as the deadliest in Great Lakes maritime history.

For Danny and Whitworth, it was a terrific find. Trotter was pleased, too. But he had another ambition, one that would stir his searching juices for a decade and a half. He wanted to find—and in some respects *needed* to find—the *Minnedosa*, the largest schooner ever built in Canada and one of the largest ever to sail in the Great Lakes.

That continued to stay at the top of his list.

The Doc

The next major player to join Trotter's A-Team came the next year, in 1987. He was Werner "The Doc" Wahl.

In any group that prides itself on its eclecticism, one guy typically stands out as the best example. For Trotter's team, that was Doc.

Wahl held a Ph.D. in nuclear chemistry. Putting the words nuclear and chemistry together as a description carried more eye-boggling heft than even, say, rocket scientist. What's more, Wahl had a *curriculum vitae* that included original research with Johns Hopkins and top executive positions with several major companies involved in nuclear diagnostics for diseases such as prostate cancer. He was also president of his own companies.

With his white beard and Santa-sized stomach, he looked more like a professor who might fit better at the front of a college classroom with a bunch of formulas on the blackboard than as a diver who could drop down to 200-foot depths.

But Wahl was always one of the guys. And he loved being one of the guys. He never affected an I'm-smarter-than-you-are attitude. Instead he was funny, a nonstop schmoozer, and grinned happily when he was teased.

The team started to cackle on the first day Wahl pulled on a new, bright orange dry suit. It was a tight squeeze across his ample belly. The team quickly dubbed his suit "the big orange condom." The Doc laughed.

Wahl also developed a lasting reputation for two other things. One, he never got seasick. And two, he'd bring onboard some of the most obnoxious, smelliest food that anyone could imagine. Sardines, headcheese, and pickled pigs feet. Guys would flee the galley for the blissfully unscented breezes of the aft deck. In part, Wahl used to bring the smellies onboard just to tease Danny, who had a notoriously weak stomach.

Also it turned out, Wahl was a good diver and had taken just about every course available. During one year, he was the most active diver in the Ford Seahorses club. He spotted Trotter early on in his diving career and he wanted on the team.

"I went out of my way to place myself in his line of vision so he would notice me," Wahl said.

Trotter indeed saw him. By 1987, he was on the team. In 1988 they discovered the schooner *Hunter Savidge*. At his own suggestion, Wahl began a new role for himself by writing a press release about the discovery. The group had never done that before. As it turned out, the *Hunter Savidge* was a great story.

The Ship: Hunter Savidge

The 117-foot schooner lay becalmed east of the tip of Michigan's Thumb on the afternoon of August 20, 1899. The wind was slack. The sails on the two masts were barely luffing. Then, all of a sudden, a white squall smacked the 20-year-old schooner. A white squall is a climatological terrorist. This fierce whirlwind strikes from ambush with no warning and disappears almost as fast.

In less than 10 seconds, every man on deck was washed over-board and the ship—with no load for ballast—dumped over on its beam ends. As the big winds started to die away, the *Savidge* slowly righted itself with the bow deep below the surface and sinking fast. In the water, Captain Fred Sharpstein looked over and saw his son, John, a member of the crew, come sputtering to the surface not 10 feet away. His sense of relief was short lived. Within seconds, John disappeared again, this time sucked underwater along with the bow. John was wearing heavy rubber boots that had filled with water, drag-ging him down, and perhaps—this was not clear—his legs had gotten entangled in some lines.

Meanwhile, Sharpstein's wife, Rosa, and the wife of the ship's owner, Mary Muellerweiss and her six-year-old daughter Etta, had been resting in the cabin when the squall hit. Sharpstein now could see that their cabin had sunk below the surface.

Only the aft end of the *Hunter Savidge* and 50 feet of one mast were still visible above the now-calm seas. Apparently the ship, in its nose-down position, was able to stay afloat because of buoyed air trapped in the rear cabin.

By now Sharpstein and four of his crewmen were clinging to the still-floating aft section. The captain was hoping that the two women and the girl were somehow still alive. He shouted their names again and again. No answer came. But he clung to the fact that people trapped in similar situations on wrecks often survived.

As it turned out, the steamer *McVittie* was headed north and spotted the floating wreckage of the *Hunter Savidge*. The captain brought Sharpstein and his sodden, badly shaken crew onboard. Then, in an act of jaw-dropping callousness, the *McVittie* captain refused to stay long enough to check the wreck to see if the two women and child might still be alive or, if not, to retrieve the bodies.

They were surely dead, he said. And he was not going to spend any extra time searching for them. He had a schedule to keep. Then, as soon as he could, the *McVittie* captain got rid of the people he'd rescued. He transferred the *Savidge* survivors to the steamer *Runnels*, which was heading to the south. Then, without even a wave, the captain nosed the *McVittie* north and ploughed toward the horizon.

The captain of the *Runnels* dropped Sharpstein and his crew of four off at the Harbor Beach Lifesaving Station. As soon as they came ashore, Captain Sharpstein frantically tried to get a crew and boats to go out and find the *Savidge*. It was not until early the next morning that he was able to gather men for the search. But on returning to the accident site, they found nothing.

Later, other freighters in Lake Huron reported seeing a floating wreck. Every time a new report came in, Sharpstein would head out onto the water, hoping against hope that he could find the ship with his wife and the mother and daughter of the owner. His searches went on not just for days but for weeks.

Trotter knew the *Hunter Savidge* story, and he had been searching for the ship for years with the hope that it might somehow still be intact.

When Trotter finally found it in 1988, the ship was nowhere near intact. The *Savidge* had suffered a hard landing at 170 feet. The hull was laid open, the anchor chain lay strewn ahead of the bow, and the masts, which had snapped off, were lying beside it. The once-proud schooner with its tall masts was now a mound of wreckage that stood only about 10 feet above the bottom.

The team dove on the wreck for weeks. They still could not positively identify this schooner, which in many ways looked like every other schooner of that period.

The rest of the team was on the verge of giving up but Trotter would not. By some powerful internal force, he felt driven to find some clue to this ship's identity.

He and Whitworth went back over the side-scans again. On this second hard look, Trotter noticed two objects off the port side—one at the bow, another at the stern. Normally, they would have ignored

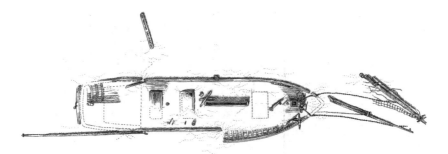

The 20-year-old schooner *Hunter Savidge* was hit by a sudden white squall and flipped upside down in Lake Huron on August 20, 1899. Some of the crew and the captain were picked up by a passing ship. But then the *Savidge* floated away, half sunk, with perhaps two women and a little girl still alive onboard. Trotter's team found the Savidge in 1988. Illustration by Robert McGreevy.

such items in a wreck that had split open with debris scattered everywhere.

They dove again. Whitworth headed to the bow and Trotter set off to track down what looked like a 15-foot board about 30 feet off the stern.

What he found—and it stunned him—was an eight-inch square board sitting face up with raised letters and the remains of red paint. It had two words: *Hunter Savidge.*

Later Trotter tried to explain what had propelled him to keep searching for this ship's identity. It was the year of his daughter Kelly's death. And Trotter sensed a profound connection to this ship where the daughter of the owner had died. John Muellerweiss attempted suicide on hearing that his wife and daughter had died. Trotter felt like he understood the father's feelings. So he felt driven to search. Once having found the name board, Trotter believed that in some spiritual way Kelly had led him to it.

Still Trotter felt an intense need to connect with Muellerweiss. Several months later, he wended his way into a cemetery near Alpena, Michigan. It was raining as he walked along carefully examining the names on the tombstones. Then, at last, he found what he had been searching for. It was the grave of John Muellerweiss.

Trotter knelt beside the grave in the wet grass. He put his hand on the stone and spoke to the dead ship owner. The long search was over, he said. Trotter told him that with the help of his own daughter, he finally had found the ship that had carried away the owner's wife and six-year-old daughter. He had found the *Hunter Savidge*. And he had left the ship as he had found it, in the cold dark waters of Lake Huron.

Rod

Rod Soja, a diving friend of Rudy Whitworth, joined the Trotter team in 1990. Lean and sinewy as his pal Rudy, the two were the greyhounds of the group. Soja, a polar opposite of Whitworth, was easy going, full of fun with an artist's keen eye and sensibility of the world.

Starting diving in 1986 at age 36, Soja loved underwater photography and he, too, began to win photo contests. When he saw Trotter's presentations at the Ford Seahorses meetings, he said they blew him away. Soja wanted to be part of that operation. As it turned out, he was a great addition to the production team. Soja not only was a first-rate photographer, but he was a musician. He could play guitar, piano, and keyboard. Another element to spruce up the Trotter shows.

Danny liked Soja especially for his quick sense of humor. His easygoing joy of life seemed to lighten the atmosphere of the whole boat. Soja, in turn, appreciated that Danny was a great audience—laughing loud and long even at his thinnest jokes.

In the season Soja arrived, the team found a good-sized ship under 170 feet of water off Port Sanilac, Michigan. Several weekends passed, the divers bringing back clue after clue from the sunken vessel. But still they could not come up with a name. Trotter strongly suspected it was the *City of Milwaukee*. But they needed to be sure.

Then Danny made a discovery. Soja tells this story, which has become a classic on the *Obsession*. Whitworth also cast an eye on these events, noting Danny's excitability, his extreme focus, and the effects of nitrogen narcosis. These were elements of his personality that would reoccur on the ill-fated *Detroit* dive.

Soja and Danny were partners on a dive when Danny discovered a name board on the stern rail. The board was covered with muck. So Danny set to brushing off the sign with his glove.

"We were about out of time," Soja remembered. "But Danny was doing his thing and did not want to be disturbed. So I helped until I saw a bit of the sign that read 'City of M—'

"That was enough for me," Soja said. "I tugged at him. 'Time's up. Time's up.' But he wanted to clear all of it. By the time we got to the mooring line, we had overextended our time."

After a prolonged decompression, Soja followed Danny to the surface.

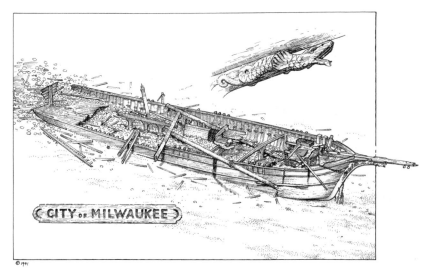

The *City of Milwaukee*, a 139-foot schooner, plunged to the bottom of Lake Huron in November 1875, some 14 years after it was launched. Trotter's team found the ship and were delighted to also discover a unique carved figurehead below the bow sprit. Danny Fader, when he was the first to discover the name of the ship, got so excited that he bubbled to the surface and exclaimed, "It's the City of Cleveland." Illustration by Robert McGreevy.

"Danny is shouting and hollering. 'We found it! We found the name! It's the *City of Cleveland!*'"

City of Cleveland? Everyone onboard was dumbstruck. Say what?

"Then I said to Dave, 'No Dave, it's the *City of Milwaukee.*'"

Danny is still bubbling with enthusiasm and on a nitrogen high. "The name board is on the starboard rail," he said.

At this point, Soja has to interject again. "No, Dave, it's on the port rail."

Looking back on the incident, Soja said, "Danny had pushed it. Maybe he was not aware that he had pushed it."

While Soja readily admits that Danny was a great diver, "a human fish," he noted other instances where Danny seemed to press a little too hard against the edges of danger.

"He would look on the [side-scan] printout and see some hunk of something way off the wreck. Then he'd go down and swim off into the ozone in search of it. He would drag his hand in the muck so he could find his way back."

"Frankly," Soja continued, "I never would have gone out without a line [tied to the ship]."

Once again, the Trotter team had made a fascinating find. That was good. But Trotter could not get the *Minnedosa* out of his mind. He worried that somehow he had missed it in all his searches and all that mowing the lawn.

"I couldn't understand why I couldn't find it," Trotter said. Newspaper reports of the day "appeared to have a high degree of authenticity and they said the ship sank eight miles northeast of Harbor Beach in about 120 feet of water.

"But they were wrong. We scoured the area eight miles northeast of Harbor Beach that had the depth of 120 feet. It wasn't there. We looked."

Rocky

In 1993 two significant events occurred for the Trotter team. A new team member signed on. He was Rocky Arsenault and his influence would permanently change the way team members dove. And at long last, after 15 years of searching, David Trotter finally found his holy grail. In a happenstance that had more to do with luck than his ever-precise planning, the *Obsession*'s side-scan sonar picked up the elusive wreck of the *Minnedosa*.

This was one ship that Trotter had to be the first to dive on. The first to touch. He had been searching for it too long to give away that privilege. With him on that maiden dive was the new guy, Rocky Arsenault.

Arsenault was a diver of the Fader ilk, only more so. They both purely loved the excitement of diving and diving deep. They had a jones for stepping up to danger's edge and even putting a toe over the line from time to time.

"I like to take risks. If it isn't exciting, I'm not doing it," said Arsenault, capsulizing his attitude in two sentences.

Yes, they were willing to do the boring stuff. Help fix up the boat in the spring. Months of tedious searching. Do chores and odd jobs here and there. And then help with the boat clean-up at the end of the season. But for them it was all about the dive.

Short and solidly built, Arsenault's full name was Maurice Richard Arsenault. His father named him after the famous hockey player with the Montreal Canadiens who was called "The Rocket." So as a kid, Arsenault also was called Rocket. As time went on, the name morphed into Rocky.

The name Rocket actually was a good fit. At age 36, he not only was one of the more colorful members of Trotter's team, but an unadulterated adrenalin junkie. When he was not diving with the Trotter team, Arsenault was out flying his own Ultralite, something he could do without a license.

Arsenault admitted that before joining the team, he did not exactly endear himself to David Trotter. Back in 1986, he was one of those guys who used to spy on Trotter, trying to find out what ship he was diving on in Lake Huron.

In that summer, one day the *Obsession* was anchored over the *McGean*. It was the first full year for Danny and Rudy Whitworth.

"I'm watching Dave," Arsenault remembered. "He's now The Guy. Top Dog. I'm bird dogging him. And I did jump him once. I pulled up right next to him. It was a cheap shot at the old man. I just rubbed his face in it.

"Here I was, some young, punk-ass rookie. And he's pissed. In those circumstances, he is a gruff son of bitch. I later realized it was better to dog him and not let him know."

Seven years passed, Arsenault matured a bit, and eventually got back in Trotter's good graces. As it turned out, "the old man" did not hold a grudge. After a long spring of paying dues by searching with the team every weekend and then diving with Trotter, Arsenault earned a happy nod from the old man.

When they finally started diving, Arsenault found he had an edge over some of the other guys. He was an experienced deep diver. Also—and more importantly—he had just started diving on tri-mix instead of compressed air. As a result, he said, "I was tearing up those underwater searches."

"That year I went from being a crock of shit to being a more noble guy," Arsenault said.

At that juncture in the history of wreck and cave diving, going down with mixed gases was viewed as not much different from filling your tanks with carbon monoxide. Tri-mix was supposed to be a killer. Diving instructors turned thumbs down on it. Dive magazines decried mix-gas diving as one step short of walking yourself up the gallow's steps.

Some resistance also came from divers, particularly old-time divers, who were reluctant to trust anything they did not know. Divers like David Trotter and many on his team had years of experience diving on compressed air. While they did not like the narcotic affect, they had learned to contend with it. They knew what to expect. For them, it was a matter of sticking with the devil they knew rather than going with the devil they did not know.

But word was getting out. Divers—using decompression tables originally developed by the U.S. Navy—were using mixed gases successfully, especially some hotshots who were cave diving in Florida.

Rocky was now on the *Obsession*, and he was touting the wonders of mixed gas. More clearheaded diving—fewer martinis to cope with. That made diving safer. You could dive deeper. Also, breathing underwater was easier with helium in the mix, less like sucking on a straw. By the end of the 1993 dive season, Arsenault had helped spur David Trotter to use tri-mix.

Let us remember that Trotter was a man of measures. He knew about calculating odds. As a diving instructor, he already was well versed on the underwater effects of many gases. He went on to do even more research. Using that background, he and the others soon were designing their own gas mixtures based on the kind of diving they were doing. They made the changes on the fly—no classroom lectures, no check-out dives. Also, they developed appropriate decompression tables. No one else was there to do it for them. As per the Trotter creed: You figure out how to do something and then you go out and do it. Now Trotter, too, was a convert.

One by one, almost everyone on the team started using tri-mix. It was a logical step because, as the years passed, the wrecks they were finding lay deeper and deeper in Lake Huron's waters. Compressed air became less and less a viable option.

Ship: The Minnedosa

"Gotcha, you elusive rascal," exulted Trotter.

Fifteen years had passed. Fifteen years of searching with his sophisticated side-scan sonar. He had scanned 750 square miles of Lake Huron's muddy bottomlands. Fifteen years of frustration. Fifteen years of finding lost ships, some very important to the history of the Great Lakes, but never the *Minnedosa*. Never the grandest schooner that Canada had ever built.

When the *Minnedosa*'s long, detailed image showed up on the side-screen readout, Trotter recognized it right away, even though it was not anywhere near where the newspaper reports said it went down. In fact, it was a full 10 miles away. And instead of lying in 120 feet of water, the great ship had bottomed out at 220 feet.

It was now 1993. For the past few years, Trotter had been trying to shake off the notion that perhaps he had missed the *Minnedosa* in his searches. He had been doing his homework. He had talked to

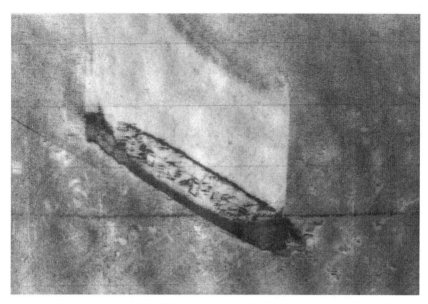

A side-scan image of the *Minnedosa* showing the hatch covers on deck
on the day it was found by David Trotter in 1993.
Courtesy of the David Trotter Collection.

Great Lakes historians. He had pursued his own research. Bit by bit,
he had culled out fragments of information.

And he had surveyed the heck out of the lake, covering literally
hundreds of square miles. Had his positioning equipment fouled up?
Had he literally passed the ship by leaving it in some hole in his search
grid?

He reexamined all the information he had gleaned over the years.
What had the storm been like? What did the charts say? What areas
had he covered already?

In 1990, he had developed a new theory. This one was based
on the fact that the *Westmount*—the ship that had been towing the
Minnedosa—showed up at Harbor Beach on the day following the
accident. If the *Westmount* had been farther south, it would have
gone down to Port Huron. That meant that the accident likely happened in more northern and deeper waters than anyone had previously suspected.

So Trotter headed toward deeper water. This did not please the
team for they knew that no matter how deep the *Minnedosa* lay, Trotter—long frustrated in his hunt—would dive to touch her. And such a
deep dive promised real danger.

Trotter upped his efforts based on his new theory. Instead of surveying only during the daylight hours, the *Obsession Too* began searching around the clock.

One weekend in 1993, a storm cropped up as the team was nearing the completion of a grid—a large area where they mowed back and forth. Driven back to shore, they returned the following weekend with a plan to complete that grid and add one more pass that would widen the search into a deeper area of Lake Huron. It also would put the *Obsession Too* in position to start the next grid that Trotter had planned.

As it turned out, at 5 a.m. Sunday—following that originally unplanned-for extra survey line that had not been part of the original grid—Trotter got a "Bingo." It was the *Minnedosa*.

Trotter later recalled that Garry Kozak, the crack side-scan expert, had once told him, "She will be found when she wants to be found."

Maybe. Or it could be that Trotter's flukish good luck was not part of the *Minnedosa*'s plan at all. Over future dives, the ship proved again and again that she resented having been found.

The team was giddy with excitement over their discovery. At first, they were unwilling to call it the *Minnedosa*. They needed to prove its identity. So for a time, they simply called it "The M Ship."

After several dives, the team found the ship's name written on the bow. Apparently Minnedosa is a Sioux Indian word meaning "waters of the rapids," although another translation is "silent waters," which would have been more accurate for its recent history.

This was very deep diving for the Trotter crew, and Danny, while still one of the most experienced divers, had to struggle a bit. In his dive logs, he frequently mentioned feeling tired. The consistent overtime at work, the strains of family life, and the long drives to the Michigan Thumb apparently were taking their toll on his judgment and ability to concentrate. Looking back, one could spot the evil omens.

On August 8, he wrote: "Went down mooring line to bow and got disoriented. Only four hours sleep."

A week later on August 29, he wrote: "I couldn't find the mooring line when I started to come up. I was down 21 minutes by this time (past the limit). I tied my safety line to the wreck and decompressed on a 25-minute schedule. When I didn't come up the regular mooring line, after awhile Rudy and Rod (on deck) thought I was dead. They couldn't see my bubbles on the surface. Rod went down to find me, thinking he would pull me back up dead. Thank God everything is O.K."

Then on October 10, again diving on the *Minnedosa*, Danny commented, "Nitrogen was making me goofy."

Built in 1890 in Kingston, Ontario, the *Minnedosa* was designed to be a star. The largest ship ever built in Canada, it was 250 feet long with four masts (the main mast was 150 feet high), and it could rip across the water at an astounding 17 m.p.h., as fast as any steamer.

It could carry tremendous payloads, but she needed a crew of 12. As a result, the owners decided the *Minnedosa* was too expensive to sail. So they shortened the masts, tore away the carved figurehead, hired on a captain and a skeleton crew, and used the hull as a giant tow barge. It would be sailed only when absolutely necessary.

A steamer called the *Westmount* was towing the *Minnedosa* south on Lake Huron on the stormy night of October 20, 1905, when the Canadian-built ship went down. In fact, the *Westmount*—a first-rate steamer—was towing not one ship but two. First in line was the *Minnedosa*, then tied on behind it was a second ship, the *Melrose*.

The wolf was out that night. A storm bared its fangs. Terrible winds. Hard rains. The *Minnedosa* was nosing up and down through the waves. According to reports, the ship was overloaded with 75,000 bushels of grain that it had picked up in Duluth. Before long, the 250-foot ship began taking on water. As this train of boats was nearing the Michigan Thumb, the *Melrose* broke free; only one hour later, the huge *Minnedosa* just vanished.

"My God, Captain, where is the *Minnedosa*?" *Westmount* mate John Black shouted against the wind.

Far to the rear and out of sight, the crew on the *Melrose* thought that their line to the *Minnedosa* had just snapped.

Later the steamer *Westmount* was able to turn, tie into the *Melrose* again, and tow it to safety. But the *Minnedosa* was gone.

At first, the *Westmount* crew thought that the line—actually a cable—to the *Minnedosa* had broken. But when they pulled it back onboard, they discovered some of the front portions of the *Minnedosa*'s prow were still attached to the end. It had been ripped loose.

What exactly happened to the *Minnedosa*? Some 88 years after the sinking, Trotter and his team were able to answer at least some of the questions.

After numerous dives, Trotter's team was able to say that it was likely that the *Minnedosa*—strung out between the steadily moving *Westmount* and the sluggish *Melrose*—was literally "pulled apart at the seams."

The team also found that the line connecting the *Minnedosa* to the lagging *Melrose* did not just break, as the crew thought.

"I could see where the rope was cut with an axe," Trotter said.

That tow line, refrigerated in Lake Huron's deep water, had survived nearly 90 years. Long enough to tell the tale. When Trotter looked closely through his dive mask, he found "a clean slice."

It's not clear why the *Minnedosa*'s axeman cut the line. Perhaps to save the ship. Perhaps to keep the *Melrose* from being pulled under as well. No one will ever know.

For David Trotter, if the finding of the *Minnedosa* was a too-long delayed delight, diving it was a much darker experience. One after another, Trotter seemed to barely escape some near-death experiences. It was almost as though the *Minnedosa*, resentful at being discovered, was striking at him.

On the first dive, he went down with Arsenault to set a new mooring line and detach the grapple from the ship. First he had to lay hands on this ship that had eluded him for so long. Chuckling into his regulator, he laid a hand on the rail and said, "I finally got you, you son of bitch."

In the late minutes of the first dive, the two men agreed to separate. Arsenault would go up the new mooring line. Trotter, who was breathing compressed air, would swim back, release the grapple, and then, as the dive boat drifted down the lake, ride it along, moving up to do his decompression stops. It was a good plan because his air was running low. And ultimately, he would be able to get oxygen from a regulator hung off the side of the boat to complete his 20- and 10-foot decompression stops.

A bit confused by narcosis and the dark silt-filled waters, Trotter worked his way back along the ship's rail toward the location of the grapple. But he could not find it. Unbeknownst to him, Whitworth had managed to release the grapple from the surface and pull it back onboard.

By this time, Trotter had swum more than 400 feet—a long, exhausting time when you are 200 feet below the surface and also have set a mooring line. His mind misty, he swam on hoping to find the grapple line. The next time he checked his time it was 24 minutes. It was late, well past the time when he had planned to start back up and begin his decompression.

His situation now had turned dire. He had no other choice but to tie off a line and ascend from where he was, even though he'd probable emerge 200 feet from where the *Obsession* was located. Hands frozen, he barely could get the line wrapped around the rail, much less clicked in for security.

Unreeling his safety line as he started up, Trotter knew that with all the nitrogen that had accumulated in his body, he was in for a long, very slow ascent. Unfortunately, he also could see that his air was running low. In a battle with his own anxiety, he determined to slow his rate of breathing. Even with slower breathing, he knew his air time was short. He would miss decompression stops and that could mean trouble.

Fortunately, Rudy Whitworth was above on the *Obsession*. He had not only tracked Arsenault's earlier ascent up the mooring line, but he spotted Trotter's bubbles more than 200 feet away. He quickly understood the gravity of the problem. He unhooked the *Obsession* from the mooring line and, with the regulators hooked to the oxygen supply hanging 20 feet down, he slowly motored over to where Trotter was coming up.

Trotter grabbed on and started breathing the oxygen, while at the same time Whitworth headed the boat back to the mooring line, with Trotter being dragged behind like a fish on a line.

It was a rescue straight out of a cliff-hanger serial in the 1940s movie houses.

The next day, Trotter and Arsenault again went down together. Once again, Trotter ended up making a long swim against a current. This time he was lugging 200 feet of mooring line and floats. He wanted to tie on a second mooring line at the bow, so divers could go up and down at either end of the ship. At one point, he began to severely over-breathe his regulator. In other words, his body was trying to gulp down more air than the regulator would allow. The effect is like trying to breathe through a straw when what you really want is a four-inch pipe.

This combination of problems was one of the forces that helped propel Trotter toward using tri-mix on the deep dives instead of his old standby, compressed air.

Finally came what seemed to be the final payback from the *Minnedosa*. Just two of the team—Trotter and Arsenault—had gone out in late October for what would be their final dive of the season. It was a prime example of how not all dangers to divers show up underwater.

Arsenault went down first; Trotter came next and quickly headed off on his own. But when Trotter got back on the dive boat he found Arsenault in a flurry of consternation. In a little over an hour, the temperature had dropped 25 degrees. "And look," said Arsenault, pointing to the north. There, sweeping down on them, was a line of dark storm clouds like an invading army. The marine radio had given no warning. But there it was.

They cranked the engine and headed southwest as fast as the *Obsession* could manage the heavy seas. But managing quickly became a problem for the 28-foot dive boat. The hull was getting hammered by 8- and 10-foot waves, first from one side, then the other. This was Don Knotts doing 12 rounds with Joe Frazier. The two wanted to pull into Harbor Beach, but the storm was trying to blast them past it. The next major refuge was Port Sanilac, 30 miles farther south, but it was unlikely the *Obsession* could survive the added distance. Harbor Beach had three entrances, three chances to get to safety. In a battle with the wind that was pushing them directly south, they had to fight their way closer to the shore.

They missed the northern entrance. Bellowing down from the rear, the storm held them in its grasp, refusing to let them turn in. Nor could they get into the central entrance. With a combination of luck, adept seamanship, and sheer stubbornness, they did manage to pull in to the southern entrance—the last one—without piling into the rocky shore.

Once at the dock, Trotter talked to the dock master, who said the storm was worse than they had thought. The winds actually were hitting 60 m.p.h.

Trotter thought to himself, "Hell, the *Daniel J. Morrell* ripped in two in 70 m.p.h. winds. And that ship was 600-feet long."

He never dove the *Minnedosa* again.

Jeff

The next year, 1994, yet another new man joined the Trotter team—Jeff Moore.

At 27, Moore was a clean-cut young guy, strong, well trained, with a smile that caught girls' eyes. And, as it turned out, he was Arsenault's buddy. And in a way, they shared some history. Just as Arsenault used to bird dog David Trotter, so did Moore's father, James.

Moore's family lived in the Thumb and, he said, his dad was an avid diver. "The question always was: 'What's Dave up to?'" Moore remembered.

"I think he jumped Dave once on [a wreck called] the *Dunderberg.*"

Moore grew up in the small town of Caro and learned to dive at age 14, but once out of high school this lad with the infectious smile sort of drifted.

In his twenties, he rambled west to Utah where he spent his winters as a ski bum at Snowbird Ski Resort east of Salt Lake City. Periodically Moore took college courses. Mostly he majored in beer, girls, and hanging out. It took him 18 years to finish his college degree in

English. He eventually got married, had two children, and got into computer programming.

Along the way, he worked hard at various jobs including selling farm equipment, became a certified ship's captain, and in his early twenties completed the grueling certification for cave diving in Florida. It was there he learned to dive on mixed gases.

He thought of David Trotter as "the Emperor of the Lakes, although he does not act that way."

And on at least two occasions, he boldly went up to his aquatic majesty and said: "I'm Jeff Moore. I think you know my dad. I want to get on your boat."

At first Trotter just smiled and nodded. The "No" was implied. Eventually, Moore made the cut.

He, too, like Arsenault and Danny, grooved on the excitement of diving. Initially he found the tedious months of searching to be barely sufferable. Years later he would come to enjoy it almost as much as the diving. As a certified captain, he certainly was qualified to handle the dive boat. But it was the underwater adventure that he loved.

And there was a lot to love that year on the *Obsession*. For it was 1994 when they discovered the *Detroit*, certainly one of the best, most intact ships that any of them had ever dived on.

And then there was the strongbox.

The Detroit

It was Arsenault who first spotted the *Detroit*'s strongbox. It was Labor Day, September 5, and after several weekends of diving. He had been nosing around the aft cabins where the water was silty, the ceilings were low, and the light was lousy.

Back on deck an hour later, he said, "I think I found what might be a safe. I'm not sure."

A safe? Cool. Let's check it out. Next to dive were Rudy Whitworth and Ron Soja.

Soja, who somehow missed what Rocky thought he discovered, remembered the dive.

"I am along the starboard side looking for photo shots and realize it's time to start back up. But I couldn't find Rudy and it's all mucky inside the ship. Then time is up."

"I see this faint light glow inside the ship. It's Rudy. The light is moving very slowly. And it's bouncing. A bouncing light is a universal sign of distress. I go in after him.

"He grabs my arm and sticks it on this big, black box. He has been dragging it [making his light bounce]. So I help him. I have no idea what we are pulling. It's a box. It never occurred to me that it might be a safe."

But Whitworth well understood what that box was. "I know the construction," he said. "Metal straps made out of steel. Brass hardware."

So Soja continued, "He and I start dragging it. Pulling, pulling, pulling."

Here they were, 190 feet underwater with nearly 200 pounds of gear and flippers on their feet. They are digging in their heels to brace themselves and pulling. Then digging in and pulling again. Finally they moved it about 10 feet, onto the promenade deck. Soja still did not know what the box was.

When they bubbled to the surface, Whitworth confirmed Arsenault's find. "It's a strongbox." Whitworth, ever precise, figured that a safe is something that is designed not to be moved, while a strongbox can be moved.

"Well," said Soja, "now that was a whole new ball game."

No one on the team had ever come across anything like a strongbox. What could be in it? Maybe it was gold. Their imaginations soared. What should we do about it? Pull it up? No, they didn't have the equipment. Work out a deal with a local museum? That seemed like a good idea. Their fantasies went into hyper drive. Maybe we could do a TV special like when Geraldo opened Al Capone's safe in Chicago.

After a month, Trotter's efforts to fully engage a museum had hardly lifted off the dime. What's more, the season was coming to an end. November in the Great Lakes is a notorious ship killer. That's when the *Fitzgerald* went down. In a big storm, a small dive boat would stand little chance of staying afloat. Also, the team was almost positive that someone else already had spotted the *Obsession* motionless 14 miles from shore—a clear indication the team was diving.

They needed to do something. And they needed to do it soon. Their conclusion: Deep freeze the strongbox.

And so arrived that fateful Sunday, October 16, their last dive of the year.

Arsenault and Moore got the call to move the safe. That choice had a nice sense of symmetry since Arsenault had originally spotted the strongbox. Both divers felt like they were under the gun.

"Psychologically there was a lot of pressure. We had a very important task," Arsenault said.

An hour later the two divers brought disappointment back to the deck of the *Obsession*. They had not been able to move the strongbox. They had taken down a single lift bag, and even when it was fully inflated, the bag did not generate enough lift to make the 200-pound safe even budge. Someone would have to go down with a second lift bag.

That someone would be Danny Fader. He was set to dive with Werner Wahl. If further work needed to be done, Trotter and Whitworth would be the next to go down.

As it turned out, Danny had only used a lift bag twice before. Both of those times were in a class, in a pool. And that was 10 years before. But he never hesitated.

"Cool," he thought. Ever optimistic. Ever enthusiastic. He was thrilled that the job had come to him, that he could play such an important role for the team.

"I can do this," he thought.

Both Danny and the Doc were already suited up. Getting them ready to go, team members performed the final prep—backpack with triple tanks, an additional tank with compressed air, dive lights, weights, lines, and, finally, a bright yellow lift bag.

Danny stood for a moment on the swim deck, a 145-pound diver loaded down with 200 pounds of gear. He wobbled just a bit under the ungainly load and then, with a long stride, stepped out into destiny.

CHAPTER 11

The Dive

From the bow of the *Obsession*, the divers could look out over the water and see first Danny and then the Doc start their long slide down the mooring line to the steamer *Detroit*.

Down, down they sped, leaving the light for a darkness that shifted in color from grey green to almost black. Their descent to the walking beam took less than two minutes. By this time, both divers had switched regulators—changing from compressed air to their bottom gas, or tri-mix.

With Wahl swimming behind him, Danny headed for the deck. In his excitement, he made his first mistake. Instead of swimming to the starboard rail and following it aft to the strongbox, he turned the wrong way and headed along the port rail. Discovering his mistake, he had to circle around and go back.

"Uh-oh," he thought, "this is going to cost me a little bit of time. Werner must be thinking, 'I wonder what's wrong with him.'"

The time loss was not big. But it did add pressure to an already high-pressure dive.

Once at the strongbox, Danny knotted on the second lift bag. It was bright yellow and stood in contrast to the black bag that already ballooned above the box.

Danny started feeding air into the bag from the additional tank he'd carried on a two-foot line hooked to his left hip.

As the air gushed in, Danny eyed the strongbox again. Somehow it seemed to be bigger and heftier than he remembered. The yellow lift bag bellied out. Bigger, then bigger still. But still the lumpish strongbox refused to move. Not an inch.

So Danny added more air. And more. "I don't think it's going to lift up," he worried. Soon it seemed that if he added any more air to the bag, the seams would tear right out. But Danny had no other choice; he kept on goosing in more air.

And then the box jiggled. At first it moved just a little bit, then it began to rise—ever so slightly—from the deck.

Now the two divers could lift the box a little bit higher, move it out over the rail, and let go. Even with the two bags attached, the box plummeted down the side of the ship and slapped into the mud below.

Swimming over the rail, the two divers followed it down and at once Danny started again to pump yet more air into the already strained lift bag. To his amazement the bag—while at any second it looked as though it might explode like a reverse water bomb—held strong.

As the divers watched, bit by bit, the strongbox slowly rose out of the mud. With another injection of air, it came up about one or two feet.

Danny checked his timer—15 minutes. Three-quarters of his scheduled bottom time was already gone.

At this point, Danny started to push the box. It was a struggle.

Somehow he had to manage to do three things at once: kick his feet with as much power as he could generate with his flippers, hold onto the box, and, at the same time, swim in a straight line away from the ship and into the silty, black belly of Lake Huron. Trotter wanted the strongbox to be at least 50 feet away from the ship. It now seemed like an impossible distance, but he would do his damnedest to get it there.

The Doc, in the meantime, had tied a line to the ship's rail and was following after Danny. This line was crucial. Without it, they might never find their way back to the ship.

Ahead, Danny clung to the box and kicked with all the power he could muster. Working this hard underwater runs absolutely counter to what most divers do. They try to expend as little energy as possible. They almost never use their arms and they kick their feet as little as possible, preferring to glide. They want to save their strength and their limited supply of air.

Soon Danny's legs were aching from the strain. Lugging that 200-pound box, the going was slow. Soon he felt his energy start to drain away.

And Danny, the human fish who only sipped at his air supply, was now gulping down tri-mix. He looked at his watch again—22 minutes. Two minutes over.

"I'm going to have to let this go," he thought. It was time to stop. And he did. But the lift bag was still full, still holding the strongbox above the mud. He couldn't just leave it like that. So he grabbed the bag with both arms and gave it a bear hug trying to force some of the air out so the box would sink to the bottom. And then he did it again.

By this time, Danny had slipped into a state of exhausted elation. Trotter, his mentor, had given him a mission. And he had done it. Others may have failed, but he moved the box off the *Detroit* and out into the invisibility of the muddy haze. It was a struggle, but he had succeeded.

At this point, Danny could only feel the quality of his success in the foggiest way. For now any margin of mental clarity gained from using tri-mix was gone.

At 200 feet, the nitrogen dissolved in his blood would have the equivalent of drinking four martinis while diving on air. On tri-mix, the effect would be reduced by only one or two martini's worth. Given the depth and his extreme exertion of swimming while trying to hold the box, Danny was narced down to his fins. His ability to make proper judgments and rational decisions had been knocked for a loop.

His watch now read 24 minutes. He knew one thing for sure. "Now I've got to get back."

He signaled to Wahl and started back down the hand line toward the ship. With all that effort in the watery darkness, Danny was not sure exactly how far he had moved the box. It later turned out to be about 30 feet from the ship, about the distance for a first down in football.

Wahl was ready to swim back, too. But then he gave the lift bag a second look and decided more air had to come out.

"I had a vision that this safe was going to float away. So I crawled up on top of the bag, squeezed with my arms, and caused it to burp." Then, climbing down, Wahl began to follow the line back to the *Detroit*, reeling it in as he went. In the darkness and swirling silt, Wahl could not see Danny at all. If he had, he would have seen things start to go very wrong.

About the time Danny reached the *Detroit*, his tri-mix tank ran dry. It was not a complete surprise. Danny had been working hard, gulping down the mix. Such things had happened to him before.

Danny simply reached down to his chest where the regulators were clustered and grabbed another regulator. Like the incident two weeks before, this regulator was attached not to his second large tank, the one filled with compressed air, but to the small pony bottle.

The instant he jammed it between his teeth, the regulator let out a blast of bubbles. A free flow. Damn.

The same regulator that had jammed two weeks ago had failed again. He had hung on to it to save a few dollars. Now it was stuck open.

The compressed air spewed out with such a force that it was almost impossible to breathe any of it. All around him, the water was exploding in fierce white bubbles. Danny clenched the blasting regulator between his teeth and tried to cull out a bit of air as he swam upward toward the walking beam on top of the ship where the mooring line was tied.

Just as he reached the line, the gushing of air blew the regulator right out of his mouth and then he could only watch as the last of its bubbles wheezed out.

Now Danny reached for another regulator. All three were there hanging in a bunch, one largely indistinguishable from the other two.

He grabbed one. He was sure it was the right one, the one connected to his tank of compressed air that should be 70 percent full. He sucked in.

It was dry. Nothing. He had no air.

At that point the veteran diver panicked. His adrenaline jumped; his heart banged in his chest and more than anything he just wanted to breathe.

Sheer panic. It had never happened to him before.

He did not think that he might have mistakenly grabbed the regulator for the now-exhausted pony bottle. Or perhaps the regulator for the empty tank of tri-mix.

He did not think to grab the regulator for the air tank hanging from his hip that he had used to fill the lift bag. It still had lots of air.

He did not think to contact his dive partner, although Wahl was still far below him, invisible in the darkness, reeling in his line.

He did not think.

One thing was sure, he could not simply stay where he was. He surely would drown.

"I'm in deep trouble," he thought. "I'll have to free ascend."

He was now about 160 feet below the surface. He knew what a free ascent meant. Surely the bends. At this depth, it was almost guaranteed that the nitrogen bubbling in his blood would climb to his brain and kill him. At best, it would block the blood flow to his joints and he might be paralyzed for life. Still and all, sprinting to the surface did offer at least a slim margin for survival. Drowning did not.

In his mind, Danny had only one choice. Go up.

He kicked his feet and the long flippers started to propel him upward, toward what was only the palest of light.

Up, up he rose, his feet fluttering. As he climbed toward the brightening light, he felt the intense water pressure of the bottom steadily begin to decrease.

At 200 feet, when he was lugging the strongbox, his dry suit had been trying to plaster itself against his body like airtight packaging around a salami. The pressure on Danny was seven times what it would be at sea level—102.9 pounds per square inch, as opposed to 14.7 psi.

As he ascended, the air inside the suit—now relieved of the pressure—was expanding. The suit now started to balloon around him. The higher he rose, the more the suit expanded. His suit was now like a balloon underwater, propelling him up faster and faster. No need to even kick now, his air-fattened suit rushing him toward the surface like a rocket.

Also, with the decreasing water pressure, the air was expanding in his lungs. He had no sense of having to hold his breath. But what he had to do—what he was trained to do—was something that might seem illogical to nondivers. But he had to breathe out. If not, the expanding air would rupture his lungs and certainly kill him. And he did breathe out.

He looked up and could see that the waters around him were getting brighter. The blackness was changing to green. The surface now shimmered above like molten mercury. But now he was ripping upward so fast through the water that he was leaving his own bubbles behind.

"My God, I'm coming up fast."

Danny's suit had a release valve, a button on the chest of his suit to allow the expanding air to escape. He banged at it again and again. But it was not enough. Still he rose. Faster and faster. Nothing seemed to brake his climb. Danny had become an underwater missile.

As he came to the 20-foot depth, he spotted the oxygen regulators that had been hung off the bow. They could save him. If he could just stop and grab one, just stay at that level, he could rid himself of the nitrogen and might be able to survive.

But in almost the same instant as the thought hit his brain, he blew past the regulators. He had tried to snag one, but with his rocketing speed he missed. The life-giving, the life-saving oxygen regulators now hung below him—untapped.

Seconds later, Danny burst to the surface. His suit still ballooned around him. From the deck of the *Obsession*, Danny looked like a bright blue Michelin Man. Like a beach ball held underwater and then released, he literally popped out of the water, shooting up all the way to his waist.

Danny's rocket ride from 160 feet had taken only somewhat more than one minute. He had missed a full 70 minutes of decompression.

Pain exploded through his body.

"Help me," he managed to gasp. His voice could hardly be heard on deck. "Help me."

CHAPTER 12

Rescue

On the dive boat, members of the team were doing what they always do. Moore, having struggled out of his dry suit, was sitting in his underwear on the back deck with Trotter. Arsenault was below changing clothes. Whitworth, who had put on his thermal underwear to get ready to make the next dive, was sitting at the wheel.

At this point, Whitworth looked out the front window and saw what looked like a small island of bubbles about 20 feet off the port bow. These were not the usual bubbles released from regulators. Those ascend in big globs. What he saw were tiny bubbles. Thousands of them, creating a 15-foot wide boiling pot of foam.

"Hey, Jeff, you've got to look at this," Whitworth said.

Both divers knew what that foam meant. Either Danny or the Doc had a free flow.

Trotter and Moore started moving toward the bow.

"Something's wrong," Trotter said. "This does not look good."

Almost at that instant, at exactly 12:27 p.m., Arsenault remembered hearing Trotter's shout. It was filled with surprise and dread. Arsenault was stunned. Trotter was always Mr. Cool. He'd never even seen him get excited before.

"Danny's popped!!"

As Danny's bright blue suit exploded out of the water, Moore remembered thinking, "He was like the Pillsbury Doughboy. He was huge." The suit was so taut that Danny's arms and legs were sticking out straight.

"He looked like a balloon that was about to break," Moore said.

"Go back down! Go back down!" shouted Arsenault who by this time was on deck. He was hoping that Danny could descend the 20 feet down to the oxygen-supplied regulators and try to decompress.

But Danny' strength was gone. Enveloped in pain, he could not make his body move. His answer was so faint it could hardly be heard across the water. "I can't."

Moore reacted like an on-duty lifeguard. Still in his underwear, he dove over the side into the 50-degree water and headed toward Danny.

As he swam, he could hear Trotter's shouts to Danny. "Don't move! Don't move!"

Any movement by Danny could aggravate the nitrogen damage.

Moore grabbed Danny's arm and managed to pull the totally immobilized diver to the rear of the boat. Even though he was shaking badly from the cold water, Moore then helped pull off Danny's dive tanks and other gear so he could be lifted into the boat.

At that point, Danny's already unimaginable pain seemed to double. The agony amped up to unbearable. His forearms and calves felt like they would explode.

At 12:33 p.m., just five minutes after he hit the surface, the divers laid Danny down on the blue crosshatch rubber matting on the *Obsession*'s rear deck. His feet were lifted to rest on a pair of dive bags. Trotter brought up a small tank with 100 percent oxygen with a plastic face mask for Danny to breathe. The tank, however, could only deliver 80 percent oxygen because the face mask had an imperfect seal.

Physicians with expertise in dive accidents agree oxygen is the best method for first responders to use in such diving accidents. Quick application often can minimize injury, paralysis, and even save lives.

As he lay helpless on the deck, the still cheerful sun now seemed to be mocking them. On this blackest of moments, the sky was blue. Danny looked as though his next breath—if he could manage to take it—would be his last.

The pain now savaged his whole body. Blood seeped from his mouth. With every breath, he coughed. The pain drove spikes into his chest and back.

"It's hard to breathe," Danny gasped.

Arsenault truly believed Danny was speaking his last words. Tears of frustration came to his eyes. He felt absolutely helpless.

"Danny was clearly deteriorating," Arsenault said. "I was afraid he was going to give it up … that he was going to die."

The divers helped Danny out of his dry suit, freeing him of the tight neck seal that was hindering his breathing.

At that point, Whitworth, who had known Danny for most of a decade, took Arsenault's place and placed the suffering diver's head in his lap. By keeping his head up, he hoped that the bubbles in this blood would not reach the brain.

Danny moaned. His chest and legs had gone numb. Whitworth could see that his stomach was distended, bulging out.

Whitworth started talking to Danny and he kept it up—a constant flow of words and questions. He did not want Danny to give up the struggle. He wanted him to stay awake and work to stay alive. He asked Danny question after question, trying to make him think and, for the briefest of seconds, to put aside the pain. All the while, Whitworth kept a careful watch on the plastic mask that covered Danny's nose and mouth. He was looking for the steady appearance and disappearance of a faint fog—the sign that Danny was actually still breathing.

For Danny, the pain seemed to obliterate almost everything in his conscious mind. His forearms and calves felt like they would explode like over-inflated balloons. The massive pressure not only seemed to stretch his skin to bursting, but at the same time was clamping down on his very bones. With every breath he coughed.

Then Whitworth saw what he most feared. Danny closed his eyes, arched his back in pain, and simply stopped breathing. His chest did not move. No fog showed on the mask.

"I thought he was going to die right then," Moore said.

But Whitworth screamed at the diver. "Breathe, Danny! Breathe! You breathe, goddamnit!" He, too, thought Danny had just slipped away. But then a faint fog returned.

It would not be the only time he just gave up breathing.

"I honestly thought I lost him three times," said Whitworth, for whom the memory of that day literally makes his hands shake.

Each time Danny's breath stopped, Whitworth was there—shouting at him, trying to penetrate the diver's encroaching unconsciousness.

"Breathe, Danny! Breathe, Danny!!" Each time his screams seemed to knife into Danny's miasma of pain, and the faint fog would return to the mask.

Meanwhile, Trotter radioed the U.S. Coast Guard.

He described the emergency. He told them to contact Divers Alert Network (DAN), a group that includes practicing physicians who are experts in these sorts of diving accidents. He told the guardsman on the phone that Danny needed to be transported immediately to Henry Ford Hospital in Detroit. It had the nearest recompression chamber.

And—contrary to his never-tell policy—Trotter gave the *Obsession*'s exact latitude and longitude coordinates.

The one thing the team on the *Obsession* could not do at that moment was cut loose and head toward shore. Werner Wahl still was down below somewhere on his decompression schedule. They could not just leave him.

During all this action, Wahl had no idea what had been happening on deck. The first time he realized something was amiss was when, after recoiling his line to the *Detroit,* he rose to where the mooring line was tied off on the ship's walking beam.

Danny was not there. He was shocked not to see him.

"He must have gone up," Wahl reasoned.

Wahl figured that Danny must have had a problem. What never occurred to him was that this diver renowned as an air sipper would run out of air. Wahl started working his way up the mooring line to begin his decompression stops before hitting the surface.

At 80 feet, the first stop, he once again expected to see Danny. But he was not there either.

"I kept looking up and I never could see him."

When Wahl reached 20 feet and the oxygen regulators, he quickly popped to the surface.

"I lost Danny. Is he onboard?"

"Yes," came the voices from on deck. "He's here."

So Wahl went back down to finish his decompression stops—12 minutes on oxygen at 20 feet and 18 minutes at 10 feet.

Once the Doc clambered back onboard, he heard the full story and that a Coast Guard helicopter was on its way.

The team fired the engine, unhooked from the mooring line, stopped briefly to pick up the yellow lift bag, which apparently had broken loose from the strongbox and floated to the surface, and started back toward Grindstone City.

Whitworth was still in back, holding Danny. Talking to him. "I was trying to keep him coherent," Whitworth said later. "I was trying to keep him with us."

"Can you move your legs? Does it hurt?"

"My back hurts," Danny said. "I've got a tingling in my legs."

Trotter at this point had been on the radio with the Coast Guard five or six times. The guardsman on the line was not giving many answers.

"When did the helo leave?" Trotter asked about the helicopter, his temper rising with frustration. "When is it supposed to get here? Has anyone talked to DAN?"

Whitworth meanwhile continued trying to coax Danny to stay awake and talk.

"Can you move your toes?" "Do you still have tingling in your legs?" "What's your wife's name?" "What's your telephone number?"

The oxygen now was beginning to ease Danny's pain, if only slightly. Once Wahl had climbed back on deck, the team was able to bring the big oxygen tank from the bow that had been feeding the regulators hanging at 20 feet. Using that tank, Danny now was sucking in 100 percent oxygen through a diver's regulator. This boost in pure oxygen helped pare back some of Danny's suffering.

Later—and it seemed like hours had passed—they heard the distinctive whump-whump of helicopter blades in the distance. It was the Coast Guard chopper. The rescuers had managed to reach the *Obsession* about 40 to 45 minutes after they were first called.

A Coast Guardsman on the radio gave Trotter instructions on how to steer the boat so the helicopter could hover above and drop a man down on a cable.

Head into the wind at 5 to 7 m.p.h. with the waves coming at about a 45-degree angle off the port side, he was told. That way, the *Obsession* could maintain a constant speed and direction.

Soon the helicopter was hovering above the *Obsession*. Its propeller wash was flattening the waves and creating a storm of water everywhere.

The dive team watched as a blue-suited Coast Guardsman dropped down from the helicopter in a sling. He brought along a small tank of oxygen.

Minutes later, a basket designed to carry an injured man was lowered to the deck. The guardsman belted Danny into the basket, with straps running across his chest and legs. Then Danny was winched up to the helicopter. It was all very efficient.

As the guardsman prepared to go up himself, Trotter told him again that they had to fly Danny to Detroit.

"You've got to take him to Henry Ford Hospital. They're the only ones with a hyperbaric chamber," he shouted over the roar of the blades. "You've got to go to Henry Ford."

The guardsman nodded, hooked into the sling, and was swiftly elevated off the deck and up into the helicopter.

Once inside the helicopter, Danny was not feeling entirely secure. Probably as a result of the tingling in his lower body, he felt like his feet were still sticking out the door. And worse, as the helicopter rose and turned to leave, Danny could feel his raw pain go up several notches.

Danny's body was reacting to a new pressure change. The helicopter now was carrying him at negative atmospheres, far less than even at the surface. What his body ached for was more pressure, not less.

Danny thought back to his dive training sessions. He had always heard that a rescue helicopter should fly as low as possible so as not to get into another negative atmosphere. He was wondering why the pilot was not flying lower.

As the helicopter lumbered toward the horizon, Trotter was on the radio again, trying to contact the pilot.

"Are you taking him to Henry Ford? Answer! Are you taking him to Henry Ford?" Trotter was furious. But the pilot ignored his calls.

As it turned out, the Coast Guard helicopter did not take him to Henry Ford Hospital.

Instead, the guardsmen flew him to St. Mary's Hospital in nearby Saginaw. Only after being examined there and given a shot of morphine, which Danny said did little to ease the pain, was he once again loaded onto a helicopter and then, finally, flown to Detroit.

From the time Danny burst to the surface of Lake Huron to the moment he entered the doors of Henry Ford Hospital, six and a half hours had passed.

Members of Trotter's team were disgusted. "We could have driven him there faster than that," they agreed.

CHAPTER 13

Chamber Ride

It was Friday, October 21, 1994. Five days had passed since the helicopter carried Danny Fader to Henry Ford Hospital in Detroit.

For five days, nurses wheeled the diver from his bed in the sixth-floor neurology section, along a hall into an elevator, down seven floors to the basement, and then into the hospital's hyperbaric chamber.

For the first two days, he was laid out on a gurney and rolled into the blue-and-white chamber, as Danny said, "like a loaf of bread into an oven." They fed him pure oxygen to get rid of any residual nitrogen in his body. Later he was able to sit in a wheelchair. Once inside the chamber, the pressure on his body was increased to six atmospheres.

For five days, doctors saw little change. Danny Fader, one of the Great Lakes' most experienced wreck divers, was paralyzed from the chest down. As a test, nurses stuck safety pins in his legs. He felt nothing.

On this Friday, Danny emerged once again from what diver's call "a chamber ride." It was his sixth.

Waiting for him was the physician in charge, Dr. Michael Eichenhorn. The doctor was not smiling. He shot straight from the shoulder.

"You will be paralyzed for the rest of your life," he said. "You have not improved as I expected. Since Monday, you have had no nitrogen in your body to interfere with the healing. The body should have been healing on its own. The reason we put you in the chamber unit all week was to see if it would help. It hasn't."

Danny was dumbstruck.

Just to make it clear that Henry Ford Hospital was done trying, Dr. Eichenhorn told him, "We are going to leave you in the hospital for Saturday and Sunday. But on Monday you will be transferred to outpatient care. I recommend Wyandotte Hospital. From there you will be discharged and sent home.

"You will not be taken down to the chamber this weekend," Dr. Eichenhorn said.

"It totally burst my bubble," Danny said. "I thought I was making some progress. I didn't expect him to say that."

161

Despite the setback, Danny—vainly, perhaps—refused to give up hope. After a nurse wheeled him back to his room, a physical therapist showed up.

Danny looked him straight in the eye. "You are going to get me to walk," Danny told him. The therapist's jaw simply dropped. He clearly thought, "This guy is in real denial."

Certainly it was the kind of determination, stubbornness if you will, seen in many hard-core adventurers.

Later that evening, his wife Jeanne came to his room along with young Dan, David and Mickey Trotter, and Rudy Whitworth and Rudy's wife, Pat.

"Look at the way I can walk," he told them.

Gripping his walker, he bumped down the hallway like a stiff-legged robot. His legs were inert, swinging like pendulums. He was generating all the power with his arms and shoulders.

"That's good, Danny," they told him. They tried to smile, to give him some encouragement.

"I had a feeling they weren't buying it," he said. "They were pacifying me. They were trying to cheer me up."

That night an Asian Indian doctor, an internist, came to see Danny. He was kindly. His voice soothed like aloe, but his message was clear.

"You are going to have to accept the fact that you may never walk again. You may have to find other work," the doctor said.

"But isn't there a chance that I could still walk?" Danny asked.

"Well, it's possible," the doctor said, "but it doesn't look like it."

Not walk again. Ever. That was not a message that Danny was willing to hear. No matter what they said, he vowed to not stop trying.

Like a mantra, he kept repeating to himself: "I'm going to walk. I'm going to get better. I'm going to work. I'm going to dive again."

From the beginning, no matter how bad things looked, Danny had clung to his positive attitude. And he prayed. He prayed hard. His rosary was never far from his grasp. His Bible stayed with him. The doctors may not think he would walk again. His wife and friends were skeptical. But no matter what, he would stay positive.

Chamber Rides

On the day of Danny's accident, it was never quite clear why the Coast Guard helicopter did not fly him directly to Henry Ford Hospital in Detroit, which had the only hyperbaric chamber in the region.

Instead, the guardsmen took him to the much-closer St. Mary's Medical Center in Saginaw.

By the time this book was being written 11 years later, the Coast Guard said all the records from that era had been destroyed.

At the time of his evacuation, Danny and Trotter's divers came to hear a number of versions. The Coast Guard helicopter did not have enough fuel to reach Detroit. The Coast Guardsmen were under instructions to take him to the nearest hospital. The Coast Guardsmen thought he was about to die, so they took him to the nearest facility.

Whatever the reason, Danny Fader's arrival at Henry Ford hospital on that Sunday evening was three to four hours later than it might have been.

The staff at Henry Ford Hospital was waiting for Danny when the helicopter finally settled down onto the landing pad. They loaded him onto a gurney and quickly wheeled him down to the basement and into the chamber.

Inside, the technician placed a bubble-like plexiglass helmet on Danny's head with a tight neck seal. Tubes ran out from the sides of the helmet, near his ears. These tubes would feed him pure oxygen.

Jeanne, Danny's brother Joe, and sister-in-law Eileen watched it all from outside the chamber. Their hearts were filled with fear. Jeanne already had begun repeating the prayer from Philippians 4:13, "I can do all things through Him that strengthens me." That Sunday had been one of the first days Jeanne had actually been able to drive following her own accident a year and a half before.

Danny could feel his family's worry. Like a miasma it seemed to seep through the chamber window. He tried to joke, to make them feel better.

But his humor could not brush away what Jeanne could see with her own eyes. "He looked so bloated. He looked like a spaceman."

Danny admitted all was not good. "I can't move," he said.

"He must be terrified," she thought. And yet he kept this grin.

Despite his jokes, Danny's mind roiled with worries. Unanswerable questions battered his conscience. "Will I ever walk again? Will I be able to support my family? How could I have gotten myself into this mess?" From his hips down, the pain was ferocious. It was, he said, like the needles and pins you feel when your leg falls asleep—but 1,000 times worse.

When the aide tucked him inside the blue chamber, Danny's hopes were high. Here he was in a hyperbaric chamber in one of the best hospitals in the state. Surely at the end of his session, he would be able to stand up and walk out of the chamber.

But after five hours, Danny could only sadly shake his head at the failure of modern medicine. His body still felt like some leaden, unheeding attachment. Something that clearly was a part of him, but that he had no sense of. He could not walk. He could feel nothing from his stomach down, except for a tingling in his legs. On the plus side, at least the teeth-gritting awful pain had subsided.

A nurse wheeled him up to the sixth floor and his new room.

On Monday, the next day, a nurse rolled him down the hall into the elevator, out in the basement, and then into the chamber. Helmet in place, like a 1950s image of a spaceman, he lay in the chamber for another five hours.

On Tuesday, the daily routine shifted. His chamber ride lasted only one and a half hours. Instead of being laid out on a gurney for the trip to the basement, he sat in a wheelchair. No oxygen helmet this time. He carried his Bible. Other people needing treatments would now join him in the chamber. None of them were divers. Two were women with bad circulation.

Outside the chamber's window, he could see a television set. It hung on the wall. Speakers were set up inside the chamber, so he could hear the music and words.

Unfortunately, the words issued from America's most perverted and bizarre, daytime television at its most voyeuristic. Jerry Springer and Jenny Jones.

"Where do they get these people?" he wondered. Danny turned back to his Bible.

His chambermates seemed to like it. But Danny said, "I was so glad to get out of there."

What he did not know was that he could ask to have the channels changed.

As the week went on, Danny found he was able to move around a bit using a stationary walker. His legs did not actually carry his weight. He got them to swing forward by twisting his body. All the movement and strength came from his upper body, the part that was not paralyzed. Yet he felt like he was making progress.

As often happens with people in crisis, Danny discovered that a lot of people cared about him. His fellow divers dropped by to chat and cheer him up. Family came. His pals from Ford showed up, some of them skipping work to see him. His phone rang constantly. Rudy Whitworth kept a flow of emails to everyone concerned about the latest on Danny's condition.

When interns came through on morning rounds, Danny happily talked to them. They had never seen anyone with the bends. Never met anyone who was a diver. Everyone was fascinated. In a peculiar way, Danny felt like a celebrity. Unfortunately, it was a celebrity based on an accident that he was not very proud of.

"Will you ever dive again?" one asked.

Unconquerable in his resolve, Danny said, "Of course."

By week's end, the nurses agreed they had never seen such a positive patient.

One of his biggest and most persistent problems was in the bathroom. The paralysis had affected him in some painful and degrading ways. A full day went by after his accident and Danny realized he had not urinated.

"You will not be able to urinate on your own," he was told. The nurse brought in a narrow, foot-long tube. A catheter. It had to be inserted where he'd never wanted to insert anything. And the process had to be repeated every three hours. He had had no bowel movements. Not for four days. The doctors ordered uncountable amounts of drugs and an extra strong enema that might have been imagined by Roto-Rooter.

The moment of relief came on Thursday afternoon while Danny was sitting in a tub of warm water. Suddenly his body just seemed to let go in an uncontrollable rush. Within seconds, Danny found himself sitting in a pool of his own excrement. His response was clearly mixed. On one hand, he was relieved; on the other, it was hard not to feel humiliated.

Then on Friday came Dr. Eichenhorn's terrible prognosis.

On Saturday morning, Rod Soja came by. He had been out of town. Always one of the happiest of Trotter's team, Soja walked in the room and started to cry.

Later that day, Danny—ever determined—went out on his own into the hallway to try lurching along with his stationary walker. He promised himself not to give up. But the doctor's words kept seeping into his consciousness. "You will be paralyzed for the rest of your life." So, too, did the skepticism of the intern, the physical therapist, the nurses, and his friends and family.

That night at 10 p.m., he got a call from Paul Ehorn. He did not know Paul. Trotter had asked the Illinois diver to call Danny because he too had suffered through a severe attack of the bends.

Ehorn described his accident, the attack that followed his attempt to crank start the engine for a compressor onboard the dive boat. Ehorn, too, had been paralyzed from the chest on down, at least for a time.

Ultimately, Ehorn said, he had improved. He now could walk around. He went back to diving. Yes, he still got pains in his legs. And yes, when he walked, he often could not feel a stone under his foot. But he was active again.

The upshot of Ehorn's message was: You can still get on with your life, even if you never walk again. You can start a new life and a new career.

Ehorn had meant the call to be encouraging.

"But it was just the opposite for me," Danny said. Now the thought was firmly planted in his head. It looks like I will never walk again. The scale of Danny's emotions, which had consistently registered optimism, tipped the other way.

"It was a turning point for me," Danny said.

In those minutes following the phone call, Danny changed his prayer to God. He stopped telling God to help him walk.

Instead he prayed, "Dear Lord, if this is the way I'm going to be for the rest of my life, please give me the strength to handle it."

And he began to weep.

A Miracle

On Sunday, he woke at 8 a.m. Two hours later, he was out in the hall-way again, lurching along on his walker with a rosary clenched in one hand. By this time, the staff had gotten used to Danny's independent ways. They paid little attention to his forays up and down the halls.

Then at midway down a hall when no one was looking, Danny sensed something new and different. For the first time since his accident, he felt something in his lower spine. Something that seemed alive.

In that moment, he lifted up the walker off the floor and took a series of quick steps, actually bending his knees a little bit. It was almost like running. Shuffling along, he moved a distance of about five feet.

Tears cascade down his cheeks, dripping onto his hospital gown. In a way it only seemed fair that if Danny was going to start a recovery, he would begin not by walking—but by running.

"Thank you, Lord," he said.

And then, to prove it was not just a fluke, he did it again. His quick steps carried him along another five feet down the hall.

"It's a miracle."

Danny, the cradle Catholic, had read about miracles all of his life. He had heard of miracles. But now he—Danny Fader—was a miracle.

Danny said that people at his church later suggested that his miracle came because he had changed his prayer. "You relinquished your will to God," they said. "And you acknowledged that He was in charge."

As he started back to his room, Danny met a nurse named Wilma.

"I'm starting to walk. I'm starting to walk," Danny exulted.

Wilma had not seen this hallway miracle. So she gave him only a weary look of skepticism.

"Oh yeah, that's good," she said. He might as well have told her that he had flapped his arms and started to fly. She wasn't falling for it.

Danny couldn't believe it. Here he'd had a breakthrough and she blew him off. "I expected her to say, 'Wow! That's terrific.'"

No matter. Danny's excitement could not be dampened. When he got back to his room, Danny was so full of his own success that he set aside his walker and tried to walk the two feet to his bed.

Now that was too much. "Boom. I went down," he said. And as he fell, his rosary snagged on the handle of the walker. Beads scattered and bounced across the floor.

Another nurse showed up at the door and helped him into bed. She, at least, was delighted to hear his news.

Danny now could truly smile for the first time in a week. "I just lay in bed, thanking the Lord and trying to pray with my broken rosary."

That afternoon, Danny went out into the hallway with his walker and did it again. Short little running steps while holding up the walker. Then after a rest, he did it again.

Danny called Rudy Whitworth to give him the news. Hardly believing it, Whitworth said, "That's great,"

Then Jeanne called. "You had better be careful," she said. "Listen to those doctors."

She knew how cocksure I was, Danny remembered.

On Monday, Dr. Eichenhorn had left word that Danny could be taken down for one last session in the hyperbaric chamber before being shipped off to outpatient care. At that point, Danny was able to move himself from the wheelchair to a gurney.

"We'll have to tell Dr. Eichenhorn," the nurses said.

An hour and a half after his chamber session, Dr. Eichenhorn showed up in Danny's room.

"I heard you are starting to walk now," he said.

But the doctor was not buying any miracles until he saw for himself. He had Danny stand up and lift one leg a little bit. And bend one knee. And then holding his hand, the doctor had Danny take a couple of steps.

Of doctors, it is often said, they may be wrong, but they are never in doubt. And so it was with Dr. Eichenhorn. Without an eye blink, he issued a new prognosis.

"I predict," he said, "that you are going to have a complete recovery."

The explanation for Danny's recovery was that with a body in shock, the nerves will sometimes build different pathways to make connections.

Danny could only shake his head in wonder. Paralyzed for the rest of his life. A complete recovery. What an astounding turnaround.

To all this Danny could only quip, "I can't pass my own urine," he said. "But when I do, I'm going to come back and piss on his leg."

CHAPTER 14

Redemption

A month or so after Dr. Michael Eichenhorn revised his original prognosis, Jeanne was driving Danny south along U.S. 23 toward Ann Arbor. It's a four-lane highway, treed on both sides with maples, poplars, and evergreens. It bypasses the town of Brighton, which has a hummock-sized ski hill and a series of hamlets such as Heartland, Lakeland, Hamburg, and Whitmore Lake.

It was their new commuting route, taking them eventually to a collection of modern brick buildings where Danny would get his sessions of physical and occupational therapy at the University of Michigan clinic, just a block north of Briarwood Shopping Center.

Danny had begun to walk on his own. He used a cane. Each step was jerky and awkward. But he no longer needed the aluminum walker or a wheelchair.

The conversation between Danny and Jeanne, which had been stilted for years by anger and resentment, now flowed. And once again they were laughing.

At one point, Danny turned to his wife and joked, "Now you're married to a robot."

To which Jeanne quipped back, "You're my little Frankenstein."

A second miracle was in the works.

Once Dr. Eichenhorn had pronounced his new, optimistic judgment, the hospital staff set Danny on a new course for recovery at Henry Ford Hospital.

Danny would not be moved to outpatient care, as the doctor had originally planned. Instead, he was scheduled for more sessions in the hospital's hyperbaric chamber—once a day for the next week. Each session lasted one and a half hours. And for his peace of mind, if nothing else, Danny learned how to change the TV channels.

Everyday he prayed and gave thanks to God. Not once, but often. And he managed to get himself down to the hospital's nondenominational chapel.

"I was so thankful to the Lord for giving me a second chance at life," he said.

This was not to say that he had completely recovered. He was still mostly paralyzed and had little or no feeling in the lower part of his body.

While overwhelming in its difficulty, frustration, and pain, Danny's feel-nothing paralysis also led to some situations where he could only shrug and chuckle.

Two days after Danny had started to walk a bit with his walker, he was out practicing in the hallway at about 10 p.m. Most of the patients were asleep at that point or watching television. The halls were deserted. Nurses did not seem to notice Danny. Given his willful ways, the nurses just turned a blind eye when he took his hallway constitutionals.

"I would walk a little ways and then my nerves would stop functioning for a while," he said. "So I would put the walker down and stop. And then when I felt I could, I'd start walking again." During these solo outings, Danny still had almost no sensations below the waist. Just how little he was feeling came to him with an eye-popping surprise that night.

"I looked down and realized that my hospital pants had come untied and were down around my ankles."

Standing there in a diaper, he realized, "I had been dragging the pants this way for a while and had no idea what had happened."

Fortunately for his sense of decorum, no one saw Danny do his diaper strut. With some effort, he managed to reach down, pull up his pants, and retie them. At that point he could only grin and lurch his way back toward his bed.

Every day, the physical therapist challenged him with new exercises. And every day, he improved at least a little bit.

When he had arrived at the hospital, Danny could move nothing below his chest. Then he started walking a bit with the walker. Now the physical therapist did not want him to just walk with support, but to go up and down stairs. Among other things, that meant bending knees that had refused to bend.

Danny wanted the challenge, the chance to heal, but he admitted, "I was kind of scared about falling." Of course, he would try.

With his hands on the rail, Danny stood on the top stair, looked down, and carefully put his left foot down on the next step. He could not really feel the foot, but he could see it settle. Then he moved his right foot down onto the same step. Success. One step down. One whole step down. Then he did it again, down to the next step. And again. He'd done it. He had gone down three whole steps. His legs were tingling like crazy.

Now came a bigger test. Go back up. And so he did. First one step. And then another and another. All three steps. Going up was much harder, but he would not be daunted.

By the time he left Henry Ford Hospital on November 1, Danny was able to work his way down a whole flight of stairs, rest for awhile on the landing, then go down another flight, and, in time, work all the way back to the top.

Danny could not walk without support. But he found—and you must understand that seemingly small advances can feel huge—that he could set the walker aside, trading it for holding the belt of someone who was walking in front of him.

His next stop was Cottage Hospital in the Grosse Pointes, a collection of communities outside Detroit on Lake St. Clair with upscale shops, manicured lawns, and fine homes including the mansions of Ford and General Motors executives.

"So this is where the rich people live," said Danny, who had grown up sleeping with his brothers and sisters in the same bed.

At Cottage Hospital, Danny got more physical therapy. His walking improved. By the time he left nine days later, he could get around using just a four-footed cane.

While his walking was getting better, other things were not. Doctors described his condition as spinal myelopathy, a compression of nerves in his lower back. That was the cause of the severe pain in his lower back and legs. It affected his walking and caused him to lose control over urination and bowel movements. He still could not urinate on his own. Release would only come from a catheter. Also, damage from the accident had left him with terrible constipation. He was fed milk of magnesia and Dufulax and had to wear adult diapers. These two plagues would stay with him for the rest of his life.

After leaving Cottage Hospital, a new phase began for his healing. On November 8, with Jeanne at the wheel, he began commuting to Ann Arbor, about a one-hour drive from his home in Highland, Michigan. They commuted every day, five days a week for eight hours of daily sessions for the next four months.

Danny had talked to some other Ford employees who urged him to take a medical retirement. But Danny was as willful as ever. He would not listen to such talk.

His goal, and nothing could dissuade him, was to go back to work. He was resolved to walk and climb as he had before.

The therapists were bringing him along. He was in a process of re-learning. How to walk. How to manage a much-changed life that could not even take going to the bathroom for granted. It was painful and exhausting. But he did everything they asked and more. Once at home, he did not stop.

Neighbors saw Danny out in his driveway trying to re-learn how to walk. He'd take a step or two and then fall, they said. But then he got up and tried again. He'd manage a few more steps, only to tumble down. And so he would begin again.

Slowly. Painfully. He began to recover. He would never get complete feeling back in his feet and legs, so the University of Michigan therapists taught him to use his eyesight to compensate for what he could not sense with his toes.

At first his exercises were simple stretches. The therapist had him lay on his back, lift one knee, and then reach around the inside of his knee and pull. Simple. But for Danny it was tough and painful. His legs were stiff. They stubbornly refused to bend. And this stretching aggravated the pain.

To give him a proper stride, the therapists had him walk like a tightrope walker along a 4-inch square length of board. Then he had to do it wearing three-pound ankle weights. And then with five-pound ankle weights.

"Close your eyes," said the therapist.

Danny closed his eyes.

"Now stand on one foot."

He needed to regain a sense of balance.

While the physical therapy continued, the therapists added occupational therapy. Every week they added more until Danny was working an 8-hour day and a 40-hour week.

To tune his hand-eye coordination, they had him build something like an Erector Set project with lots of nuts and bolts and angle irons. The therapist told him to assemble it and then take it apart. Now do it again. And each effort was timed. So he got faster.

They had him lift weights starting at different levels and usually ending up above his head, as you might lift a box to put on a shelf. They had him pick up a wooden box and carry it around the room, avoiding obstacles. And after he did that, well, they added weight to the box. Eventually it weighed 50 pounds. Danny could feel the raw pull on his damaged lower spine.

He walked on a treadmill, faster and faster and at steeper and steeper angles. He did resistance training for biceps, triceps, and for the quadriceps in his legs.

And finally he did very job-specific work—fitting pipes, working with pipe elbows and nipples. Pushing, pulling, reaching high, working low, screwing one fitting into another.

By the end of four months of these daily workouts, Danny began to feel that he was in the best shape of his life. But his recovery was turning out to be more than just physical.

In the late 1960s and early 1970s, a time of youth revolution and urban upheaval when the country was trying to extricate itself from Vietnam, the allusion was often made to the Chinese symbol for crisis. It read literally as "dangerous opportunity."

Truly for Danny and Jeanne, this moment was just that—a dangerous opportunity. To their credit, they made the most of it.

Unlike any previous time in his life, Danny now was entirely dependent on Jeanne. For him, it was an eye-opener.

Every weekday Jeanne drove him down to Ann Arbor for his eight hours of therapy and then drove him back. This went on for four months. Put another way, they spent something close to 300 hours together, just the two of them. No interferences, no interruptions.

What they did with that time was talk. And talk and talk.

At first it made Danny cranky. He had always run things his way and he still wanted to be in control. He wanted to make the decisions. He felt like he—not Jeanne—should drive the car. But the simple truth was he could not do it.

At times, he got so frustrated he even made nasty remarks to Jeanne. He didn't like the way she drove. Didn't like the speed. The way she passed other cars and so on.

But that irritability passed. More and more, Danny began to rediscover the importance of Jeanne in his life. Their words flowed, back and forth. What else could they do? They were hermetically sealed twice a day in a box on wheels. They had no choice but to talk. And talk brought new understanding. At one point not so many months before, the couple had been on the brink of divorce. Now that was changing.

They talked about important things. They talked about nothing much at all. They talked about their fears and anger. They talked about the gospels and the Bible. They talked about giddy times in the past and hopes for times to come. Their words became a soothing balm on what had been an incessant burn of anger. They talked about whether Danny would ever go back to work at Ford's. They wondered if he would ever get his job back. They talked about their son, Daniel. At times, Danny would just break down and cry. But for the most part—and this was the best—their talk was once again filled with laughter.

"I would crack jokes and she would joke around with me. It was fun. We rekindled that old closeness," he said.

Jeanne could see and feel the changes. Knowing from her own auto crash, she said, "Accidents can make you introspective. You realize how precious life is. And what is important in life becomes very clear."

And so it happened to Danny.

"I started to look back on how selfish I was," he said.

These were months of re-educating themselves in things that they thought were fully under control. At the same time that Danny was re-learning how to walk, he and Jeanne were re-learning how to talk to the one person each of them had been able to tell anything to.

"He was struggling to regain his health," Jeanne said, "but we made it a joyful time. It was a wonderful few months. We spent quality time together. I could make him laugh. And he could make me laugh.

"That time really drew us together," she said. "Now we really support each other."

Danny would say later, "Our marriage is now the best it has ever been."

As the priest had said at their wedding, their marriage boded well because of their faith and their laughter.

On March 27, 1995, six months after his accident, Danny Fader returned to his job as a pipe fitter at Ford.

He brought with him four boxes of doughnuts for his pals at work. They knew he had struggled hard to make this comeback. What they did not know was that Danny Fader had not only regained a semblance of his former active life, but with it he rediscovered a wonderfully happy life with Jeanne.

For these things, he felt truly grateful to God.

CHAPTER 15

Gold Fever

Three years had passed since Danny's accident.

In that time, Danny had achieved a semblance of recovery and returned to work. Trotter and his team continued to search for lost ships. But they did not go back to the steamer *Detroit*, even though the strongbox—as far as they knew—was still sitting out in the mud.

Certainly the team could have gone back to the *Detroit* at any time. But in a visceral way, it felt wrong.

"It was just too painful to consider," Trotter said. "In our minds, the strongbox and Danny's near-death experience were intimately linked. That safe could have contained $50,000, but it almost killed Danny."

To be sure, for those three years Trotter's team never stopped wondering about that heavy metal box for which so much had been sacrificed. Was the box still there? As Trotter knew it would, word about the *Detroit*'s location had gotten out. The local dive charter guy certainly knew it. And after all, he had put the exact latitude/longitude numbers out over the radio when he called the Coast Guard. Other divers since had dropped down into Lake Huron's darkness to take a look at the ship.

In his programs given at divers conferences, Trotter even had mentioned the strongbox. But no one on the team even whispered where it was hidden. Concealed well away from the ship in the murky darkness, Trotter felt sure no one had found it.

Now one big question remained: What was inside?

Perhaps nothing at all. But in a mix of logic and optimism, why lock a safe with nothing inside? So maybe it did hold something. Historic papers. A ship's log. And maybe, just maybe, it held a cache of pre–Civil War gold coins.

With three years gone and Danny having resumed much of his life, curiosity tightened its grip on Trotter and his crew. What for years had engendered only painful memories now was starting to nag. An unscratched itch. An unfinished opus.

On the morning of August 12, 1997—in an almost spur-of-the-moment decision, Trotter and his group agreed.

Okay, let's do it today. No special planning. No preparation. Just a decision.

Some decisions seem to come at their own will, uninvited. And often ill-timed. So it was with this one. While the day of Danny's accident was ironically gorgeous, this one was thoroughly unsavory. The weather was sour and obstructive. Even though it was mid-summer, a pestering rain gusted across Lake Huron. It was cold. They squinted at the horizon with their chins tucked inside the collars of their jackets. The grey-blue waves hit the shore in three-foot-high ranks. They would eventually grow to almost six feet.

But the decision had been made. There was no stopping now.

As Trotter backed the dive boat into the water at the Grindstone City marina, it was clear a number of changes had been wrought over three years.

He now had a new boat. Like the original *Obsession*, this boat was an aluminum Marinette. But it was bigger—32 feet long instead of 28. It could carry more gear and divers, cope with nastier water, and still could be towed behind Trotter's Ford van. Trotter named it *Obsession Too*.

Also, the team makeup had changed. Rocky Arsenault and Jeff Moore were still onboard. Still young, still strong, but now—with four seasons under their weight belts—they had adopted the air of veterans. Others were new to the *Obsession Too*. On this day, they included Frank Troxel, Mike Nalepa, Ken Lalko, and the newest diver—who would join them for the first time that day—John Makuch.

As most marine engines do when they are trying to make a waveless crossing of a harbor, the *Obsession Too* sounded like it was muttering in its sleep. Soon they were out beyond the breakwall and into the open waters of Lake Huron. The engine pitch grew to a muscular thrum and soon the dive boat was cruising at a hull-banging speed.

Just over an hour later, they tied onto the mooring line that stretched down to the side-wheel steamer 200 feet below.

First things first, they had to actually find the strongbox. They knew about where it lay, but not exactly. Moore and Arsenault—members of the original team—went down to search.

Starting from the *Detroit*'s starboard paddlewheel, Moore made a series of sweeps using a line tied to the rail. After several pendulum swings, he found the box wedged into the mud. It was about 30 feet from the ship.

Carrying a three-eighths-inch polypropylene rope on a reel, he knotted the line securely to the box. Unreeling the heavy line as he swam, Moore headed back to the mooring line and up to the surface with Arsenault. At this point, Moore figured he had played out between 300 and 350 feet of line.

Lifting the strongbox would be not only hard work, but tricky. If the *Obsession Too* had a power winch and steel cable, it would have been one thing. But it had no winch and no cable. Instead it had six very excited divers who had not entirely grasped how much muscle-straining effort it would take to haul in more than 100 yards of line that was tied to a 200-pound metal box.

Also, the strongbox lay only about 30 feet off the side of the *Detroit.* The team faced a real risk that the box, while being lifted, could slide into the ship and snag. So they decided to do things to avoid that nasty possibility.

One, the *Obsession Too* would start its engines, untie from the mooring line, and try to move away from the ship as the box was being raised. And two, the crew would pull like galley slaves for at least the first 50 feet of line, just to make sure the strongbox cleared the upper works of the steamer.

This would be a brutal task. Just lifting the strongbox would have been hard enough, but to do it while pulling against the power of the boat would make it doubly hard. And yes, it was raining. And cold. And the deck was bouncing up and down.

Still in their dry suits, Moore and Arsenault were standing on the swim platform, an almost water-level platform at the rear of the dive boat. The others on deck arrayed themselves along the line as though readying for a tug of war.

"Okay, ready?" The engine growled and kicked in gear, and the *Obsession Too* pulled away to clear the strongbox from the wreck.

"Heave! Heave! Heave!"

Shouts went up. So did swearing, grunting, and laughter. Orders flew up like birds released from a cage. Do this and that. Hand-over-hand they pulled. And pulled. The wet line cut into their hands.

The box was obdurate. But foot by foot, they heaved it higher, all the time wondering how the box could be so unimaginably heavy and the rope so very, very long.

As if the muscle-grinding pulling was not bad enough, Moore and Arsenault soon took full cognizance that the three-eighths-inch poly-propylene line was not really designed for this kind of work. As they pulled, they watched the line get thinner and thinner.

"It was as tight as a guitar string," Moore remembered. And it was getting tighter and thinner all the time.

After a long struggle, the team could finally glimpse the box below the surface. They stopped for a breather, collapsing on the deck. At last we've got it, they thought.

But then Moore looked back to the box, just to be sure that it was still well tied as the *Obsession Too* drifted down the lake.

That's when he spotted a heart-stopping problem. Their rope to the box was fraying, being sawed away little by little as it passed over the edge of the swim platform. Of the three-strand rope, one strand had snapped and a second looked ready to shred.

"It's chafing!" Moore gasped. "It's cutting through. We're going to lose it."

If the rope completely separated, that would be the end. The box would drop like a cannonball. And the team—now having drifted far from the *Detroit*—would have little hope of finding it again. Not ever. To make the line-shredding problem worse, the dive boat was being bounced around in a three-foot chop.

The team held the line fast. And then Moore, as quickly as he had jumped in to save Danny, was in the water with a second, thicker rope. He quickly tied it to the box. Now able to breathe a little easier, the team pulled the strongbox to the edge of the swim platform.

Now came the challenge of lifting the box up and onto the swim platform. Once out of the water, the box would be even heavier to lift. The 200-pound box would then, without the water's support, weigh a full 200 pounds. And the lifting job was aggravated by the bouncing of the boat.

But somehow they did it. The team pulled. And Moore and Arsenault grabbed the box with their hands and managed to muscle it up onto the platform. Once there, it was tied down.

It had taken more than 45 minutes of heaving, sweating, and swearing to get it up. Hands red and raw, breaths coming in gasps, everyone onboard sat back for a minute, shook their heads in relief, and laughed.

But now another element in the team's total lack of planning came home to roost.

Just as they had neglected to bring a winch to hoist the strongbox up from the bottom, it also never occurred to anyone that they might need some special tools to actually pry open the strongbox.

After all, this was no ordinary box. With heavy metal straps and a sturdy lock, it was designed with the sole purpose of keeping people from breaking into it. This was a safe that could be moved. But what would actually be kept safely inside, if any kid with a screwdriver could pop it open?

As for tools onboard, all they had was Trotter's toolbox for the boat. Arsenault and Moore hit it for anything they thought might help.

"We pulled out six-inch chisels and mallets and drill bits," Moore said. "But what we needed were a five-foot crowbar and a six-pound sledgehammer."

But never mind; the gold fever that had been simmering for hours now kicked into a rolling boil.

While the other team members looked on, Moore and Arsenault attacked the strongbox like crazed five year olds under a Christmas tree. They banged and whacked and pried.

Arsenault grabbed his weight belt and started hammering on the box with the lead weights. It was an onboard shark frenzy. Tools began to fly this way and that.

Trotter was laughing, thinking it does not get any better than this.

A six-inch chisel. Overboard.

A pry bar. Into the drink.

A crescent wrench hit the water with a glub and disappeared.

John Makuch, who was on his first outing with the team, could hardly believe what he was seeing.

"Who are these guys? They're nuts."

After more than half an hour of tool-flinging, knuckle-banging work, the door to the strongbox gave way. The frenzy was done. A silence swelled on the back deck. After three years, after near death, after hours of struggling to raise and open the strongbox, the moment had arrived. The team gathered to look.

As the door to the strongbox eased back, Makuch said Moore's and Arsenault's eyes "were as big as dinner plates."

With the door open, all anyone could see was water. It was black and it stank the foul stink of the muddy bottom of Lake Huron.

Moore jammed his hand inside.

"What do you feel?" Arsenault asked.

"It's cold. It's real cold," Moore said. His fingers stroked the bottom, wiped along the sides, and finally probed into the corners.

"I don't feel anything."

"You don't feel nothing? Nothing at all?"

Arsenault then jammed his hand into the stinking liquid. Nothing.

At that point, they started to laugh. And laugh.

"What a bunch of knuckleheads we were," Arsenault said.

Then Makuch walked up, reached into his pocket, pulled out a handful of coins, and tossed them into the box.

"Just so you don't come up completely empty," he grinned.

Now their three years of questions finally had been answered. It was a relief. It was a letdown. It was a disappointment. But the itch had finally been scratched. At that point, they untied the strongbox

The empty strongbox on the swim platform on the *Obsession Too* in 1997.
Courtesy of the David Trotter Collection.

and shoved it over the side. It hit with a thuggish slap and then burped as it went under. In seconds, it was gone.

In retrospect, one might wonder whether pulling up this empty box was worth Danny's near-death experience and what would become a lifetime of pain and disability.

The simple answer must be no. No box, in fact nothing in this world, would be worth Danny's suffering. But this resounding negative largely misses the point for adventurers and others who find a life satisfaction in pure acts of daring.

What if the circumstances were different? If Danny had not had his accident, would it then have been worth it? If he did have his accident and the box was filled with gold, would that have been worth it? These questions bring us to the matter of success.

Typically, the general public will confer its approval on an act of daring *if it succeeds*. The success makes whatever sacrifice worthwhile. If it fails, they condemn it. But this is a conclusion for people who do not dare. People on the sidelines. For the people on the *Obsession*, including Danny Fader, this was not the point at all.

They did not dive for gold. That was never the motivation. They dove, at least in part, because diving holds risks. Risks that in themselves convey a sense of valor and worth. If a mountain climber happens upon a gold nugget, well, he'd be delighted. But once again, it would not be the reason for his passion to climb.

The success for the diver, particularly these deep wreck divers, is in the diving itself. It is taking the risk. Exploring the unexplored. Discovering the unknown.

For them, to dare is to live.

Epilogue

In the ensuing years, each of Trotter's team took a somewhat different course.

Werner "The Doc" Wahl no longer dives.

In the spring following Danny Fader's accident, Wahl had two heart attacks. Doctors installed a pacemaker and he retired the following October 1 on his birthday. Then he and his wife moved to Florida. They now live in Jacksonville, just a short walk from the water. He works with an investment club, but has not given up his love of the water. But now he spends his time fishing.

Rudy Whitworth never dove again with David Trotter.

He and Rod Soja used to commute together from their homes west of Detroit to go wreck hunting with Trotter. On their three-hour drives to and from the launch sites in Michigan's Thumb, they talked long and earnestly about their wreck diving. Together they worried about the fact that the ships they were finding were deeper and deeper, and as a result more dangerous. Both men were very lean of build so the longer decompression times for deep dives were, for them, especially cold.

Following the trauma of Danny's accident, Whitworth made a firm decision and dropped out of Great Lakes wreck diving entirely—but not from warm-water diving.

For years now he has been traveling the globe to dive at some of the world's most exotic locations, including the South Pacific and the Far East. His underwater photography—stoked by colorful fish and corals—continues to win prizes and show up in calendars and in magazines.

Rod Soja continued wreck diving with Trotter for a year and a half after the accident.

But like Whitworth, he became more fretful about dives that were often going below 200 feet. As he said, they were "on the cutting edge of danger." Also without Rudy, Danny, and the Doc onboard, wreck diving was not quite so much fun as it had been in the past. So he, too, gave up Great Lakes wreck diving but, like Whitworth, continued for a few years to ply the warm waters, mostly in the Caribbean where he has shot lots of first-rate photos. Several years have passed now since Soja hung up his scuba gear. Now he has a new passion: golf.

Rocky Arsenault, the adrenalin junkie, continued to dive with Trotter for several years, then took a break, and starting in 2006 came back for more diving with the Trotter team. Trotter says he is one of the rare ones to stop wreck diving and then return to it later. After his extended layoff, his first dive was down 200 feet on tri-mix. He was nervous beforehand, but it was like he had never missed a season.

Jeff Moore has become a hardcore wreck diver and one of the mainstays in Trotter's group. An English major in college who is now working with computer technology, Moore has helped Trotter write many of his discovery reports. The handsome young guy married a pretty woman. They have two rambunctious kids. And his wife says, "I like it when Jeff dives. We get along better."

David Trotter

By this time, David and Mickey Trotter had suffered another emotional jolt.

A young girl named Megan Boljesic, from Mickey's fourth-grade class, had virtually adopted the Trotter family. Like their lost daughter Kelly, she was bright, energetic, and an excellent student. They took her into their family, virtually as a daughter. And since Megan wanted to go to college, the Trotters planned to make sure that she got that chance.

But then, in a cruel twist of fate, she too died—killed in a reckless automobile accident. Like Kelly, she was 16 years old.

For the Trotters, it was an anguish revisited. Their wounds left by Kelly's death had never healed. Now this. The Trotters and Megan's uncle set out to seek justice. The accident had been caused by a young immigrant who had flouted the law before. The Trotters and Megan's uncle took him to the Immigration and Naturalization Service court and eventually had him expelled from the country after a two-year legal fight.

To this day, Trotter remains bitter and angry about the accident that killed Megan and the man who caused it. The anguish, he said, was terrible for him and for Mickey. In a rare display of anger, Trotter said, "God forgives, I don't."

As for the Trotters' two sons, Jay and Ross, they suffered the same sort of anguish as their parents, but they went on to graduate from college, entered business, and now have families of their own.

The Trotters, in the meantime, changed their working lives. David was offered a promotion at Ford Credit that he had long coveted. But he said "no thanks" and retired. A couple of years later Mickey retired, after 27 years of teaching elementary school.

Did Trotter also back off of wreck hunting? Not an inch. As Arsenault once said, "he's a lifer."

Now in his mid-60s, Trotter is continuing to explore the big inland waters. Every year he discovers new virgin shipwrecks. And every year his reputation grows as the most proficient wreck hunter in the Great Lakes and one of the best in the world. Many believe that his ever-growing collection of lost-ship discoveries is unlikely to be matched anytime soon—if ever. At this writing, he has discovered nearly 90 lost ships and surveyed more than 2,000 miles of Lake Huron—not to mention some hefty chunks of Lakes Erie and Michigan.

Accolades for Trotter have been many, but one of the most profound for him came from Garry Kozak, widely considered the world's best side-scan operator. After Trotter had discovered a 1930s biplane deep in Lake Huron, Kozak—noting the difficulties of the find—said, "You know, David, that is a great pickup."

As much as Trotter loves diving, he loves shipwreck history more. "Where else," he said, "can you, in three or four minutes, travel back in time to see things as they existed. There underwater, it is as though time stopped."

And he loves bringing that history alive for people who may never get to see such hidden marvels. He quotes John Steele, who made a comparison to the old days when divers used to strip the wrecks. "When you dive with a crowbar," Steele said, "you dive alone. When you dive with a camera, you take thousands with you."

Trotter had brought his cameras from the very beginning when he found and dove on the *Daniel J. Morrell*, the ship that had split in half. It was his first and one of his most important discoveries. At that time, filming was not particularly in fashion. Most divers were still in a seek-and-grab mode.

Over the years, he has improved his technology for his presentations. At first he used 35 mm Nikons to shoot underwater slides. He now uses sophisticated digital video equipment. He also has joined forces often with Robert McGreevy, famed for his marine drawings and paintings, particularly his meticulous underwater renderings of wrecks. Several of McGreevy's art works are in this book.

Wish List

Trotter often is asked, "What is the most interesting ship you have found?" His answer, while glib, is accurate: "The next one." And he has some fascinating finds on his wish list.

"You know," he says slyly, "there are other strong boxes and other treasures out there on long-missing ships."

Here are three:

On November 13, 1863, while the country struggled in the midst of its great civil war, the nearly new 163-foot *Water Witch* went down in a storm off Saginaw Bay. All hands—estimated at between 20 and 28—died. Trotter said that he has some evidence the *Water Witch* was carrying a strongbox filled with specie, that is, gold coins. He estimates that its worth today is in the thousands. It's likely the *Water Witch* was badly battered and now is strewn across the bottom of Lake Huron. Trotter said, if found, he can use the unique engine type to identify it. Then will come the challenge of finding the strongbox.

The gales of November earned their foul reputation in that year of 1863.

One week after the *Water Witch* sank, the steamer *Keystone State* went down in Saginaw Bay on November 20. Once again, all hands were lost—33 men. The *Keystone State* was big, one of the largest steamers on the lakes at that time. It was carrying a load of farm implements, hardware, crockery, and, yes, a safe with $3,000 in gold. That's $3,000 in 1860 money.

Finally, Trotter has his eye out for the *R.G. Coburn*. The 194-foot steamer, just one year old, lost control of its rudder during a storm off Saginaw Bay on October 15, 1871. It was carrying 30 barrels of high-grade silver. Wallowing in the trough of the heavy seas, the barrels broke loose and smashed into the sides of the steamer, opening holes where the freezing Lake Huron water rushed in. Thirty-one passengers and crew died.

As it turned out, the *Coburn* was owned by Eber Ward, the same man who owned the steamer *Detroit*. And as with the *Detroit* and his other ships, the *Coburn* was self-insured.

Trotter always has a wish list. As a result, since 1996 when we last left his trail of discoveries, he has made a number of important finds.

The *G.F. Becker*, a 39.6 foot tug that was built in 1928 and went down in heavy seas after apparently hitting an underwater object on September 30, 1931. Trotter and his team found it in 1996, largely intact in 220 feet of water.

Designed to tow barges, the *Becker* was recruited for heavy use in building the Ambassador Bridge that spans the Detroit River from

Detroit to Windsor, Ontario. It also was rumored that smugglers used the *Becker* to ferry cases of liquor between Canada and the United States during Prohibition.

Interestingly, Trotter's divers were able to uncover some strong clues that the *Becker*'s sinking was no accident. It might well have been scuttled to collect the insurance. Among the salient clues was that the tug was found nearly 60 miles from where the captain and the single crew member said it had foundered in Lake Huron.

Secondly, all the three-quarter-inch glass in the portholes just above the waterline were uniformly smashed, as though with a hammer. These openings would have allowed a mass of water to rush in. By comparison, glass in the portholes on upper levels of the boat was unscathed.

Finally, the captain reported that he was forced to abandon ship because, after hitting an underwater object, damage to the rudder and propellers made them inoperable. But upon examining the rudder and propellers, Trotter and his dive team found no damage at all.

The captain, George Klemm, and a single crew member survived the wreck in a lifeboat and were picked up by a passing ship.

In 1998, the team found the steamer *City of Detroit*, which went down in a brutal storm off Saginaw Bay on December 4, 1873, while towing a consort, the *Guiding Star*. When the *City of Detroit* suddenly lost power in the huge waves, the captain ordered that the line between the two ships be cut. The *Guiding Star* survived, but the *City of Detroit* went down with all 19 crew members.

In 1999, they discovered the *Metropole*, a 118-foot steamer that plunged to the bottom on the relatively calm day of August 8, 1903. The crew discovered water leaking into the bilge that could not be stanched. Everyone onboard abandoned ship and eventually made it to safety at the tip of Michigan's Thumb. Apparently the *Metropole* was ill-fated from the start.

The ship was originally built as a 100-foot steam barge in 1883 and named *Sakie Shepherd*. She was designed for fishing and excursions. Twelve years later, in April 1895, the *Shepherd* sprang a leak in Lake Erie and went down in 50 feet of water. It was not so deep that the ship could not be raised and put back into service. But her bad luck continued: she caught fire three years later while tied to a dock at Courtright, Ontario. She was declared a total loss.

But that fire was not the end of her. Two years later, new owners towed the *Shepherd* to Detroit and rebuilt it, adding 18 feet to its length. It was relaunched in 1900. With this whole new start, the *Shepherd* also got a new name—the *Metropole*. Unfortunately, the

The *Frank H. Goodyear*, as she sits on the bottom of Lake Huron. The owner's luxury railcar can be seen amidships. Illustration by Robert McGreevy.

new name did not alter the ship's luck. She went down for the last time three years later.

In 2002, the team found the *W.C. Franz*, a 346-foot Canadian freighter built in 1901, which plummeted to the bottom following a collision with the 4,279-ton steamer *Edward E. Loomis*. Apparently at the last minute, the *Franz* veered off its course directly across the bow of the *Loomis*. Four crewmen on the *Franz* were killed and 15 were rescued.

One of the most significant ships ever found by Trotter's team was the *Frank H. Goodyear*. The 436-foot ore boat was not only distinctive, but its sinking helped prompt a change in navigation practices in the Great Lakes. The *Goodyear* also was one of the rare ships on which Trotter's team actually found the bones of a crewman.

In the foggy predawn darkness of May 23, 1910, the eight-year-old *Goodyear* was downbound off the tip of the Michigan Thumb with a load of iron ore from Duluth. Its destination was Cleveland. Suddenly, the 534-foot ore boat *James B. Wood* appeared out of the darkness going full speed, ramming into the hull of the *Goodyear*. The crew of neither ship saw the other before it was too late.

When Trotter's team got down to take a look in 2002, they found a 12-foot hole gouged in the side of the *Goodyear*, big enough to swim through.

With its tonnage of iron, the *Goodyear* went down in less than five minutes with 18 passengers and crew, including two women and two children. Five people survived.

The *Goodyear* was a ship that seemed to have a grudge against David Trotter. In an eerie way, it seemed to resent having been found.

Of his six dives on the 250-foot-deep *Goodyear*, Trotter suffered free flows on the first four dives. He managed to resolve them all underwater, later having two of his regulators entirely rebuilt. Unfortunately, they would free flow again. And then, on this sixth dive, his ear drum burst at 160 feet while he was descending to the bow holding his camera.

That ended his diving for that year.

Trotter's advice for anyone who has ever burst an eardrum: Do not dose it with Swim-EAR, the stuff used to dry out ears after swimming. One, it did not help. And two, the fluid flowed through his pierced eardrum and into his inner ear and hit him with a searing pain as bad as any he had ever known.

The *Goodyear* was originally owned by and named for Frank Goodyear, who was a member of the same family of auto tire fame. But Frank's fortunes came instead from mining and railroads.

Since Goodyear himself used to sail onboard from time to time, the shipowner arranged for a private luxury railroad car set up amidships. It sat crosswise to the length of the ship. In the car was his private bedroom, sitting room, guest rooms, and a bath with ornate brass fixtures. He traveled in style.

Frank Goodyear died three years before his namesake ship went down. Its new owners took over not only the ship but also the railcar. They used it as quarters for some of the crew.

One of the surprises for Trotter's team was discovering a skull and bones of one of the crew members lying in a protected passageway for the stern cabins. The *Goodyear* was not only the last resting place for the ship, but also for a member of the crew. Realizing that it was a gravesite, the divers touched nothing.

However, they felt it was important to mark the spot in some tasteful and appropriate way. So they ordered a special plaque to be placed near the hallway where the bones had been found. It will remain there for any divers who might follow the Trotter team.

It reads: "In memory of those men and women who lost their lives aboard this vessel on May 23, 1910. May they rest in peace."

Finally and most notably, the collision and sinking of the *Goodyear* prompted shipowners to finally and formally establish shipping lanes in Lakes Huron and Superior. These lanes would separate the upbound and downbound ships. It had taken more than 100 years of collisions to reach this resolve.

In 1911, the Lake Carriers Association set out recommendations that upbound (meaning north for Lake Huron and west for Lake Superior) ships should stay closest to the shore, which was also the fastest route. Downbound ships, which were loaded with heavy iron ore and needed deeper water, were to stay two miles farther out. Four years later, in 1915, the Canadian Lake Carriers Association adopted the same lane separations for the two heavily traveled lakes.

Separate lanes were not established for Lake Michigan until 1926. And it was not until after World War II that lanes were set up for Lakes Ontario and Erie. Eventually all these lanes would be separated by not just two, but five miles.

This is not to say that these resolutions by the owners of the largest lake ships stopped all collisions. They did not.

For the ship captains, staying in the shipping lanes was strictly voluntary. If they were late for a delivery deadline, well, to heck with the lanes. Furthermore, many smaller ships—particularly lumber carriers—were not registered members of the major lake carrier associations. So they felt no sense of obligation. As a result, the watery crashes did not stop for a number of years.

More recently, Trotter and his team found the 165-foot barkentine *H.P. Bridge* and explored it in 2005. The three-masted ship—faster at the time than even the side-wheel steamers of the time and only five years old—went down in a late night fog on May 11, 1869. It sank quickly into Lake Huron after being run down by the propeller ship *Colorado*. All the crew escaped safely to the *Colorado*.

The *Bridge* is of special interest to the divers because it is remarkably intact. It sits upright with all three masts and cross-arms in place and it has a handsome carved figurehead of an eagle—from an era when figureheads were rare. The bell on the foredeck is still shiny, and bricks sit where they were originally stacked three-deep on the deck. And in the captain's sea chest, the divers even found an old stovepipe top hat, the kind that Lincoln used to wear.

So Trotter, while he does not foresee any early retirement from wreck hunting, does recognize that the grand old days of finding a wreck every weekend are fading. With much of the Great Lakes waters increasingly explored, he expects that discovering virgin wrecks will become a rarer and rarer experience. No, he says, the glory days of wreck hunting are not over. But he knows that the end may be in sight.

The barkentine *H.P. Bridge* was sunk after being rammed by the propeller ship *Colorado* in a fog on the night of May 11, 1869. Trotter and his team found it in Lake Huron in 2005. Artist Robert McGreevy re-creates what the accident might have looked like.

The barkentine *H.P. Bridge* sits upright on the bottom. You can see in artist Robert McGreevy's rendering the crossarms still in place and how the decks were stacked with a load of bricks. Illustration by Robert McGreevy.

In his career, Trotter has been involved in and often led the way for making changes that now are considered standard parts of wreck diving—sophisticated positioning equipment, first loran-C and now GPS; improved sonar gear; technical diving using multiple gases; and the change of attitude from wreck stripping for souvenirs to creating a photographic and historical chronicle.

Certainly Trotter has not been alone. He often cites a sense of pride of having known, worked with, and dove with many involved in Great Lakes shipwreck hunting. These include members of his teams over the years and right up to today, with special feelings for Danny, Rudy, Rod, the Doc, Rocky, Jeff, and John Makuch. He also feels fortunate to have been involved with such shipwreck hunting stalwarts as John Steele, Paul Ehorn, Chuck and Jeri Feltner, and Garry Kozak. Together, he feels, they have built a strong legacy of discoveries and innovations that future shipwreck hunters can build upon.

It's unclear how much longer Trotter will continue to search. But at a future time, perhaps on his fiftieth wedding anniversary to Mickey, he does plan a break when the two of them will go on a world-class tour. It will be one of many thank yous for Mickey's years of selfless support for this admittedly obsessed man.

As for **Danny Fader**, his determination to recover continued unflagged despite some setbacks.

Following his rehabilitation, Danny managed to stay with Ford as a pipe fitter for nine years. Toward the end, however, his damaged body began to deteriorate. He was forced to go back again and again for rehabilitation. He could no longer climb and suffered mightily when he had to walk long distances. Finally the recurring pain outdid even Danny Fader's resolve. He accepted a retirement. Now, some 13 years after the accident, Danny continues to endure real pain in his back and legs.

Not surprisingly, Danny's miraculous recovery redoubled his already strong faith in God. He attends Mass daily and often more than once a day.

In the years immediately following his accident, Danny and Jeanne took several pilgrimages to famed religious shrines. The couple went to show their devotion and to give thanks, but also to pray and for healing and strength.

"God, I sure would appreciate it," Danny would pray, "if you could create another miracle to heal my lower spine and other problems."

The first shrine they visited was Ste. Anne de Beaupre in Quebec, Canada, which has a reputation for healing that dates back to the construction of the first chapel in 1658.

Next they traveled to Medugorje in Bosnia-Herzegovina, where an apparition of the Blessed Virgin Mary appeared to six children over a period of time starting in 1981.

In 1996, they visited Our Lady of Fatima Shrine in Portugal, where in 1917 three children saw the Blessed Mother of God, who asked the people to pray the Rosary every day. Thousands came soon after and reported a miracle—that they had been able to look directly at the sun and watched while it danced.

In 1999, Danny and Jeanne flew to Mexico to visit Our Lady of Guadalupe Basilica on a hilltop just northwest of Mexico City. In 1531, the Virgin Mary appeared to a native man, Juan Diego, and she asked him to tell the local bishop to build a church on the spot. To prove her reality, she left an image of herself imprinted on cheap cactus cloth called atilma. This cloth, which by rights should have disintegrated within 20 years, can still be seen today almost 500 years later. And over the years, thousands of miracles have occurred at the Basilica.

In 2000, the couple visited Jerusalem and went to the Diamond Jubilee in Rome. On every trip, they brought their son, Daniel.

As for the marriage of Danny and Jeanne, it might be described as the second miracle. The marriage recovery was no short-term accommodation while Danny commuted to rehab. It has grown stronger and stronger over the years.

They rediscovered that they were each others' best friends. As in the early days of their romance, they continue to be able to tell each other anything and everything.

So their open, airy lakeside home is constantly filled with talk—and yes, laughter.

"Our marriage is the best it has ever been," Danny has said.

Over the years, Danny stayed out of the water, but it did not mean that he had given up all thoughts of diving. He simply put these thoughts away, like an old favorite book that had been relegated to a box in the basement. Especially on warm, sunny mornings, his mind would drift back to those heady days onboard the *Obsession*—his cave and his mountain.

With the passing of a decade, Danny's diving days became almost surreal in his memory—days aboard the *Obsession* when his everyday cares were swept away. Days with the piquancy of danger and yet with an uncomplicated sweetness. Those were the times when he was healthy and strong and all life was painted in vivacious colors. But it seemed doubtful that he would ever dive again.

Then, at the beginning of February 2007, just after the manuscript for this book had gone off to the editor, he did it. After 13 years, he pulled on a scuba tank and dove.

David Trotter and Danny Fader at Danny's 60th birthday party in October 2006.
Courtesy of David Trotter Collection.

He and Jeanne had joined their church group on the *Norwegian Jewel* for a cruise of the Eastern Caribbean. On the first day, Danny spotted a sign-up sheet for a shore excursion to scuba dive at St. Thomas, the third port on the ship's itinerary.

Jeanne told him to go ahead. After all, he had been talking about it for years. Doctors had told him that the nerve damage had already been done. It was unlikely he could do himself more harm. And with a careful dive, he would be safe.

As for Danny—although he had some trepidations—he was avid.

At the ship's sign-up desk, the clerk asked Danny if he had dived in the last year. He fudged his answer and talked about diving in the Great Lakes. In minutes, he had signed on.

Out on the boat, Danny made not just one dive, but two. The first went down to 70 feet and the second to 45 feet, where he saw—of all things—a sunken ship. It was not much of a wreck. It was an old drug runner and was badly broken up, Danny said. It was not the kind of find that Trotter would even bother to dive on.

But Danny emerged from the water with a grin so broad its beam might have been spotted back in Michigan.

It's unlikely that Danny will become the diver that he once was— the human fish, the explorer of wrecks where the waters are deep, dark, and deadly.

But one thing was sure. Danny Fader was back.

Acknowledgments

After some 40 years as a writer, reporter, editor, and author, I have found the best parts of my work life have been the people I've met along the way. And it has been especially true with the research and writing of *Shipwreck Hunter*.

In some very warm ways, I feel like I have been taken in as at least an auxiliary family member by the principals of this book. This was especially true with Danny and Jeanne Fader, and also with David and Mickey Trotter.

As a researcher, I still am breathless with the Faders' openness and absolute candor, their detailed memories, and their willingness to discuss not only proud moments but also their most painful ones. At the outset, I thought this book would be a pure adventure story. But once talking with the Faders, I found that telling their story would make the book much deeper and more significant. I can only salute them. The odds they've faced—and faced together—at times seemed insurmountable. But surmount them they did—with laughter, tenacity, and a deep sense of religious faith. To my mind, they are true heroes.

It was my special fortune to work with David Trotter. He, after all, is the best—the lord of the shipwreck hunters. What a terrific subject for a writer. He and I had known each other for more than a decade before I started this project. During that time, I wrote several stories about him and his discoveries for the *Detroit Free Press*.

David has been wonderfully helpful with this book, coming forth with not only his own story—which held some true tragedies—but because of his accumulated knowledge of all matters of wreck hunting and diving. He was my go-to guy on all technical matters.

Everybody who knows Mickey loves Mickey. And I count myself in that number. She is a joyous presence who has been David's mainstay and his most enthusiastic supporter.

As you might guess, this book was based on hours and hours of interviews. And then on more hours and hours of follow-up interviews. And then more interviews after that. And then once a draft was finished, the Faders and Trotters read through the whole thing and made scores of helpful comments, additions, and corrections.

It must be said, however, if this book does contain errors—and at this length they are nearly unavoidable—they are mine. And mine alone.

Also special thanks to Paul Ehorn, who also was remarkably forthcoming. I gave Paul the section of the book about his diving life and legal hassles and he too made a number of important corrections. To my mind, the Great Lakes diving community owes him a huge debt of thanks. If any wreck hunter finds himself at legal odds over ownership of a found ship—and these issues come up regularly—he or she can thank Ehorn that they have some recourse when faced with charges.

My gratitude to Charles Feltner, whose sage perspective gave me a clearer sense of Great Lakes wreck diving history. I am sure he and Jeri must have spotted me picking up my socks after a several-hour interview in their Dearborn home. They had charmed them off.

Thanks, too, to members of the Trotter team who also submitted to lengthy interviews—Rudy Whitworth, Rod Soja, Rocky Arsenault, Jeff Moore, and John Makuch. Werner "Doc" Wahl was not only a sharp, detailed, and funny interviewee, but he and his wife graciously invited me to stay in their home while I was in Florida.

Thanks, too, to John Steele, whom I visited and interviewed at his home in Wisconsin.

The divers who managed to scuba down 530 feet in Lake Superior to the *Edmund Fitzgerald* were hard to catch up with. I tracked down Terrence Tysall in Orlando, Florida, at his parents-in-law's home. Mike Zlatopolsky, better known as Mike Z., apparently is constantly on the go. But I managed to meet him at a restaurant off an Interstate 94 exit at Kalamazoo, Michigan. He also graciously provided the photo of their dive group that appears in these pages. With a little phone detective work, I caught up with Randy Sullivan, who captained the dive boat, at his home in Sault Ste. Marie, Ontario.

Gratitude also to Valerie Van Heest, the leading expert on the disappearance of Northwest Flight 2501.

Since a book such as this involves both contemporary and historic matters, I did a fair amount of library research. For help during these delvings into microfiche, weathered photo copies, and yellowed news clippings, I extend my heartfelt appreciation to staffs of the Burton Collection at the Detroit Public Library, which has a healthy file on Eber and Clara Ward, and at the Great Lakes Marine Collection at the Milwaukee Public Library, which holds folders of material about John Steele.

On a personal level, special thanks to my son, Christopher, and daughter, Teresa, who have been supportive. But also because they took time out of extremely busy lives to travel across country to prop up my morale when I suffered a rather sudden hearing loss from Meniere's syndrome in the summer of 2006. At this point I am doing fine with the assistance of hearing aids and some clever pharmaceuticals.

A thank you to Linda Kato who can turn a phone call into a vote of support.

And finally, thanks to the staff of Ann Arbor Media Group. First for their faith in the book. Second for leaving me alone to write it. And finally, for kicking me in the butt when the writing started to take longer than it should have taken.

Bibliography

Ange, Michael R. *Diver Down: Real-World Scuba Accidents and How to Avoid Them.* Camden, Maine: International Marine/McGraw-Hill, 2006.

Bernstein, Peter L. *The Wedding of the Waters: The Erie Canal and The Making of a Great Nation.* New York: W.W. Norton & Co., 2005.

Canadian Museum of Civilization, *Rene-Robert Cavelier de La Salle.*

Chowdhury, Bernie. *The Last Dive.* New York: Perennial, 2002.

Feltner, Charles E., and Jeri Baron Feltner. *Shipwrecks of the Straits of Mackinac.* Dearborn, Michigan: Seajay Publications, 1992.

Harrison, John MacLean. *The Fate of the Griffon.* Chicago: Sage Books, 1974.

Heden, Karl E. *The Great Lakes Guide to Sunken Ships.* Boston: Branden Books, 1993.

Keiley, Jarvis. "Rene-Robert-Cavelier, Sieur de la Salle." *Catholic Encyclopedia.* New York: Robert Appleton Co., 1910.

Kurson, Robert. *Shadow Divers.* New York: Random House, 2005.

Madsen, Axel. *Cousteau: An Unauthorized Biography.* New York: Beaufort Books, 1986.

Michigan Shipwreck Research Associates, "The Disappearance of Flight 2501," *Joint Archives of Holland Quarterly*, Spring 2005.

Milligan, Jessie, "LaSalle: Historic Hero—Or Demonic Despot?" *Fort Worth Star-Telegram*, October 21, 2003.

Moehringer, J.R. *The Tender Bar.* New York: Hyperion, 2005.

Munson, Richard. *Cousteau: The Captain & His World, A Personal Portrait.* New York: William Morrow and Co., 1989.

Powter, Geoff. *Strange and Dangerous Dreams: The Fine Line Between Adventure and Madness.* Seattle: Mountaineers Books, 2006.

Sander, Phil, "Christmas Tree Ship," *Wisconsin's Underwater Heritage*, Wisconsin Underwater Archeology Association, December 1998.

"Story of La Salle and the Griffin, The," *History of the Great Lakes*, Vol. I. www.halinet.on.ca/GreatLakes/Documents/HGL/.

"Trials of La Salle, The," USGenNet. www.usgennet.org/usa/topic/colonial/pioneer/chap2.html.

Toronto, University of, "Cavelier De La Salle, Rene-Robert," Dictionary of Canadian Biography Online, Library and Archives Canada, 2002.

Trotter, David, and Mickey Trotter, "The Morrell Encounter," *Wreck Diving Magazine*, Issue 11, 2006.

Wahl, Werner, "Treasure of the Great Lakes!? The Discovery of the Sidewheel Steamer *Detroit*," Undersea Research Associates, Canton, Michigan, Unpublished manuscript, November 7, 1994.

Walsh-Sarnecki, Peggy, "Diver Won't Quit Quest for Truth," *Detroit News and Free Press*, December 31, 2005.

Wangermann, Bill, "The Great Storm of 1913 Decimated Great Lakes Shipping," *Sheboygan Press*, September 6, 1905.

Wikipedia contributors, "Great Lakes Storm of 1913," *Wikipedia, The Free Encyclopedia*, http://en.wikipedia.org/w/index.php?title=Great_Lakes_Storm_of_1913&oldid=113026182.

Willis, Glen, "The Great Storm of 1913," http://www.pointeauxbarqueslighthouse.org/preserve/shipwrecks/1913storm.cfm.